THE
POWER
of *the* HUMAN
HEART

OUR JOURNEY TO 2012
AND BEYOND

*A Message of Trust, Triumph
and Transformation*

by
Amber Dawn

SOURCE PUBLISHING
CALIFORNIA

Printed in the United States of America.
First Edition.

ISBN 978-0-578-077444

Book design: Jane Brunette
Cover art: Jaiv, and Step JurJahn

Excerpts from "2012 and Human Evolution" by David Wilcock
are used in Appendix II with permission from David Wilcock.

Published by Source Publishing
www.newdawn2012.com

To all those, known and unknown,
who have helped me on my journey;

and to all the beautiful people
who feel the winds of change
as we awaken on Earth at this time,

I dedicate this book,
with love.

～

Here's to the crazy ones, the misfits, the rebels,
the troublemakers, the round pegs in the square holes...
the ones who see things differently --
they're not fond of rules...
You can quote them, disagree with them, glorify or vilify
them, but the only thing you can't do is ignore them
because they change things...
they push the human race forward,
and while some may see them as the crazy ones,
we see genius, because the ones who are crazy enough
to think that they can change the world,
are the ones who do.

~ Steve Jobs
US computer engineer
& industrialist

Table of Contents

A Change of Heart

True security comes not from clinging to the known
and predictable but from trusting the process of life,
welcoming change and growth at all times.

~ Read on the back of a motor home

ONE OF THE MOST frequently asked questions between travelers is, "Where are you from?" This simple query leaves me honestly stumped for a reply. At times I try some smart answer, such as looking up at the stars and musing, "I can't quite remember…"

Finally though, I am required to give the standard and lengthy explanation, "I was brought up in numerous countries, none of which felt like home, so it was easy for me to keep on moving. I have been traveling, never really settling in anywhere, for the past 25 years."

I gathered many puzzle pieces on that long and winding road, and the picture that they form gives me a lot of trust in the wondrous process of Life. The book you are now holding in your hands is a summary of my journeys and where they have brought me to. Here is the essence of the experiences made, the awareness gained and the truly inspiring information discovered along the way.

Life bombards each of us with all the opportunities we need, to experience, to grow, and to fulfill our dreams. I feel fortunate to have had, without great funds, an unusual and varied life. One could call it lucky, for although my life was not necessarily easy I was, at least in some ways, free. I have lived for the last quarter century now with no alarm clock, no fixed schedule, and no socks.

You may imagine that a traveling life has more than its share of fun and freedom. It certainly has more than its share of changes, chances, and challenges! I can promise you, as a professional nomad, it isn't all calm waters, apple pie and cherry blossoms! Perhaps you can benefit from the insights it has given me, without having to spend days organizing trips, nights waiting at airports for delayed flights, or years living out of travel bags.

Take this book as a kind of shortcut, if you like. It saves you time, money and agro. See it as a package deal, no strings attached. You get, from the comfort of your armchair, a lifetime of hard-earned experience and information, plus entertainment on top, all boiled down and conveniently packed in book format, to digest at your leisure. You get the gemstones without the digging, and the benefits without the heartaches. I'm sure you have had enough of your own! As you wander through these pages you may recognize parts of my journey as similar to yours. You will likely find some confirmation of your own feelings, and perhaps some reminders of who we are and what we came here for.

Our life stories, however different from each other, have led us all to a similar place in life. We have lived and loved, lost and learned; we are looking within, and looking out, wondering what the future holds in store. It is no coincidence that we are all on the planet at this time. *None of us got here by mistake.* Many of us are aware of a change in the air, of an increase in speed, and that these unsettling times hold great promise.

A lifetime of traveling has obliged me to be responsible and discerning, to be accepting and adaptable, to let go and to trust. I share here the trials and triumphs of my journey that transformed my outlook on life; how traveling pushed me to expand, and compassion opened me to love. I share my confidence and my vision, the result of my lifelong enquiry into the beyond. And I offer the knowledge and insights that can open our minds and empower our hearts for the road ahead.

From the moment I set pen to paper this book threatened to explode into a multidimensional affair! It has taken my constant focus and the combined efforts of my family and friends to hold it down, grappling to keep it in some manageable format. Following the laws of our expanding universe, it just kept on expanding!

This was, precisely, why I hadn't attempted it earlier, despite the frequent insistence of others that I really *should* write a book. I had plenty of counter arguments for why I *shouldn't*. I type with two fingers. I abhor computer work, sitting at a desk, pressure, decisions and deadlines. I felt that, with so many billions of people on the planet, surely I could worm my way out of it.

So I would respond with any number of lame excuses. "Why me?" was a common one. "I have no time" was perhaps the most pathetic. And, "Maybe in 2013" was one of my favorites but, admittedly, really defied the point! Eventually though, someone who commanded consideration found me, pinned me down, and said "Yes. You. Now. Siriusly.[1]"

Gulp. "It's not about hearing what you want to hear," my partner had wisely said, "it's about hearing what comes to you."

We were staying at a recording studio complex at the time and upstairs "The Musical Nomads" were relentlessly rehearsing a catchy tune. Only the chorus came through the ceiling, again and again and again... It was a real earworm:

> *There's always a word that needs to be heard,*
> *There's always a story to tell and I hope you will share it*
> *There's always an ear that wants to hear*
> *It's a brand new day.*

"Okay, okay," I resigned, "I do get the hint!"

I knew better, by then, than to argue with destiny. It is bigger than we are. Having turned down numerous signposts in life there are some messages you just can't ignore. Whether we feel up to the task at hand or not, life always knows when we are ready.

This epic story is not so much about my own travels as it is about that awesome journey we all embarked upon when we enrolled into life on this planet: our collective journey through sorrow, struggle and victimhood, to seeing that the world simply mirrors the accumulated pain our souls brought to heal. We came to realize that *we actually create* our own reality and that the hurt we attract

---

[1] *Not a spelling mistake*

is a reflection of our own unloved shadows. It is through understanding, acceptance, and compassion, by opening our hearts to embrace all we are, that we open the door to a new world.

What we see around us is the world we have created, the world that mirrors all that we believe. It is the world we are now changing, simply by expanding ourselves. For humankind has always strived to reach further ~ it is written in our genes and in our souls.

We are now rapidly discovering how much more we, and our lives, can be. We are beginning to understand the energetic laws that govern our world, the degree of interconnectivity and the power of our own influence. We are just beginning to glimpse our human and planetary potential. Very soon we shall be offered an unparalleled chance to recreate our world reality, to go to a totally new level of awareness, a new level of existence, which is beyond victimhood, abuse and suffering. It is already in the making.

～✑

MY EXPERIENCES from life on the road greatly broadened my perspective of people and the planet. They led me from intolerance to acceptance, from judgment to compassion and from insecurity to trust. They guided me from worry to peace of mind, and from hurt to understanding, gratitude and self love ~ a never ending road. While others keep reminding me that my life has been far from the norm, I have never felt that I have done anything exceptional or extraordinary. I am simply being led, as we all are, through a great journey of remembering; motivated, as we all are, by the innate search for peace, happiness and love.

Between the covers of this book I have brought together many facets of humanity's growing awareness. I am not pretending to know the whole truth, or your truth. I am simply painting the pictures that make sense to me, which have given my life clarity, direction and greater peace. Perhaps you will find some pictures that suit you, or use the colors I provide to make your own.

Amongst other material, I share my experience of the law of attraction, my understanding of the role of suffering, and the keys to dropping victimhood. I describe my openings to unconditional love, and instances of finding myself "in the now" ~ the timeless zone between our thoughts ~ and some portals that take us there. I speak too of the changing ages and how they affect our daily lives. I describe "the Quickening" foreseen by the Maya thousands of years ago. I give numerous examples of the interconnected nature of our world and of our multilayered existence. And I portray my own discoveries of my energetic being and the energy world: that which lies beyond, or rather within, our physical reality.

Now if some of these concepts are new to you, don't worry. Some were new to me until recently and indeed to most of us. This knowledge is part of the awakening of the human race from its unconsciousness. We are like kids with a new toy, figuring out how our world really works. Many of us can feel an undercurrent of change on our planet and that something extraordinary is in the making. It is a most wonderful time to be alive!

Indeed, Earth and its inhabitants are undergoing a boost in evolution. Old issues are being forced out and new information is coming in fast and furious. Our personalities, relationships and beliefs are changing rapidly, being both dissolved and expanded. Everything that is unloved is being pushed to the surface.

Many have found themselves in the last years going through a zone of turbulence, feeling out of balance or plainly unhappy. Many may feel insecure as the media threatens us with stormy waters ahead. The planet is expressing our instability. Knowing what we are going through, and where we are headed, encourages us on our way and makes the bumpy journey a lot smoother. Looking around for clues, fulfillment and peace of mind, we find ourselves beautifully supported by all those who have cared to share their knowledge. And as we open the door to welcome it, we open the door to our own inner wisdom.

Now there is plenty of far-reaching information available these days and I must admit I love that and I will get into some of it in the latter chapters. But I have met plenty of people on my travels who were pretty advanced in some areas but not so very steady on their feet. Western civilization tends to encourage our intellect but ignore our emotional base. And it is tempting, for sure, to take refuge in our "higher" parts. Yet I have found it to be most essential, before we climb too high, to check out our basement first. Life is speeding up technologically, intellectually, biologically and energetically. To prepare and steady ourselves emotionally we need a solid foundation: a strong core of self worth and deep-seated trust.

Traveling has shown me how grounded the more intuitive races on the planet are. They have largely retained their intrinsic connection ~ to themselves, each other, and the planet we live on. Many have a distinct softness which portrays this centeredness. This quality is essential in these times. We need not learn it but simply uncover it within ourselves. Where will we find it? It lies in every human heart. To grow in love, to deepen this sacred connection, is the one reason we are all, all together, on this planet. We are all here to heal our hurts and our hearts, in preparation for, and participating in, a great shift ahead.

Any reluctance to embrace the future comes from the hurt and fear we still carry ~ due to not realizing that life has always been, and will always be, our friend. Hence, more conceptual information may seem daunting or unrealistic, until we have regained trust in ourselves and in the guiding process of Life. Eventually, through linking the pieces together and understanding our own pasts, we come to see the interactive nature of our world, and how everything is geared towards our individual and global evolution.

Whoever we are, wherever we live, we are all driven by one single motivating factor: our search for happiness. And this search, this irresistible lure, brings us again and again to look at ourselves as the source of our own reality. Thus life rather cleverly leads us from trying to figure out, "So what went wrong this time?" to our own self discovery and our own expansion. The greatest relief is when we finally realize that *nothing ever went wrong*. Every experience, enjoyable or not, brought us one step further on our way. This lifetime is a journey of awakening, a journey of expansion and refinement; a journey from separation to oneness.

There are three words you are going to find repeatedly throughout these pages: life, experience, and journey. There are just no other words that portray their core meaning. This is rather symbolic, because there really is no substitute for this human life, our experiences, and our journeys.

We are a truly wonderful species, trying bravely since eons, through trial and error, to make sense of the game. And after some dead ends, some U-turns and some one way streets, we are finally finding our way out of the maze, without any guide book but the human heart.

WE CANNOT DENY that change and growth are an inevitable part of our human existence. Yet many have had more than enough of being told how we can endlessly improve ourselves, enough of fighting with their demons. The idea that we are hiding bad traits and monsters makes most of us not want to look within!

What if the answer to finding peace in life lies not in a wearisome class focused on improving one's character, but rather in full acceptance of who we already are? There are no faults in the design. Both our egos and our minds have been vital tools in our evolution, isolating us from each other and from our whole selves, encouraging our individual development as living seeds. Similarly, the strife we endured also played its role in bringing us to where we are now: mature human beings ready for the next step in our collective evolution. This step is nothing less than the flowering of the human soul.

So it is not about improving who we are; it's about finding who we are, and being more than just okay with it: loving it. It's about our own self discovery, our own reunion with ourselves, and our return to wholeness. We need to air our love here; to see that we are, and always have been, okay. It is only our own judgment, and that of society, our mirror, that has split us. Therefore it is now only with self love that we can really face our shadow parts without condemning, and thus dividing, ourselves further. And as we look around with newly found compassion, we find that within each of us lies no wrongdoer, but rather a split and hurt soul protecting itself from anticipated pain.

Through complete acceptance of ourselves, others and the world, we reclaim our wholeness. In our wholeness we regain the trust and joy of our early childhood: powerful, playful, and open. It is the state of original innocence we never lost, but just misplaced for a while.

Freed from the bonds of victimhood, from blame and from the

survivalist mindset, we unleash the power and playfulness of our creative energy. We embrace our fullness: the parts that have been locked away ~ *and no, it need not hurt to find them* ~ and the parts we have not yet dared to be ~ *and yes, it is okay to dream!* This fun adventure of self discovery is what life is all about. And as we awaken ever more to all that we are, we become ready for the unveiling.

We shall soon all be granted the awareness of what lies beyond the veil. We are about to discover that we are not just a physical body but an energetic being of eternal and infinite nature. And from that viewpoint we shall acquire a vast inner understanding of our world, our interconnectedness and our oneness. How we integrate and maintain this awareness depends solely on the openness of our hearts.

We hardly ever feel ready for change, yet life has an uncanny knack of knowing exactly when we are. We are being offered, and handed the keys to, a fully new paradigm. A new world, if we can take it.

All we need is to come to terms with life, to recognize that it is not a random mistake and that the world is not unfair. For if we are closed through insecurity, how can we dare to trust in anything new? Until we are at peace with the past, we cannot embrace the future. Until we overcome victimhood, we cannot trust that life will not hurt. Until we love ourselves, we do not believe we are good enough. Until we release judgment, we fear failure, and may even fear punishment.

We finally come to see that all our sorrows and struggles have never been due to mishap or misdemeanor, but have simply been guiding our individual growth in an ever-evolving world. We will examine the role of suffering and its untold benefits: how it has kept us in balance, strengthened our vision, and opened our hearts; how it has awakened in us the awareness of choice and that we are, indeed, creators. We shall see that our suffering has been part of the perfect plan and the mirror for our own belief in hurt. And as we are now uplifting ourselves out of this current mindset, not only do we outgrow the need for further pain, we thus change what the world reflects back at us.

It is, daily, our true feelings that influence what we attract. As we shift our own feelings *at the very base* by developing our self love, we open increasingly to recognize the holistic and supportive nature of life. This outlook greatly affects both our understanding of events and what we receive. Indeed it is the depth of our self worth ~ our self trust and hence our trust in life ~ that is the gauge of our ability to believe in, *and thus create*, a better world for ourselves.

These times are calling for a massive healing of hearts, for which we are each here to do our part, for ourselves and for all humanity. When the puzzle pieces of our lives are brought together, this shift of feeling can occur rapidly, even overnight. It is then, in understanding and deep gratitude, that we both look forward to and help create the amazing future that awaits us as soon as we accept the invitation.

And when this change of mind and heart occurs, from resistance to acceptance, from judgment to compassion, and from fear to love, we discover that our freedom lies in trust, transcendence and celebration. For it is in knowing ourselves to be innocent, seeing that life has always served our evolution, and feeling that the world is our benevolent loving guide, that we can welcome change and go with the flow. It is in making this very shift in our core beliefs that we transform the vibration on this planet to a new frequency, thus ~ through the power of our hearts ~ creating a new world.

This is our sacred journey.

Sacred Journey

Our life stories, however different from
each other, have led us all to a similar
place in life. We have lived and loved,
lost and learned; we are looking within,
and looking out, wondering what the
future holds in store. It is no coincidence
that we are all on the planet at this
time. None of us got here by mistake.

CHAPTER ONE

The Little Story of Me

Your childhood may not have been perfect…but it's over.

~ *Popular wisdom*

BEFORE WE LAUNCH into the joys of a nomadic lifestyle and of our collective journey here on Earth, let me introduce "the little story of me." If it comes across a bit gloomy, back in the early days that is precisely how I felt!

I do not have any memories of my youngest years, spent largely in the sun-baked climes of Mexico and Africa. So to begin at the beginning, my life, as far as I can remember, started the first day at school. This daunting event took place in chilly Scotland and I was freezing. My school years are a long, vague blur. The next event that really stands out to me is the day I left.

As a child I couldn't easily relate to the world around me. I could clearly recall a different place: one of cooperation, gentleness, closeness, and care. I couldn't understand why people were grumpy, rough, or didn't smile back. I was nostalgic for that other space; things didn't feel quite right here and upset my young sensibilities. I couldn't make sense of the competition and the pushiness, the striving to be better and putting others down. I felt there was more to life, so I couldn't take the card games, the "bored" games, the ball games or the social games seriously enough to have much fun. At times I thought, "Please, could somebody stop the planet? I would like to get off!" Nobody ever did.

I was reflective and reluctant. In gym class I always snuck back to the end of the queue until, inevitably, the teacher would spot me and make me come forwards to jump the horse. I was pretty sure I had been pushed into life in the same way by my spirit companions: "Go on, you can do it!" I was scared it would hurt and, with that attitude, of course it did!

Having bravely made the cosmic leap to the earthly plane, I was quietly hanging on in the birth canal waiting for the most favorable astrological position in which to make my worldly appearance. The nurses, however, were late for lunch. So they yanked me out with forceps, hung me upside down by my feet, and whacked me. This cemented my feeling that life here is not fair. I had done nothing to deserve such treatment and yelled my protest. The nurses totally missed my point and coolly responded, "Healthy baby, strong vocal chords."

I readily confess that, after such a rough start, I had for long years a bit of a victim view of life. It seems that many of us did, for it was the global mindset at the time. I certainly didn't feel I had chosen, or had any control over, my life. What most shocked me was the insensitivity and violence humans could display towards each other. There didn't seem to be many more like me on the planet and I wondered how I had got myself in here. It wasn't until much later that I recognized my own streak of insensitivity, in trying to help others, in a hardly diplomatic way, with truths they were not yet ready for. Disappointment was my pet pattern and the world, being our mirror, was always happy to oblige.

Early on I developed chronic bronchitis. It would flatten me, on cue, every time we spent the holidays at my grandparents' lovely island home in Jersey. I would lie in bed all day, alone, wheezing. This frequent holiday mode enabled me to find, deep within myself, a quiet, peaceful contentedness. It would spare me having to keep up with my sporty, achiever type, cousins. My dear grandmother was also not the cheery, cuddly, apple pie type. She was a large, imposing and intimidating woman, weighing some 300lbs, and she didn't favor me one bit. *"Little girls* ~ i.e.: under the age of 21 ~ *should be seen and not heard."* I felt squelched in her presence.

Unbeknown to me at the time, the bronchitis was a physical manifestation of my feelings. I felt restricted in my expression, that I couldn't breathe, and that I was being held down and stifled in some way. This was not my grandmother's fault, it was just how I reacted to her, and it baffled the poor doctors who said the sea air should be so good for me. The symptoms of restricted breathing reoccurred, in stifling social surroundings and difficult personal situations, over the next 30 years. Eventually, and this is the beauty of experience, I understood where it was coming from. The "sickness" became my guide. Noticing it arising, I would recognize my true feelings, and either change my environment or, better still, my reaction to it. The symptoms would then subside right away. This is one of the great things about us humans: we may be a bit slow on the uptake but once we do get something we can be pretty good at making quick shifts!

So all in all I was a timid, fragile, and serious child, and for my first 20 years I was way too shy to open my mouth. My friends now can hardly believe this, for once I had got over that initial hurdle I spent the next 20 years making up for it! That was another quick shift, motivated, as much of our progress is, by the "negative" feeling of isolation. One day I just decided I wanted to be more open, and set about shaking off my shyness. This released some of the strong, bright and cheerful character that was smoldering within. Much of our real work here is overcoming the patterns of insecurity that hold each of us, and humanity, back from expressing our inner brightness and beauty. These days there is a wealth of information on how we can reprogram our minds and feelings and when I first came across it, having done it, I knew it to be true.

For years, I happily blamed my upper-middle-class upbringing for the fact that I was so non expressive. A model child, I was always too polite to voice my truth; perhaps because, on the rare occasion I did, it came out brutally honest. Finally the bronchitis taught me that I really had to open up the flow and to get things off my chest. It led me to realize that the restrained social milieu I was brought up in was just the reflection of my own "stuck ups." Life on the road did away with those soon enough. Nothing stays stuck in India!

My mother came from the gracious, over-cultured background of ballet. My father had a colonial youth of nannies and etiquette. It is therefore hardly surprising that emotions at home weren't exactly free flowing. While my dad's parents were in Argentina during the war he was sent off to school, at the ripe old age of five, in nearby Switzerland. It was, after all, as his mother wrote, "only three weeks away by boat...!" I was also not a hotshot on feelings myself. I grew up in a kind of isolated bubble, not feeling very much at all. It seems that this was a protective layer to shield me from my own sensitive emotions, for if I had really allowed myself to feel them I may very well have become desperate.

FOR SOME OF US, a large part of our childhood, or our life, may be spent finding out what we *don't* like or want. This is not as unfortunate as it seems at the time! It helps us to realize what we *do* want, and thus serves to strengthen our desire, our focus and our vision. It is beneficial to recognize that, rather than a random raffle ticket or an awful mistake, we have actually chosen the perfect family and environment for this purpose. Well, "chosen" may not be quite the word, but we at least slotted into what we needed, like it or not!

It seems that I needed emotional isolation and an unconventional lifestyle, for that background strengthened me through introspection, challenges and upheavals, and stretched my outlook and my heart. And so I went from being shy, withdrawn and reluctant, to being open, grounded, and going forth into life. The hardness that came from my insecurity gave way to a softness that stems from trust. Over-activity gave way to quietness, infringement to acceptance.

For much of this earthly life though, I felt I must have read my galactic map upside down and ended up on the wrong planet. It certainly wasn't all peace, love and pancakes! I could agree that Earth was a pretty place to visit, but couldn't imagine that one would really want to live here. At first glance, it seemed to be a correctional center for juvenile delinquents. Looking closer, it was rather a loony bin for misfits! Some see it as a survival planet. Yet life brought me to realize it is really a perfectly designed playground that cleverly steers us to grow in love. We are here to heal our hurts and our hearts.

THERE IS ONE RARE MOMENT in my normally dysfunctional middle class childhood that really stands out. I was in my early teens, and my father and I were out sailing. We were heading back towards a glorious sunset above a little Spanish bay. Live music wafted towards us from the harbor. There was silence between us and the sea was very quiet. The silence seemed to hang in the warm air, echoed by the still waters.

And then a strange thing happened. It felt as though time had stopped, as though we had moved into a zone of slow motion. It was very surreal. I was overcome by a tremendous other-worldly sense of bliss and peace. I wondered about this occurrence for many years. A lot of water has washed under the bridge since that day, but this single memory has always been etched in my soul.

Throughout my life, I have been blessed with more of these magic moments. They come spontaneously, through letting go, through silence, through shock or grief, and through the words of mystics: portals into the ethereal. These gaps are windows into another dimension: a space that is always here for us when all else stops. They remind us of where we come from and where we always belong to: the behind-the-scenes reality which, I suspect, we shall all be experiencing in our lifetime.

If I think of all the crap I learned in high school,
it's a wonder that I can think at all...
That lack of education hasn't hurt me though,
for I can still read the writing on the wall.
                    ~ Simon and Garfunkel, lyrics

MY HIGH SCHOOL, in France, was hardly a cheerful place. It consisted of two huge grey blocks, aptly situated between a hospital and a cemetery. It fit so perfectly with the average picture of life: you are born at the hospital, do your time at the school of life, and end up inevitably, rich or poor, down the road at the cemetery!

I was never your stereotypical teenager, crooning over boys or pop idols. I was reading about Near Death Experiences in *Life After Life,* by Dr. Raymond Moody. Admittedly I missed out on some of the fun that can be had here! Needless to say I was always the odd one out, but I later came to see that not fitting in had supported my individual growth.

I used to visit the old graveyard sometimes in my lunch break. It fascinated me. I would read the moss covered tombstones and wonder about all those many different lives. There were young mothers and children too. I pondered all the suffering that had been felt, questioned what the purpose could be and what lay beyond.

On the search for the meaning of life, I took philosophy classes. One day, while we were dissecting what someone had said in ancient Greece 2,500 years ago, the whole class started to laugh. The afternoon sun had cast the shadow of the teacher's long nose across the blackboard. From then on, in every class, whether it was sunny or cloudy and whatever the time of the day, he insisted we close all the blinds! I was the hardest hit by the absurdity of this new rule because, in every class, I would choose whichever desk would get the most sun during that hour. The sun's warmth kept me going, class after lifeless class. I was a rational atheist, but I could appreciate how sun worship may have originated. It symbolized for me a bright, nurturing, impersonal energy sustaining all earthly life-forms, and always there for us, even if obscured by clouds. I was later to find out that the sun is really so much more. Not only does it nourish our physical existence, keep us warm, spare us from getting SAD, and give us light, it also transmits evolutionary information to the DNA that builds our very cells.

It became clear to me through this incident that studying philosophy wouldn't give me the answers I was looking for. It puzzled me that such a well-studied man could be so insecure. It baffled me that one could be so scared of one's own shadow, looming far bigger than its source of origin. With what we all know now about the collective shadow phenomenon, it makes a bit more sense! (We will throw more light on our "shadows" in chapter 14.)

Other classes were also not fulfilling my growing curiosity. It hadn't taken me long to figure out what was really wanted of me in school: not to express my individuality, but to fit in with the norm. I played the game, because regurgitating what we were told to believe got me top marks. However, near the end of school, out of interest, I wrote an intelligent essay that did not fit the political views of the establishment. Instead of the usual grade A or B, this cheekiness was rewarded with a D. D for dumb. My economics teacher was perplexed at how his pet student had flunked so badly on her final homework!

Although I had it easy enough, I deeply disliked the critical, competitive and elitist nature of the system. Back in primary school I felt sorry for the less academic classmates who the teachers pointed out as being bad. I told my parents this wasn't fair on those kids because they must have other good qualities that maybe I didn't. They replied that, "Life is not fair." And, in those days, I believed it.

I relate all this, honestly, not only to display my humanitarian streak but also to point out that I have a well functioning brain! I feel I have to say this here because towards the end of this book we will explore some rather far-out information and, if you are still with me then, I would like you to recall that I am, really, quite normal. I do not see angels, chat with my spirit guides or have tea with the ascended masters. I am actually rather down to earth, and yet there is very little by now that I do not deem possible. Of course you don't *need* to believe anything I say, it is enough if you too can allow yourself to wonder.

A fast-firing brain, however, is not the answer to life either. In third grade we underwent common sense intelligence tests. I got 99 out of 100 questions right. I cried in class because I failed one and it was such a silly mistake. Now, that is embarrassing and shows a serious lack of self appreciation! It demonstrates that however well we do in life, through self judgment we weaken ourselves and can be easily pushed off balance. Our self love is a core factor for our stability.

We can appreciate ourselves for whoever we are; even if we appear to fail dismally in the eyes of anyone else. We did not come here to learn to be perfect. We came here to learn to love ourselves, anyway. Now there's something they didn't teach us in school!

ALTHOUGH IT SEEMED like it never would, the last day of high school finally came. My philosophy teacher said I should keep studying the ancient Greeks. My French teacher said I should study literature, and my math teacher totally agreed with her. My economics teacher was still dumbfounded, my gym teacher tactfully said nothing, and my heart told me to go traveling. And so I did. My dad, B.A., M.A., who had been to the top English colleges, agreed with Einstein that I'd learn more on the road:

> *The only thing that interferes with my learning*
> *is my education.*
> > ~ *Albert Einstein*

Fortunately all those years of "learning," the dates, the "facts" and the figures, dissolved into the mists of time the moment I left school. It didn't take long for the real education to follow suit: how to wake up to the alarm, listen to the boss, stay put in our class and believe everything we are told. You know, the really important stuff. And thus I plunged, headfirst, into the sea of life, after 12 years of very academic schooling, knowing nothing at all. I certainly didn't know my heart from my head, my left brain from my right, or myself from Adam.

It's not that one can't develop some of this awareness in the school ground. Those who were less studious than me were in fact ahead in those areas, for it is through life's experiences that we come to know ourselves. To make up for lost time in this field, I soon quit the nine to five and attended a crash course in the school of life: India. For at study or at work one is just so distracted by the full schedule, so engaged by everyday issues, that the "trivial" concerns of who we really are, and what we truly came here for, simply do not arise.

CHAPTER TWO

India My Love

~~~

If I were asked under what sky the human mind has
most fully developed some of its choicest gifts, has most
deeply pondered on the greatest problems of life, and
has found solutions, I should point to India.

~ *Max Mueller*

BEFORE I HIT THE ROAD, I bravely attempted a normal lifestyle and a couple of respectable jobs. But between handling the housework, the shopping and the bills, the office phone ringing, the telex machine jamming and the paperwork piling up, I would gaze out of the window and wonder what the big wide world had to offer. As I was hurrying out of the wind and rain one day, my umbrella got stuck in the office doorway, highlighting my feeling of frustration and restriction. It was the last drop: "I'm out of here!" So one chilly Parisian spring morning I boarded a Syrian Airline flight to New Delhi.

I had heard that India is the most spiritually orientated country in the world so it seemed the fitting place to continue my search for the meaning of life. I arrived at dawn and the sunlight was softened by the dusty haze, giving the warm air a promising mystical feel. I ignored the crowds of touts that didn't quite fit into my rosy picture of a semi-enlightened population, and took a rickshaw into the city. As we drove past the ramshackle shelters on the roadside, patched together out of bits of tin and plastic, waves of shock and awe engulfed me. 24 years later, the scene is still vivid. With no bathrooms, obviously, families were out on the streets, having their morning bucket baths. And worse.

"Is India nice?" I have often been asked. Well...there are many superlative adjectives that may partly describe the full feature, action packed, epic 3D movie that is India. "Nice" is not one of them. "Mind-boggling" comes close. It is extraordinary, awesome, overwhelming, horrifying, powerful, eye-opening and enlightening. India is a crash course in Life.

I was not a born "believer." As I saw it, I was far too logical for that. I had been brought up atheist, thank God. Yet it didn't take me long in India to feel, and see, that there is more to this world than meets the eye. I should tell you, at this point, that I never smoked any substance that could alter my perception. A friend once gave me a try. I didn't inhale; I coughed uncontrollably and wheezed for three days. End of story. My experience with alcohol was the same short-lived. So I remained very rational, very clear-headed, and didn't leave too many brain cells along the dusty road.

My first partner, with whom I left to India, had lived there for seven years. He took me on tour. We spent one year traveling the length and breadth of the country, through dusty towns and holy sites, barren plains and high mountains; through the coconut palm-clad south and the hippie-clad beaches. We slept in trains and in temples, in villages, pilgrim shelters and chai-shops. On beaches, rope beds, mats, and hard floors. It was nine months before I had a hotel room door I could shut and say, "*This* is *my* private space!"

On my first day in India we had gone straight from the city, on a crowded local train, to a nearby village. I will courteously spare you the details of that journey. We arrived at the simple home of my partner's friends, conspicuously poised on a bicycle rickshaw. The whole village came and stood, sat and squatted around us, mouths wide open, watching us drink chai tea. Most had never seen a white woman before and there was nowhere to hide from their unabashed stares. The next morning at four there was a sturdy knock on the door. My partner reported, "The village women want you to walk to the toilet field with them and then to bathe in the river." I flatly declined. We went later by ourselves down to the river. A baby's body lay naked on a sandbank. Death in India is not hidden behind closed doors.

TWO WEEKS AFTER LEAVING my cultured and protected middle class life, I was engulfed in the largest religious festival in the country. The "Khumba Mela" is an enormous mass gathering held every four years. Millions come from all over the motherland to cleanse their karma in the dubious waters of the Ganges.

I remember sitting at one camp watching a dreadlocked "sadhu," who was stark naked and covered in ash, smoke a huge silver chillum, while a band of guys wearing short tunics and peacock feather hats played devotional chants to God on extremely off key instruments. I had to pinch myself! This was not the world I knew, of intellectual conversation and table manners. Mere weeks earlier I could never have imagined such a scene, yet here I was, plunked right in the middle of it. It was an eye-opener to the different realities on one planet. I could feel my mind and my tolerance level being stretched daily. My partner informed me that marijuana is not seen there as a recreational drug but as an enhancer of consciousness. A "sadhu" is a "spiritual seeker," and worshippers of Shiva could buy their weed at government shops as part of their quest for enlightenment.

It's an understatement to say that the Indian mind works very differently to the western one. Concepts that may be challenging for us are commonplace for them. They understand that diversity is not different from oneness. So the many colorful gods of Hinduism actually describe the many aspects, the multiple facets, of the one godly energy. Obviously, as soon as one tries to describe God one fails miserably, so one can anyway only portray a feature. Hence, the more the merrier! And although, like all of us, they tend to get caught by the illusion of separatism, the Indians are still extremely tolerant. The vast majority of Hindus, Muslims, Sikhs, Christians, Buddhists, Jews, and other religions in India live happily side by side. Only the good old media, reporting the rare cases of fanaticism, would have us believe otherwise.

India is Earth's cradle of spiritual quest and, since the '60s, the search for a deeper understanding of our physical life has led many seekers to journey there. There is a common, and ambiguous, spiritual teaching, "The material world is an illusion." We used to joke that this becomes laughably apparent in India. Indeed, everything starts to fall apart moments after you bought it!

Along this line there were, specifically, two little events at the Mela that really made me start to wonder. One sadhu had given me two unusually large "rudracks," a "holy" seed. At bedtime, I put them into my money belt along with my camera, which I always slept with, deep inside my sleeping bag. The next morning the seeds ~ and only the seeds ~ were gone.

The second surprise came later when I had my photos printed. Out of shyness and respect I hadn't taken many close-up pictures, but one elder sadhu stood out to me. Just as I clicked he saw me and put his hand up in a gesture of refusal. I wondered whether his hand would be blocking his wizened face. When I had the pictures developed I was mystified. The photo I had taken before him and the one after were side by side on the same negative strip. His photo was simply not there.

Of course one can disregard the facts and say, "well, maybe this and maybe that." Maybe. Me, I had no explanation. I had to start an "open" box in my logical mind where I store things I just cannot sort. The box is pretty crammed these days. It is not easy for our western trained minds to accept that we do not know. Nor to allow the mysterious, to accept that there are happenings we cannot explain, and a subtle world we cannot even describe.

Donkey years later, someone loaned me a book, "First Light." Carol O'Biso, a rational American lady describes her visit to New Zealand to bring old Maori statues, called "Tiki," to an exhibition in the US. The Maori believe that a spirit lives within each Tiki. She, a logical westerner, did not. For the catalogue, each Tiki was classified and photographed singly. Yet the largest, most powerful Tiki was not on her negatives. I was glad for this confirmation that I hadn't lost my marbles.

INDIA IS ONE OF THE TOUGHEST CLASSROOMS, but the reward is priceless. Once you get past the surface, once you can accept the hustle and the bustle, the chaos and the poverty, the dirt and the dust and the noise and the smells, you start to feel the powerful spirit of the country. The air is vibrant. It is an almost tangible field.

It seems to come from the unwavering faith of so many people for so long. It doesn't matter that they appear to be praying to many different gods, or that the rituals are excessive and imposed by authoritarian priests. What matters is that they all believe, they all pray, they all offer, every day, their devotion.

India teaches surrender. It's too huge, too crazy and too strong. You just can't fight it. It's a country of extremes: too hot, too crowded, too noisy… and what can you do about it? Absolutely nothing. You can leave of course, and many do. Things just don't work like they do in many other countries and after a time you stop asking, "Why is the bus so late?", "Why is the shower cold?" and *"Why* is the electricity off, *again*?"

The answer is simple: It just is.

And after a time you have less expectation, less frustration, and more appreciation. Everything that works is something to be grateful for, rather than something to be taken for granted. That was India's gift to me.

I learned gratitude the hard way, but I was a fast learner. One day early on in my visit, after a few hours of sitting on the bare and bumpy wooden train seat I exclaimed, "My legs are sore!" In reply, my eyes were drawn to the far corner of the carriage. A man was sitting there, with no legs. I hastily revised my comment, "Thank god I have legs to be sore."

In India you discover that anyone can be your guru. What did all the beggars teach me? You can't take on the suffering of the world. Nor are you asked to. You can't help everyone. Nor do you need to. We each have our own life, our own learning. If a beggar makes you feel guilty about your status, if that makes you feel you have to give, then you may be missing their present to you: gratitude for all you have.

On the desk of the New Delhi tourism office was a sign: "You do not come here to change India, you come here to change yourself."

Years later, in Thailand, I was struck by a very crippled young woman on the pavement. Amidst the superficiality of busy Bangkok, she emanated an outstanding peaceful and loving energy. I wanted to tell her, in my very limited Thai, that she was beautiful, but it is a tonal language. The word "suay" means either "beautiful" or "bad" depending on a subtle pitch of the syllables. I didn't dare get it wrong. Once again, in the face of her radiance and fulfillment, it was I who was on the receiving side.

The word surrender has to us a negative connotation. But in fact it is most beautiful, because it is a doorway to the beyond. Surrender is full acceptance, allowance and approval of the way things are. It is the recognition that there is absolute intelligence behind the workings of the universe. It is our devotion, our total trust and our complete let go.

I came to understand that surrender is a portal. There is no more resistance, no more struggle, no more push. It opens the door to loving the world and to your own self love.

I knew a pretty Nepali woman, a housemaid. She was always smiling. She was older than me and looked younger. She had borne ten children. Seven of them had died.

Such people show us the power of surrender.

A Tale of Trust

You gain strength, courage and confidence by every experience in which you really stop to look fear in the face.
~ *Eleanor Roosevelt*

I LEFT INDIA DEEPLY MOVED in my feelings and beliefs. My souvenirs were faith, a sense of humility, and an everlasting appreciation for the easiness of my life and every hot shower I have ever had.

During that intense year of pilgrimage, I had become tired of bogey yogis and smarmy swamis trying to get into my bed. My first partnership died a natural death and I spent the next year living in gentle Nepal, on the far side of Pokhara Lake, just watching the mountains. It was a most magical and powerful time, 1987, the beginning of the winds of change.

It was there that I met my long-term partner, with whom the rough and bumpy ride of self discovery began in earnest. Inexorably linked, as all our journeys are, with the evolution of humankind. At the ripe old age of 25 another relationship was not on my list and I did my very best to resist it. However we seemed to have some sort of soul agreement, although I couldn't figure out what is was! He was a tall, expressive, and spontaneous German. More precisely, a tall *order, explosive*, and spontaneous *combustion!* It was some 20 years later that I understood more of the picture.

He is my soul mate in that we share the same tastes, the same understanding of life and the same vision. We were worlds apart in our emotional setup. I was light and cheerful, he was deep and depressed. He was rather intuitive, with some brilliant insights, but also very volatile. After a most normal upbringing, he had, at the tender age of 22, a natural experience that was rather mind-blowing. Over a period of seven weeks he found himself shifting in and out of this reality, going through death on some level while remaining in his body. His small town life had not quite prepared him for this and it left him, not too surprisingly, rather un-grounded. It is impossible to relate the experience, but the Tibetan Book of the Dead, which describes passing through stages of the afterlife in no clear language, made perfect sense to him after that. After this cosmic revelation he found himself unable to reconnect to his daily life. There were also essential rungs missing in his re-lationship to himself: the internal ladder that enables us to take such a trip to the stars and to bring the experience down to earth. It was therefore most difficult for him to integrate this new aware-ness into his former personality.

Our courtship was not a quiet romantic affair, but rather high flying and high voltage. In due course, as it naturally happens, I started to feel distinctly peculiar, especially in the mornings.... I has-ten to add that pregnancy, childbirth and babies were the scariest things I could possibly imagine! The result of the home pregnancy test was undecipherable. That evening, engulfed in apprehension, I looked to the sky for an answer, as one instinctively does. It was sunset and there was just one single cloud above the snowy peaks: a large pink dove.

I had never written a poem in my life but words flowed out of my pen:

Little sister, come and see
everything that's happened to me,
All the spaces I have been
and the wonders I have seen.

Now it all seems long ago
from this mundane life we know,
But let me take you through the door
to the world I was in before,
And I'll show you a fairyland
where love and truth go hand in hand,
Where magic, luck and mystery
are commonplace as you can see,
Realities that lie beyond
this earthen land to which we bond.

And you will bring back to this side
memories you cannot hide,
Old wisdom which you'll long to share,
for it's a higher world than here,
A land where heaven touches earth,
Creation has a new rebirth,
And we shall know what it is to Be,
a part of nature's harmony,
And laugh in love with the rising sun,
just thanking Spirit for what is done.

So little sister, come and see…

I resolved to take the dugout the next day and paddle across the lake for a check up at the local clinic. Life, however, had other plans. A good friend had been busted in Kathmandu for someone else's pot and we had to go there immediately.

We were young, wild and free... and just a little bit silly. We had overstayed our visas and by chance, on arrival in Nepal's medieval and atmospheric capital, underwent a most unlikely passport check. We were arrested without dinner and chucked unceremoniously into small, dark, and dank cells. I was not amused. On the contrary I was rather alarmed at first, and hardly able to communicate at all with the six local women with whom I shared the hard floor space. That was all there was to share on first impression. But they were as human as the rest of us, and they fed me. Very different from the many young, sweet and personable English backpackers you meet these days on the road, I was brought up aloof, stemming from bourgeois insecurity. In that cold stone cell one day, my heart was so moved by one of the women crying that I overcame my shyness. It was the first time I had ever put my arm around another person in a gesture of warmth.

After two weeks I was released. I flew to India and the midnight moon greeted me as a smile in the sky. I slept that night in a little hotel in the main bazaar wrapped in bliss. Nothing makes you appreciate your freedom as much as having once lost it.

By then, I was no longer feeling sick and lay aside the urgency of a check up. I headed up to the cooler mountains and one day, when I was near a foreign run hospital, I did a urine test. It was negative. What a relief. The notion of abortion didn't disturb me, but it was great that I didn't have to undergo it.

A couple months later I did a long hike with my young brother in the highlands of Zanskar on the Indian-Tibetan border. We met only nomadic shepherds on the way and they pointed out the untrodden route to our local guide. It was a rather grueling hike over the high snowy Baralacha pass that pushed us at times to the limits. I was grateful to ride over the pass on the small pack horse which was belly deep in snow. From the top, the white peaks of the Himalayas reached in all directions as far as the eye could see.

Although summertime, it was cold at that altitude and we always slept fully dressed in our tent. We finally reached Dharamsala, the headquarters of the Dalai Lama in India, a bit the worse for wear. For the first time in a month, I could strip off and have a shower. My belly was, quite unusually, a small round lump.

Now, I hadn't seen my German boyfriend since we were ar-

rested, as he had been flown back home. So I couldn't be pregnant.
I wasn't particularly worried, but I thought I better have it looked
at. The Tibetan doctor had me lie down on the bed and felt my
belly. It was just as well that I was lying down. "Six months," he
said in his simple English.

"Six months to live?" I queried jokingly.

"Six months baby," he said.

This was not an acceptable answer. I was not six months
pregnant! It just couldn't be! My belly was tiny. Childbirth was my
biggest dread in life and it was simply not an option. However, at
six months, abortion wasn't either.

I spent the next two weeks with violent diarrhea. On my fifth
run to the toilet one morning a fellow traveler asked, "Have you
had a shock recently?" I admitted that, indeed, I had. "Diarrhea
comes from not being able to digest the situation. That's why
everyone gets it when they come to India." Considering how emotions affect our bodies this made total sense. "Having a baby is
easy," she breezed, "all you have to do is relax."

"I'm a very relaxed person," I blurted.

"Are you?" she replied amused.

I have noticed repeatedly that we never feel ready for the next
step, but life seems to know exactly when we are. I do hope you
have noticed that too.

When I finally accepted the situation things got a whole lot
better. I started to feel wonderful, very happy and totally fulfilled.
My brother and I celebrated with a three day camel trek, sleeping
out in the desert under the full moon. The tranquil ambience was
broken only by the camel bellowing its protest when the cook tried
to force feed it with his inedible stodgy porridge.

I was sure straightaway that the baby was to be born in a
small quiet ashram I had visited in South India. My partner
arranged to meet us there. The gentle, elderly English father of the
ashram was not so sure: "This is a holy place, a spiritual community." That sounded perfect to me. I simply knew it was the place.
One of the elderly sisters reassured me, "Well, if it just happens
here…what can you do about it?"

We were given one of the two huts by the banks of the wide
holy river, the Ganges of South India: a simple room without the

flash mod-cons of electricity and running water. It was a beautiful, peaceful atmosphere in the secluded ashram grounds and I loved my short pregnancy. In the evenings we would go to the little temple and listen to the brothers chant and sing sacred songs to the sounds of the sitar.

There was one lady staying at the ashram who had assisted midwifery in Africa. She gave me a few valuable tips, perhaps the most precious being: "Don't let anyone fill your head with all that could go wrong!" In the west, putting the focus on our concerns hinders the natural process. She said she would be happy to hold my hand, but in due course she had to leave. She reminded me that some women think they have indigestion when the contractions start. How silly of them I thought.

My partner assured me we could do it without her. "Millions of women give birth every day. The body knows exactly what to do." He trusted in the universe, I trusted in him. I also felt, from the unlikely circumstances of the pregnancy, that this child was damned determined to make it here. That our friend was busted on the day I had planned to do my first pregnancy test, that I was imprisoned so I couldn't follow that up, that the urine test was negative, and that my belly was hidden for a month under layers of clothing, seemed like a lot of coincidences.

The day after our prospective midwife left, Durgananda, who lived in the other hut, invited us over after lunch. He was an unconventional, cosmopolitan Sri Lankan with a fun sense of humor. The ashram ladies wouldn't let me eat papaya because it is abortive. So he treated me to papaya and chocolate. In India, everyone wishes you to have a boy. "It's a girl," he assured me, "I've predicted many babies. I've always been right." Soon after I felt like my belly was going haywire. "I've got indigestion; maybe from the chocolate, I'm going to lie down for a bit." He laughed.

I coached myself through the next few hours. The words kept running through my head. "All you have to do is relax. The body knows exactly what to do. All you have to do is relax." Right. In those circumstances you are being asked to relax! It's all you have to do. Very funny! But she was right. Evening fell and we lit a couple candles. She had told me, "Don't push too early. Wait until the inner ring is wide enough for the head to pass through." When my gallant partner, armed with torch and tape measure, checked to see if the ring was wide enough, he exclaimed: "The head is already through! Now, all you have to do is push it out!"

Well, there are times in life you think you are doing your utmost. You think you are giving your best and yet it doesn't quite do it. This was one of those times. I pushed. And I pushed. And I pushed again. Repeatedly, the head came partly out and slipped back in again. Then one time my partner said, "The head is going blue." And then, I really pushed. I gave it everything I had left, which wasn't much. You don't care anymore for yourself; you realize that in order to give new life you will have to go beyond yourself. Birthing is like a death of the ego: in order to become more you have to surrender yourself totally. And so I did.

A baby girl popped out, long and skinny with big feet. She was wide eyed, clean and almost beautiful. We waited until there was no more blood passing through the umbilical cord before we tied a bit of string around it and cut it with our nail scissors. The Sri Lankan dude passed by our hut with a pot of chai and cookies: "Anyone for tea?" I have to say, his timing was impeccable. We sat all together on the bed in the quiet candlelight. The dude, my partner, my 20 year old brother and I, and this bright little spirit newly arrived on planet Earth.

> *They come through you but not from you,*
> *And though they are with you yet they belong not to you.*
> *You may give them your love but not your thoughts.*
> *You may house their bodies but not their souls.*
> *You may strive to be like them, but not seek to make them like you.*
> *For life goes not backwards nor tarries with yesterday.*
> *You are the bows from which your children as living arrows*
>   *are sent forth.*
>   *~ Kahlil Gibran*

SOME DAYS LATER we named her Chandra, which means moon in Hindi. Durgananda laughed, it was the name of his mother. The Indian ashram brothers came around to greet her. One of them played her soft music on his guitar which mesmerized her. Another one said to her, "Never forget."

Babies, not yet having developed a mental approach to the world, are totally in the moment. Not having started to identify, to separate, name and classify, they experience things directly, without the filter of the mind. They are still in oneness. Hence their radiance, their magic, their wholeness. As I lay next to her once, I shifted for a moment into that spacey feeling and noticed, "Wow, so that is how her world is!" It is a state we will all again experience.

Those days I didn't know she was to be my greatest guide in life. In laughter, in love and in "let go." Those days I didn't know very much at all. I thought life just happens to you and you take what you get.

So there I was, in India, with a baby and the grand total of $300. To top that off, my partner was a constant source of spice in a life that already hardly promised to be boring. Great start!

CHAPTER THREE

The Myth of Death

In the end these things matter most:
How fully did you live?
How much did you love?
How well did you learn to let go?

~ Buddha

AS IT HAD BEEN ONE of life's great surprises for me, I wanted to surprise my parents with the baby. I sent letter after letter asking if they would like to come to India, or not, but no reply came. I guess they just didn't want to say "no." Those days, communication was slow. We lived at 6,000 feet in the Himalayas and would have had to go to the capital to make an international phone call. Eventually, I just posted a photo of our child, writing on the back, "The marvelous mini milk monster." Shortly after, I sent a letter describing the childbirth. She was already five month young. I knew the story would appeal to my dad's sense of strength and adventure. His type of gal! I looked forward to his praise, and also, to giving him something he could feel proud of. It felt like my gift to him.

For weeks no post came. Finally, on the last day of the annual village fair, mail arrived at the tiny post office. We walked back through the festivities and up to our quiet little two room home. We sat on the old wooden chest by the window overlooking the wide valley, and the sounds of the celebrations reached up the hillside.

I had three letters from my family which had taken three weeks to arrive. I opened my sister's first: her familiar, tiny scribbled handwriting filled two pages. My eyes fell instantly on one little line in the midst of it all: "Daddy had an accident." I looked up and said, "My dad's died."

"Nonsense," my partner replied.

It was then that the sounds of the long horns being blown in the village square, marking the end of the festival, rose up into the spring air, carrying with them across the valley the end of my childhood.

I cried everyday for a year, nearly everyday for two, and on and off for seven. It didn't help that I had clearly experienced my own life ~ my sense of identity, my energetic existence ~ as not depending on my physical body; that my higher part knew he was still alive; that I met him in dreams. I was, in my smallest part, heartbroken. And through that pain I became aware of my inner child. Through that pain I learned to feel compassion.

The little child in me felt alone, unsupported, and it missed its father's admiration. My letter describing the birth hadn't reached in time for him to read it. I missed the sense of closeness we felt but never expressed; and, most of all, I felt I hadn't done enough for him.

The last mail I ever received from him, in reply to the photograph, arrived, oddly enough, shortly later. It had crossed with mine. It read, "I know you will be an excellent mother." The card was a sailboat at sunset: "True love sets free."

There is something about tragedy that brings you down to the ground. It humbles you, forces you to surrender. What saved me from falling apart was my baby, so bright and funny and full of radiant smiles.

Interestingly, during the weeks before the news came, I had felt an omnipresent foreboding of death. The feeling was so strong and sad that, worried for my baby, I even refused to take the bus along the narrow mountain road to the town. It shows our deep connection to those we are close to.

Our newborn actually came close to leaving us a few times in that first half year. And again I somehow had, not a constant worry, but an underlying sense that she may not survive the first 6 months. I received the news of my dad's passing six months and one week after her birth. I felt then as if either she or he had to leave as part of my life's screenplay, and that my father had chosen to leave for my benefit instead of her.

Life goes on

DEATH SOUNDS DARK and scary and is likely associated with our worst feelings. So the topic of what lies beyond may not be your usual cup of tea, but it is mine. And the irony, the apparent paradox is, that by considering and studying death, we find wonder, peace of mind and even joy. We make truly illuminating and inspiring discoveries about our life: the real us, what is within; and some of our purpose here, which leads us to live both more fully and at peace.

These days the topic of what lies beyond, and our feeling towards it, is of considerable interest. And this is not because, as some would have us believe, we are all going to abandon our bodies in a global catastrophe! Rather, we shall experience great revelations without having to leave at all.

Since my father's passing I have thought about death on a steady basis. A morbid obsession, you may say, waste of a life. But you see, there is no opposition between life and death. "Life" is when I am in a body, and "death" is when I am out of one. That is the only difference. It is just another stage of life. The "I" remains the same.

Now we may not all have had the chance to experience this. I feel very fortunate that I have, and I will attempt to share that with you. It is not an obvious concept to convey because we are so identified to being only our bodies; and also, because our language stems from this physical reality, it cannot really portray the immaterial spaces of other dimensions. Many have tried, and there are some excellent descriptions. We can't grasp them with our minds, but we can allow the feeling in.

> *You are never more alive than the moment after*
> *your body closes down.*
> ~ Stuart Wilde

*In a singular burst of euphoria, my mind, my heart and my soul
opened simultaneously to complete cosmic awareness. And it
shall be the same for you, no matter how spiritually evolved you
may be or not. Our humanness simply cannot conceptualize the
breathtaking sense of wholeness that reunites with your spirit in
what we refer to as death. Seeing death as the end of life is like
seeing the horizon as the end of the ocean.*

~ Dannion and Kathryn Brinkley,
THE SECRETS OF THE LIGHT

Death looks gruesome from the point of view of the body or
the ones left behind, but to be out of our body-mind is a really enjoyable state. We should rather use the term "afterlife," or more
precisely: "life-continuation." Life and death walk hand in hand.
It is simply the voyage beyond the horizon. We only seem to disappear to those standing on the shore. They may see a door clos-
ing, you have just moved into another room.

I understand when people say, "That's just wishful thinking,
out of hope." They may feel the topic to be out of reach, ungraspable. They may not dare to consider it or believe it, out of fear it
may not be true. Some are afraid to look at it out of fear of "judgment day." Others believe they are better off not to know, don't
need to know, or say, "We can't know." I dare to say, that due to
many having been there and back, we can at least get a glimpse.

The reason to look into death is not morbid curiosity or abstract interest. It is just being realistic and responsible. Seen from
a traveler's perspective, we came here on a limited visa. To consider our next destination is quite essential for our lives because in
doing so we enable ourselves to live fully, with far less fear. The
end of one's life is not something one has no feeling about. We are
either scared of it or it is something to actually look forward to.
This does not mean you are rearing to go, and neither am I quite
yet; but we can be more prepared, when such changes occur, to
enjoy the happening.

Fear lives in the gap between "us" and "something else." So
as we become familiar with something that is at first foreign to us,
we become at ease with it. We have all experienced this: with a

new person, a new place or a new country. So, in familiarizing our-selves with the topic of our "life-continuation" we become a lot more comfortable with the whole idea. You may feel a bit peeved that you have to leave home, but how often have you moved house? Life goes on.

Take it from a brain scientist. In her book *My Stroke of Insight: A Brain Scientist's Personal Journey*, Jill Bolte Taylor describes the insights that followed from her stroke:

> *I wondered how I could have spent so many years in my body and never understood that I was just visiting here. This cellular mass of my body had provided me with a marvelous temporary home. It was clear to me that my body functioned like a portal through which the energy of who I am could be beamed into a three dimensional space. . . .*
>
> *I felt like the genie liberated from its bottle. I felt I would never be able to fit the energy of me back into this skin.*

DEATH IS NOT AN END, IT IS AN EXPANSION. It is not a sleep, it is waking up. It is shedding the layer that separates us from the whole, to reveal that which we have always been. It is the redis-covery of our expanded self.

We associate our body with our life: it is the vehicle through which we have been able to express ourselves on Earth. We can't eat chocolate without it, but we can experience the vastness, the magnificence and the perfection of our eternal spiritual identity. That makes up for the chocolate, doesn't it? Be sure that you have thoroughly indulged and enjoyed your body while you have it. It would be a bit of a shame to have to come back all over again just for the chocolate!

It seems to be not all that difficult to leave this home, for mil-lions seem to manage, more or less successfully, every day. The trick of course is to enjoy it. Dying is like childbirth: a natural process, a transition from one phase to the next. You made it into this life and you will make it out, as billions have done before, and you have likely too. It makes sense that throughout our eternal spirit existence we have materialized in and out of form before. We don't need to know *how* to do it. "Just relax…" Trust that we will feel comfortable with where we are going, because that is where we come from. In fact we are neither coming nor going. We simply always *are*.

I met a young woman once who had worked at a clinic for elder people; she told me that the last words half of them say, or yell, are: "I don't want to die." This fear can be avoided. I have been on the other side, and so have many, many others. Countless "Near Death Experiences" (NDEs) have been written about. These are not just brain fantasies because these people are often clinically "brain dead." I urge you to not put the topic off. Read what they have to say! We are alive, we stay alive. You are no deader than when you leave Disneyland. You just used up your ticket to ride.

> *The year was 1975. Back in those days I was one cocky, 25 year old guy who could anticipate a punch, fieldstrip a rifle, and fix a '57 Chevy. Beyond that, quite frankly, I didn't give a damn! I'd never heard of a near-death experience and would not have believed in it even if I had. I never gave any thought to that kind of crap, until the day…*

Dannion Brinkley was struck by lightning, not only once, but twice in his life. He had:

> *…one death and two near-death experiences. Once I was clini-cally dead for 28 minutes… that's dead, nothing near about it. Needless to say, after three times on the other side, I finally saw the light! A lot of things took time to penetrate my thick skull…*

He and others share the highlights of their experiences in a beautiful 28 minutes long film, "Infinity: The Ultimate Trip." It is well documented through Near Death Experiences, which are quite commonly known to doctors and nurses, that at death we leave our body. There is, throughout thousands of accounts, a common theme:

Oh my god! I'm not really dead ~ am I? I mean, my body is dead
~ but I'm floating. I can see my body on the bed...the nurse is
pulling a sheet over my head... everyone is crying. I want to
shout, "Hey, I'm not really dead! I'm alive!"
*   I'm ejected out the top of my head... like a pinpoint of light,*
my energy, my soul... It's as if I shed my skin, like peeling a ba-
nana. It's wonderful to feel so free....no more pain. As I leave my
body, in one whoosh, I seem to grow a little, my light expands...
                    ~ Michael Newton, JOURNEY OF SOULS

We are then pulled by a magnetic force through a kind of tunnel towards a brilliant loving light. Our guides, soul mates, family and friends greet us. When you "die," you are not finished, ended, terminated, obliterated, wiped out, extinct, extinguished and nonexisting! Your life energy is exactly that: *life* energy. You *are* the ongoing energy of life. Life goes on, and on, and on.

～○

Imagine the universe beautiful and just and perfect.
Then be sure of one thing: the Is has imagined it
quite a bit better than you have.
                    ~ Richard Bach, ILLUSIONS

THE FEAR OF DEATH, and for some hell, has been used to control us. How can we overcome this fear? Is it not that, at any time of our lives, we ought to be ready to go in peace?

   Peace comes when we start to see that life is, surprisingly, fair. We have designed our lives with opportunities for our expansion. To make the game spicier they may well be disguised as obstacles. It is the ultimate perfect set up: we can experience different realities depending on our attitude and our viewpoint. We get the world we believe in, and the ability to change it. Karma is not a system of punishment and reward but simply the consequence of our thoughts, feelings and actions. We have all been in hell sometime: caught in the mental and emotional space of doubt, resentment, depression, guilt or hate. The only hell we have to worry about is the one we create for ourselves and for our co-cells. We are, here and there, our own and only judge.

One day your life will flash before your eyes.
Make sure it is worth watching.
~ *Source unknown*

Make your life the kind of book you would like to read! For after leaving this plane we will be treated to a panoramic life review. In that flash we will understand all the whys and "hows." You may very well find that what you consider to be your weaknesses are indeed your strengths, that your "failures" were all for the best. We are always right where we are, even if it doesn't feel like that at the time. When all is said and done, the only judge you have to face is yourself.

So the reason we want to develop compassion for others weaknesses is not to win brownie points. When you get to review your life, in every minute detail, you would like to have compassion for that less conscious person that you too were. For we will see our exchanges with others not only from our own feelings, *but also from theirs*. As in any movie the emotionally charged parts stand out most. Because of our single viewpoint and our rather selective memory, we could be in for surprises, sadness, shocks or sheepishness.

If we are the critical type we will judge ourselves harshly and give ourselves a tough time about our "failings." We may even feel for stringent lessons the next time around. Is it a wonder then that we are all anxious about a potential "judgment day?" Don't kid yourself, because it's not a matter of being religious. It is simply our smaller part being worried about our own possible criticism. This trait is what undermines our sense of worthiness.

We grade ourselves from the perspective of what we had intended to do here, and from knowing the love we are here to display. Do your best to remember what you wanted to experience in this life. To express more love is *always* a good start. I am not threatening you with hell, only with your own disapproval! You won't get anything worse than that.

Fortunately, at our spectacular life review we have our inner coach, our own wiser part, embodied perhaps by a spirit guide, to console us that we didn't fail *too* miserably. Can we match that love? It's all not that serious really, it is the play of life and this is our sand pit! In the end it is less about what we did, than *how we truly feel* about it. This feeling is our resonance. It is the vibration of our feeling that either resonates with the love of our higher self, enabling us to merge with it or, heavy with blame, causes continued separation.

Perhaps we gave ourselves a thumbs down last time and therefore came back to give it another shot! Hence our shaky self esteem, our striving, and our longing for approval. One man reported from his NDE that from the point of expressing unconditional love he had done a horrible job. Years later he was still not over it. It is like putting glasses on and suddenly we can see clear: "Oh, so *that's* what it was all about... Can I try again?"

Once we have seen, then we know, and from knowing *we* judge: this is good, this is bad. That is why judgment is part of death, of our seeing from behind the scenes. If our heart is open we will have compassion, if not we will give ourselves a hard time. It is the same in our daily life: all hell is created, in some way, from our own judgment. With compassion we realize that none of what we felt to be our "mistakes" and "misdoings" was of a bad, sinful, or evil nature but simply out of our unawareness. We did the best we could at the time. Would you blame a baby for not having a beard? So no condemnation of ourselves or others is relevant, only acceptance.

Give it a trial run: dig up some well buried episodes of your past. Having misunderstood and blamed at some time, are you now able to forgive? To love that teenager doing nonsense, that small child always within us, trying so hard to find happiness and approval?

Make yourself at peace with who you are and with everything you did and did not do. Most likely, whatever we all accomplished, we won't feel it was enough! Much of what we wish we had done is finally for our own and other's approval. Seriously consider taking a shortcut: sidestep all that work by just approving of yourself, as you are, now.

When I loved myself enough I redefined success
and life became simple.
~ Kim McMillen, WHEN I LOVED MYSELF ENOUGH

We can always compare ourselves to those who seem to have, or to be, more than us; but why would we, except for inspiration? We are here to love ourselves, as we are, where we are, and to know we are okay. Suddenly the world around us looks brighter. The pushing stops, the trust begins. You are not defective, insufficient, and in the wrong place. You are beautiful, just as you are, and so are all the mirrors around you.

We are all human and have, in different disguises, the same issues around self approval and trust. How much acceptance and compassion we have for ourselves is a vital factor in both our daily life and our onward journey. This has never been truer than in these times: for *our feelings* determine the reality we recreate. Fortunately the influx of information and light coming in now is most conducive to our growing in understanding and love. Soak it up, relax, and keep your daily life in perspective. When faced with something larger, the small stuff quickly fades to various shades of insignificance.

AFTER MY FATHER DIED I met up with my family. It was then that I was granted another glimpse into the eternity that words cannot portray. It was a hot day and I walked out with my brother and sister down to the river. We stood there, on its banks, in silence. My mind went blank in the still summer air and it seemed a vast space opened up around me. I felt therein the enormity of our soul journey, how connected we were through the ages, and how life had brought us together once again. The silence felt sacred, not empty but full of knowing. The river flowed slowly past, inexorably, the river of life that takes all with it. It was a long time before anyone spoke.

∽

I HADN'T SEEN MY FATHER IN YEARS and that was hard enough, but for my sister it was worse. She was staying with our parents at the time of his parting, and she was pregnant and moody. One evening she didn't respond to his "Good night." The next day he left early morning to work and never returned.

It feels tragic, irreparable, but what do we know? Perhaps it was part of the script. Years later I watched an interview with Jessica Schab. At sweet little sixteen she had told her dad that she hated him and he had died that night of a heart attack. You can imagine how she felt. She later learned that there was a soul arrangement between them: because they were so attached to each other, she would have to give him a sign so he would know when to leave her. I wrote that to my sister.

Still, my dad leaving so unexpectedly made me feel we want to love while we can, and to always stay even with people so we have no regrets. Don't leave anything nice unsaid. Whatever your differences, when some-body dies you will just want that person to know that you love them.

The first time I met my father after he had passed on was, as it often is, in the dream space. My heart soared when I saw him standing there. I threw my arms around his neck saying, "I love you, I love you." Then I jumped back and exclaimed, "Oh, but you're dead now! I cry so much when I think of you, what should I do?"

You can guess what he replied! "Just relax."

Looking back at my own grief I often wished I had taken my dad's departure lighter. I forgave myself that weakness a long 20 years later when I told a very close friend about his death: "I was 27 when he died. I took it really hard."

Zephyr, 26, looked right into me from across the room, across the space and the years that seemed to separate us, and quietly said, "Of course you did."

I am guessing I am not the only one in the world who can be hard on herself. This is why we yearn for approval: because we judge ourselves. Instead of beating ourselves up for what we think we are not, it is high time to love ourselves for what we are. We are all earnest individuals seeking to do our best in this seemingly confusing world. Take note that to be our best includes times of not being at our best. Because it is not about forcing anything, not about being good or better, but about being and loving *the totality* of who we are.

Understand your inner child, your weaknesses, the insecure parts within yourself, and give them some love. And with time you will realize we are not alone in a cruel and random world. We are always connected to our expanded self, to the whole, and to the cosmic laws, which are, truly and honestly, fair and loving. This may not be obvious at first glance, but if we are willing to tilt our heads a bit, to twist our necks and to peer through the smoke-screen, we could be in for a big surprise.

CHAPTER FOUR

Beyond the Veil

If the doors of perception were cleansed,
everything would appear to man as it truly is ~ infinite.
~ William Blake

LET'S STEP BACK IN TIME to my early days in India, with my first partner. After some months of traipsing around the country we went to Kodaikanal, a laid-back southern hill station. A welcome break, or so I thought, from the intensity of new impressions and input that floods one when traveling in India. One day, my partner went for a long walk and I strolled down to the village for lunch. I found a quiet little place boasting "Special Mushroom Soup" and avocado toast. It was certainly the tastiest mushroom soup ever, a dark flavor, a bit heavy on the pepper. I was back at our old colonial room when my stomach started churning. I was feeling more than a bit queasy and I guessed it was the avocado at battle with the mushrooms and cream. As it became more intense I started to worry if those "locally grown mushrooms" were in fact safe to eat. Finally it calmed down and I laughed at my own insecurity.

When my friend returned I was sitting on the edge of the hill-side, gazing across the wide valley to the blue mountains on the other side. "You know what," I said flippantly, "I could fly over there. And the funny thing is, my body would drop down and everybody would think I was dead." I chuckled wholeheartedly at this idea. "I wouldn't be dead of course, because we don't die."

He knew this of course from Hindu teachings, yet still he looked oddly at me, "Are you okay?"

I had never felt better. As if my blinders had been removed, hidden secrets were arising from the depths of time. I felt such peace, at one with the world. I watched the sun set ever so slowly and "oohhed" and "aahed" at the glorious show of changing colors in the sky.

The clouds had depth and content, ever morphing. I wondered how come I had never noticed that before. My partner, a bit put out by my over-enthusiasm, went inside to light a fire. I noticed that the boulder next to me was made up of many colors: reds and greens and gold. How could one possibly paint that? I picked up a small stone and looked at it from all sides. Every little detail was enhanced. It was fascinating to me and I seemed to get absorbed for ages, like a young child, just gazing into it.

Finally I got up, a bit wobbly on my feet, and sort of floated indoors. I felt almost weightless, walking lightly across the vibrant grass where every blade stood out clearly. The room was dimly lit. Fruits were glowing in a dark corner, as if from their own inner light. I curled up on the sheepskin in front of the fireplace, transfixed by the flames flowing, dancing and caressing the wood. I sank inwards. Words seemed to emanate from the fire. "You are not Amber... of these parents... this address... You are the spirit inside of you, immortal, everlasting."

I closed my eyes and felt myself dissolve, gently shaken apart. Everything I thought I was floated away. I was not solid, or separate, anymore. As though a vast space opened up within me, my being expanded, spanning all dimensions back to source.

I felt myself a part of something indescribable, infinite, otherworldly, endless, eternal. An inseparable part of the All, and all that is. What a beautiful feeling! So relaxing, so familiar. Of course, this is who I am! It is who I have always been, and will always be. I didn't know how I could possibly have ever forgotten the obvious: I am an energy stream, a vibration. I am flowing, fluid, like colors swirling and patterns dancing, touching and shaping other streams around me. We are all related, all connected and intertwined, as we blend and merge and intermingle.

When I opened my eyes everything else was fluid and seamless too. I could sense the aliveness in all around me. The cushions, the candles, and even the walls lost solidity, shifting as though

made of jelly, their once limited and fixed boundaries flowing outwards. My friend had put on the Moody Blues and the familiar
songs took on a totally new dimension. Time expanded. Each song
seemed to last an hour. I could hear every note, every instrument,
their harmonies enhanced by their individuality, and I drifted on
them to divine inner spaces.

I thought my body was probably dying. I remembered an
aunt saying how at peace she had felt as a child when she was
drowning. The mushrooms must have been poisonous! I felt I
should be, maybe, more worried, but I realized dying didn't matter,
I was still me. Simply without my body, my borders and my concerns. Not only was I still very much alive, I was fully reunited with
the totality of my being. It felt much more like I was being born.

I wondered why there is so much separation made between
the states of being alive here and being alive on the other side. It's
pretty much the same, just less solid. Of course, if you are not
aware of the being that you are inside your body, then death
sounds like a pretty terminal condition.

I decided to tell my partner. It was difficult to move my
awareness back into my body and away from that state of utter
peace and bliss. I made a huge effort to pull myself together and
realized I was actually pulling myself apart from my wholeness,
separating again from the essential world. I was re-identifying
with my limited personality, reasserting my old identity, putting
on my coat.

To my surprise, when I told him I was dying he started to
laugh. His face was very strong and bright, distorting, his spirit
shining through. I felt, "Oh well, if he doesn't care, I certainly
don't!" He then told me they were "magic mushrooms" which
grew up here, and that I shouldn't worry, we could talk in the
morning. Morning seemed a million years away but that was fine
for me. I closed my eyes, let go, and returned back to bliss land.
Fusing back into the oneness, at one with my vast being.

For hours in front of the glowing embers, I explored the morphing and flowing within me and the revelations that surfaced.
On the long, slow return to earth, I languished in the feeling of
peace and laughed at the oddity that was my body.

Dawn found me feeling very open, fragile, as though newly born. The world had now crystallized back from its energetic landscape to its usual solid state and the rocks, however hard I peered at them, were plain grey.

My friend filled me in:

There are various sacred plants that induce a spiritual, mystical experience as one's awareness shifts out of one's mind to a larger part of our being. One goes through a psychological "death" as all the parts that form our limited ego identity ~ our name, our profession, our personality ~ are unceremoniously removed. We are left with the eternal infinite being we have always been. Thus reunited with that all-knowing level of consciousness, some exclaim: "I am Jesus!" Mystics who are already in that place of wider awareness do not even feel any effect. In ethnic societies shamans would take these substances in order to gain knowledge of our inner energy world and thus be able to inform and guide their people.

It's called a "trip" because one appears to journey on it to another dimension. Of course you are not going anywhere, just seeing what is within. Psychedelic substances free our mind of its ordinary patterns and structures that allow us to see only the world of matter. One thus becomes aware of the energy field that is within everything. You do not "hallucinate," you have simply shifted your viewpoint; and this changes your perception of the world. You are going deeper inside, seeing the same reality from a different perspective. You are peering behind the scenes.

Albert Einstein and other pioneers of modern physics described the energetic nature of our reality which is being widely confirmed these days by science (as we will see in chapter 25). It is very multi-layered. We can access one level, the astral plane, in a lucid dream: our landscape takes on a very bright, vibrant, luminescent quality. It is similar when we die: the outer, physical layer drops off and we rediscover the light-imbued energetic nature of our being.

This light-energy, or life-energy, is in everything but more easy to grasp in a fresh fruit, a flower or a butterfly, than in our coffee mug or the wall. Since they are less dense, the aliveness shines through. We can see it in a young child's face more easily than in a politician's.

In an altered state of consciousness we shift to where the veil is thinner. We see that the world is really less solid than it usually appears. We finally understand the cryptic teachings: "The material world is illusion." We glimpse the energetic existence that is the base of the physical world. Because matter is less dense the world has a more luminous quality. Forms are still there but less solid, more fluid.

It can be a bit disconcerting to watch normally reliable objects and faces becoming floppy and flowing out of the confines of their normal contours. It's rather funny to have something lose its shape in one's hand, or have the dough one is kneading expand uncontrollably and attempt to flow off the baking tray! In that dimension its energy is no longer strictly bound by the physical laws of our limited time-space reality, and nor is ours.

We normally perceive the world as solid, separate bodies, yet when we can widen to also know our energetic inner being, we become aware of our non-locality, because, in fact, we exist everywhere. A friend described tripping with Timothy Leary: "I looked out at my VW beetle and I knew it took me from here to there but in that state of consciousness I couldn't quite make sense of that. I knew that I was everywhere and therefore there was really no difference between here and there. I was with some friends, and at one point, being out of my body-awareness, I didn't know which one of us I was, and I knew, too, that it didn't really matter."

We come to recognize that we are, indeed, linked to everyone and everything. Without the mind our sense of time also stops, and it seems such a funny idea to cut infinity up into tiny boxes and call them hours! Being more in the present, I perceived time very much slower. I was also fully aware of the presence of eternity, the zone of no-time. Our Being spans many dimensions, many levels of consciousness. I know these are far out concepts, yet it validates what physics tells us about non-locality and the relativity of time. A good description is that the interval of one hour, or one day, remains the same but the amount of happening, the feeling of time, within that interval varies, depending on our point of perception, our degree of awareness.

This is not as far out as it seems. We will see in later chapters why we all have these days this feeling of greater intensity. It is not really that time is moving faster, but rather that as our consciousness expands we experience more happening within a set time frame ~ a day, a week, or a year ~ than ever before.

A mind-expanding substance is a window, not a door. It can show us places but not take us there, refresh our memory but not permanently enlighten us. It is only to be taken in the best circumstances as it can be otherwise unsettling. Every trip is different, depending on our state of mind, our emotional steadiness, our focus and the brand. Always check with your doctor before use!

I am deeply grateful for this most insightful experience that broadened my understanding of life, as it has for many mainstream and influential members of our society, including artists, writers, musicians and scientists. On the dullest of days I look around, knowing that just beneath the surface the place is brimming with conscious energy. I remember that whatever is going on in the world is backed by this field of live intelligence.

If you have ever seen a "Magic Eye" book you may be able to imagine how there are other invisible dimensions within our one. Staring at the flat 2D pages one is amazed to find fully in-depth 3D pictures hidden within. It is interesting to note, that in order to see this other dimension, you do have to take your focus off the picture on the page. It is the same with our apparent world picture.

OVER 20 YEARS AFTER MY TRIP I found science and spirituality coming together as Jill Taylor Bolte, brain scientist, described her mystical experience from undergoing a stroke. Reading her book *My Stroke of Insight: A Brain Scientist's Personal Journey*, I exclaimed: "This is it. This describes the same experience!"

No longer capable of perceiving temperature, vibration, pain or body position, your awareness of your physical boundaries shifts. The essence of your energy expands as it blends with the energy around you... Those little voices inside your head reminding you of who you are and where you live become silent. You lose memory connection to your old emotional self and the richness of this moment, right here, right now, captivates your perception. Everything, including the life force you are, radiates pure energy. With childlike curiosity your heart soars in peace and your mind explores new ways of swimming in a sea of euphoria. Then ask yourself, how motivated would you be to come back to a highly structured routine?

I liked knowing I was fluid. I loved knowing my spirit was at one with the universe and in flow with everything around me. I found it fascinating to be so tuned in to energy dynamics and body language. Most of all I loved the feelings of deep inner peace that flooded the core of my being.

I relate these stories because death, and sometimes life, can be disquieting if we are not aware of this version of reality. Indeed, we don't need to leave our bodies to experience the rest of our being. In fact it seems likely that we shall all be granted such an illuminating insight.

NOT THAT LONG AGO, in Tonga, I had a most interesting meeting. Picture me sitting in an internet café, checking my email. I suddenly look outside and see a young guy walking past. I feel to rush out and say hello... but I think, "You can't just rush out 'cause there's a cute blond guy walking past and say 'Hi'." So I didn't. The next day, I saw him at his backpacker's reception, and again I resisted the urge to rush across the street. When I went there some days later, he had left. I reminded myself that one can't really miss things in life and, if they are really meant to happen, they will.

A couple weeks later I flew out to the capital, Tongatapu. From there I had another flight to Fiji. I walked into the airport and there was only one other foreigner there. Guess who? This time I went up and said, "Hi." We connected well on the plane and went to stay at the same resort. One day I saw a small cross around his neck and asked him about it. He told me his story. As a rational German, he had never believed in anything "spiritual." Then one day, he was at a backpackers in New Zealand, sitting quietly on his bed. He was not stoned in any way. Something happened he could barely describe. As though Grace had descended on him, he became aware of the multiple levels of his being and how they were all finer and finer layers of personality. At the base of all was just pure being, and that Being was everything. He sat there with a big smile on his face the whole time, 20 minutes or so, in a state of total peace and bliss. I told him, as others had, that this was the state of Oneness that Zen monks would meditate a lifetime for, while facing a blank wall!

There is a picture that comes close to explaining our inherent wholeness and godliness: God is the ocean, we are each a droplet. The drop has the same properties as the ocean. When the drop enters the ocean, there is no more distinction between it and the ocean. It is still a drop and yet is has reconnected to the whole, it has merged. They fuse into one. It has been said: the drop becomes the ocean.

The most graphic description simply cannot portray how blissful it feels to be immersed in that space of peace and oneness. Little black squiggles on paper just can not describe the multidimensionality of the universe! It is impossible to convey that this lies all within us. It is similar to going inside the tiny tent described in one Harry Potter book to find a massive, multi-storey palace unfolding within.

> *To see the world in a grain of sand*
> *And heaven in a wild flower*
> *Hold infinity in the palm of your hand*
> *And eternity in an hour.*
>
> ~ *William Blake*

MANY OF THE BEAUTIFUL PEOPLE I have met around the globe, with perspective, awareness and values, have used sacred plants at some stage that have shown them the other realms. I can totally understand the desire to escape this one and therefore to use drugs regularly. But we chose this realm to develop approval, so escapism doesn't really help us out there. Psychedelics are an eye-opener, an inspiration and a teacher, but in the end we have to make the journey on our own. Otherwise it would be too easy, like cheating. Habitual use prevents one from enlightening and strengthening the lower rungs that enable us to reach those realms by ourselves. To build high we need a solid foundation, and we are aiming high. Or so it looks to us from this end! It's probably not, just a big step for man and a tiny step for humankind.

Once we know there is so much more, we tend to ask, "Why are we enclosed in this limited time-space reality?" The reasons are manifold, interwoven aspects of a vaster, multilayered, cosmic picture.

How our human race first got into this separated reality is of course debatable. Perhaps it is the fruit of natural expansion, wonder, exploration and creation; a meandering dream-journey that took us increasingly further from source and hence increasingly into matter, density, doubt and a sense of disconnectedness. At earlier times we have been more aware of our inner connection. Yet, sensing that this separation is part of a natural cycle and the universe is unfolding as it should, how does this stage of our history serve us?

Being isolated from the whole is the way we grow individually. In the same way a child needs to leave home to find itself, this separation and our experience allows us to develop our uniqueness. And as we discover the potential of *our creative power,* we become harmonious instruments for the expression of consciousness on Earth.

Consciousness cannot be imposed on matter, anymore than our own knowledge can be imposed on someone else. Only through experience can it become *incorporated.* Hence we are the bridge, the link between awareness and matter, the living tools that channel spirit into form. It is through our lives that we are each founding the relationship in which the light of consciousness gradually seduces the physical realm with its charm.

It is the same relationship we are building within ourselves. Our three-dimensional perception limits us to living in our smaller part, isolated from our larger self, so we may become aware of our own small, unloved parts ~ that we have isolated. Life here steers us to feel the density of the resistance, the disapproval, and the hurt we carry, and by integrating these aspects of the earthborn psyche, we deepen our acceptance, compassion, and trust. As we finally unite with these separate parts, as we embrace our wholeness, we become reunited with our greater being, quietly waiting for us to feel the love.

If our true purpose and identity were revealed too early we would likely be overwhelmed. We are currently sheltered in this dream reality, protected from seeing too much too soon ~ for if we saw the glory of it all at once we could crumble in comparison. Seeds await, enclosed, in the darkness of the earth, and one spring day they burst forth.

We can trust that when we are ready, the door opens.

CHAPTER FIVE

Soul Journey

~~~

We live only once… but that's forever.

~ Step JurJahn

THREE YEARS AFTER I had left the office life and boarded that first plane to India, I had that mind-expanding experience, my daughter's birth and my father's death behind me. After this eye-opening insight into the beyond, my inquisitive mind kept gathering puzzle pieces, but one does not grow from transcendental knowledge unless one can integrate it and use it for the benefit of one's smaller being.

I had seen that life and death are like night and day. "Death" is when we wake up. I concluded the following. It is not the events of our life that matter, but what we have gained from them. Not what we achieve, but who we become through our endeavors and experiences. All we take with us is what we have become, and the only way to become more is to love more.

Life is the same on both sides of the coin; it follows the same logic, the same fundamental laws. This is not just projecting our world into the hereafter; it goes the other way around: this physical world is a reflection of that one. It is founded on the energy worlds; like the outer layer of the onion, it depends on the inner layers to exist. We are, first and foremost, an energetic being. It is the underlying, all pervasive energy world that governs how things work here on the physical level.

Hence we move through the spirit worlds in exactly the same way we do here: what we are, how we think, feel and express ourselves, creates our reality. It is *our energetic vibration* that draws us into the appropriate situation. We go where we fit. That is how we ended up here together, after all. So we don't have to worry how we will proceed from this Earth when the time comes, or what will happen to us next week, or in 2012, for everything follows energetic laws and takes care of itself. All we need to take care of is our "vibe:" our emotional resonance.

We each bring into this world a certain possibility, an outline, a rough sketch of our potential destiny. Through our actions, our thoughts and our feelings we color in this sketch. We thus enrich our painting, which becomes our signature, our boarding pass, imprinted with the colors of who we are. The essence of what we have become, *created*, through the experiences of this life ~ our resonance ~ is our blueprint. It is, energetically, the river we ride to our next destination, the pathway to our individual and collective destiny.

Some live in the great hope that we will be wiped clean when we leave. Sorry to disillusion you guys but, to a large degree, we remain us! This is why we want to come to terms with ourselves. There is no absolution ~ for there is no blame ~ except for our own.

> *In the ecology of the soul, you are not allowed to leave without the darkness, as the last thing that's needed is billions of bits of unclaimed psychological sewage floating around the celestial lost and found department.*
> ~ Stuart Wilde, THE ART OF REDEMPTION

We take some personality with us, at least to the next level. After a friend had died, I happened to meet him in my dream body on a "beach." I was surprised to see him. "You look good," I remarked.

He replied with his usual pride, a bit put out, "I always look good!" I had to laugh, it was so typically him! We talked a bit until he had to leave, into a space where an elder being awaited him.

Picture yourself like a tall multi-storey building. You are living on all floors at once, but while you are in the ground floor, you, your body part, is not aware of the rest of you. You actually span the whole building, in more and more glorious levels up to the top floor which is divinity. The bottom floor cannot talk to or understand the top floor. Still they are all one. When we leave our bodies, we usually don't get to become enlightened right away. We are the same old us, just without the lower floor. That floor stands empty, while we have just moved upstairs.

This picture generally works for our linear minds. However, more accurately, all that you are is rather enfolded within you, expanding to infinity. This is something our linear minds have more difficulty to grasp! We are the spirit of life. The part of us in body, in form, is unaware of our larger part, which is fully immersed in the infinite and the eternal.

We are multilayered beings currently limited to seeing only our first floor. Looking at it from another angle, what we think of as us, here on Earth, is just the little part of us that was not in full agreement, or in love, with itself and the world. Such a feeling is energetically dense, equivalent to, and thus creating, this density of matter that is the material plane. So it is the energetic quality of this part of me that brought it into the physical world. Whatever is not in the light vibration of love, like the heavy resonance of judgment, blame and guilt, drops to the bottom floor. For the lower the frequency of the feeling, the greater the density it creates. We experience this in our daily lives: when we raise our own vibration, through our acceptance, trust, and love we enter a lighter feeling, a brighter reality. The exact same shift happens on a larger scale. It is through this change of frequency, of our collective vibration, that we are already creating a new world paradigm.

We are all here at this time to brighten our ground floor, our foundation. From this ground floor, we can access the cellar of our being, our shadow: the unloved, unacknowledged parts that have been stored away and buried within, our stored pain. We can bring into this cellar, that is our subconscious, the light of our awareness and the warmth of our love which we receive from our higher floors. It is thus that we build the link that reunites us with our expanded being. Dannion Brinkley reports from his extended near death experience:

> *Even more astonishing for me was the fact that, as multi-dimensional beings, there are aspects of us, in the totality of our being,*

that are doing this powerful work in several places at the same
time. I don't know about you, but I found those were some pretty
wild and cosmic perspectives to grip!

    I always thought one life held quite enough spiritual
intrigue for me to handle. Then to discover that we co-exist with
ourselves in multiple lives on multi-levels of consciousness was a
huge leap for me. Nevertheless, I knew it was true. And you
know, it sure helped me to understand why we need so much
sleep at night. Think about it. With all the work we're doing on
so many levels, no wonder we feel tired all the time!

    Through our multilayered existence, on those subtle levels of
our being, we have far more exchange with others, than we are
aware of here. We often work things out together in those planes,
such as pointers and "chance" meetings, which explains a lot of
synchronicities. Seeds are planted, and we receive tips and guidance through inner hunches. Sometimes we can remember significant encounters that occurred in the dream plane. My first year in
India I met a very gentle, powerful, well-traveled Indian yogi. His
passport showed him to be way older than he looked. Sometime
later in Nepal I saw him one night in a dream, but it had such a different quality to it that I instantly asked him, "Is this a dream?"

    He replied, "No, this is a meeting." He had come to ask me a
certain question, I answered and he left. After numerous encounters, I came to accept that we can rendezvous in the next plane.
Just behind the thin veil of the solid world, we each have an energetic body-mind which moves by focus and intent.

    One day my partner had shown me a new hibiscus flower in
the garden. "It's apricot color," he said.

    "It's rather peach," I replied, and tried, unsuccessfully of
course, to explain the subtle difference. The next morning I awoke
out of a vivid dream encounter with a close friend. He was sitting,
as usual, in front of the computer, in what we named the "comput-
eroptus addicticus" chair. I asked him if the color was peach or
apricot. Ever the diplomat he replied "Yes."

    I asked him again and he came up with another smart an-
swer. "But really?" I insisted.

He looked at me with eyes far brighter, far more vibrant, than in physical reality and softly said, "Amber, it really doesn't matter." I realized instantly from the vivid brilliance of his eyes that this wasn't just a normal dream, and woke up laughing over the truth of the message.

CHAPTER SIX

The Joys of Traveling

*In order to live freely and happily you must sacrifice
boredom. It is not always an easy sacrifice.*
~ *Richard Bach,* ILLUSIONS

AS IF BEING A VISITOR to this planet isn't quite challenging
enough, one can complicate one's life even further by frequently
moving around the globe. I lived my early years in numerous
houses, five schools and six countries. Thanks to this upbringing,
and because none of those places felt like home to me, traveling
came naturally.

The nomadic lifestyle is not quite as glamorous as you might
imagine, yet it is certainly an efficient training ground for these
times. I joke that, even though travel has become a lot easier these
days, the plus points of this itinerant lifestyle still are:

> ~ *Much of the time you have little idea where you are going
> until you get there.*
> ~ *It makes you acutely aware that you are always a beginner,
> and a visitor.*
> ~ *It reminds you there is so much more to life, and always more
> ground to cover.*
> ~ *Rather than preparing for what you do know, you frequently
> have to prepare for what you don't.*
> ~ *The best-laid plans usually have to be thrown out the window.*
> ~ *You constantly, and often rapidly, have to figure out new situ-
> ations you find yourself in.*
> ~ *You can't settle long into the feeling of having reached some-
> where, knowing that you always have to move on.*

~ You repeatedly have to leave your comfort zone, everything you just have become familiar with, behind.
~ You have to make numerous choices everyday, the outcome of which can make a considerable and possibly drastic difference to your comfort, your security, or your digestion.

I therefore fully appreciate that traveling is not everyone's ideal way of life, however I have it in my blood and in my stars. And for those who have adopted this unsettled lifestyle, the nomad is precisely, despite appearances, what his name suggests: No mad! At times I do, indeed, get weary of moving; but still, the benefits are unbeatable. It keeps one flexible and open-minded. It steers one to become responsible and discerning. It develops both our self reliance and our appreciation of others. It is a great training in acceptance, adaptability, and widening. We learn to let go and trust in the outcome.

Every time you step into an Indian bus, at times hurtling down snaky mountain roads in the dead of night, you deliver your life. You frequently recognize it is not in your own hands. A memorable horse ride took me once along a very narrow track that was cut into the mountain edge along a ravine: on one side was the steep rock face and on the other a plummeting drop to the icy river. Atheist that I was, I prayed! Indeed, I have lived much of my life on the edge, and these situations have made me often grateful for my life. I will narrate one of the scariest incidents, for its comic value.

One night in India, when sleeping by the beach, I woke up to see a bare-breasted bandit holding a machete to my partner's throat while requesting him, "No violence, please!" This was rather comical in the circumstances, but I admit the humor was lost on me in that moment. My partner was quick to reassure him, "No, no... don't worry... no violence." The dacoit, one of five such men, then asked where our money was.

"We keep it in the village," my partner lied, "it's not safe out here."

The bandit agreed: "You are right, it's not safe out here." My heart was thumping so loud I was sure he could hear it. "Is that your wife and child?" he asked. I was praying that our seven year old daughter was still asleep and wouldn't pipe up in reply.

"Yes," my partner answered curtly.

"Good they are sleeping," he said in his broken English.

This incident reminded me of a really humorous Argentinean group I met once on the roof of a bus. Indian bus roofs can be a popular place to ride as they offer more air, space and view than inside. As we started the long climb over a high altitude pass into Ladahk, the bus driver got us all down, saying it wasn't safe. So we sat in the back of the bus and one by one we crawled out of the window and back onto the roof. The panoramic view from up there, of the snow-clad Himalayas and the Tibetan style steppes dotted with little shrines, was just too memorable to miss. At the end of the trip, one of the Argentineans gifted me with his parting words: *"Whatever* happens in life, don't lose your sense of humor!"

ONE GROWS TO TAKE such a varied life for granted, yet I am often reminded that most days traveling are unusual to some degree. You often don't know where you will spend the night and sometimes don't know where you are when you awaken. When this happens I savor this rare feeling of just being alive on Earth, and try to hold my brain off from figuring out which place or country I'm in.

Life is everyday different. It's here today, gone tomorrow. You become well aware that everything changes. You learn that there are twists in life that don't care for our best-laid plans, and that always help us somehow on our way. This encourages you to be flexible, spontaneous, and to leave attachments constantly behind.

With such freedom comes responsibility. Amidst many options you make multiple choices daily and realize how they affect you. You may well end up wet, cold, tired and hungry. I didn't always make the most enjoyable choices but that's how I found out! So increasingly, you learn to listen out for tips and follow inner guidance. You learn to look ahead and you learn to quickly change course.

Every day you meet new people and face new situations. You live much in the open, exposed, and you encounter, often at close quarters, all types of people. Usually the British talk about the weather, the Americans talk about money, Indians talk about

God, and Australians about fishing, and no one talks about their feelings. Yet whatever our diverse viewpoints and opinions that appear to keep us separate, you discover that at the base we all *feel* the same.

Living less sheltered and more exposed, you become aware of your own vulnerability and you often see the fragile and warm side of our multicolored human race. Perhaps your flight is delayed, once again. You set up camp in the airport amidst your fellow passengers, who are happily snoring in various languages. Some locals share their dinner with you and a small child curls up in your lap.

Years ago I received the following mail from a fellow traveler:

> *I remember that great 'trip feeling' I had brought home with me...what's left now? Pictures, memories, songs, sadness... Sadness, because traveling we meet so many beautiful people, all the time; everybody is open-minded and wants to change the world... Here, it's routine, disillusion, and fun is all about getting wasted... I guess, if you're used to that, you can not realize how much better it can be.*

If you haven't experienced other cultures then you may not realize just how much we are influenced by the particular ~ and often peculiar ~ mindset of our own nation. By the education, the social conduct, the language, the media and of course, the weather! Interacting with a range of people from around the globe, you soon notice that there are many other ways of exchanging, thinking, and feeling.

I greatly enjoyed living in non-western cultures where people are mostly more relaxed, smiley, and gentle. It is very heart-opening. Largely because their societies are less separatist, competitive and pressuring, these races are still more connected, trusting, flexible and intuitive. More in the moment and in the flow, they are less fixed on timings. You learn that to be waiting doesn't really matter. You have to be *somewhere* anyway so you might as well relax *wherever you are*.

You come to see how adaptable we humans are and how easy it is to change your circumstances. It may take a long time to decide where to go next, yet once you have made that step, onto the plane, within a day you can wake up somewhere totally new. The novelty is always exciting.

You are in the plane above the cotton wool clouds, leaving the last page behind. The next page is a totally blank sheet. The cities' skyscrapers look like huge tombstones, and you marvel at the amazing patterns of Earth's rivers, fields, deserts and mountains. And as you rise above the clouds you are greeted by the sun and you remember that it is always shining. The awesome views remind you how small we are, and whatever we can outwardly achieve here, however high the mountain or social ladder that we climb, is nothing that we can take with us. What counts in the end is not measured in meters, or in dollars, but in the beauty and richness of our soul.

Traveler's Tales

I ONCE MET A MOST EXOTIC, olive-skinned girl and was wondering where she could be from. "I'm English," she said.

I tried another approach, "And which blood are you?"

"Oh," she replied, "A positive."

So I rephrased my question! "What are your ethnic origins?" She was a most unlikely combination of Burmese, Greek and Bolivian. Cultures are intermingling worldwide making for the most beautiful children. Humankind is naturally coming together, blending and thus expanding. While some old cultures are being absorbed, a new race of world citizens is being born.

This is not only happening on an ethnic level. I have kept contact with people from all over the world and I see how everyone is observing the same phenomenon: a great expansion of the human mind is taking place on the planet. In some progressive pockets it is openly apparent, whilst in other places it is not. Yet if we look deeper it is there too, as an undercurrent throughout the population. This is a collective awakening that has nothing to do with anyone's level of education or social position. It has to do with the changing seasons.

ONE FUN ASPECT OF TRAVELING is that people on the move are rather open. The time you have together with fellow travelers is expected to be short, so you make the most of it. You meet a lot of ordinary people, all sorts, and they tell you the intriguing things they have experienced. They are not trying to sell you anything, nor is it, as you could imagine, a social game of who has got the bigger and better story. They are just seeking answers to the curious incidents in their life. Among the very many stories that got me thinking, here is just a handful.

In a small beach resort in Sri Lanka, many moons ago, I saw a tourist reading a book underneath a palm tree. Over an hour later he got up, placed his book on the chair, and walked away. He hadn't done five steps when a coconut smashed the seat of his chair. He told me he had felt a sudden urge to get up and stretch his legs. Another traveler had pitched his tent under some trees. In the middle of the night, from deep sleep, he suddenly sat bolt upright. In that very moment a coconut crashed through the canvas of his tent onto the pillow behind him.

Someone else told me how a psychic had foretold his mother of an incident he would have a few years down the road. This occurred, along with precise details, as predicted.

I know one young guy who fell off a 15 meters high cliff. He separated automatically from his body as it fell, understandably not wanting to go down there, and found himself in a space of utter "out-of-this-world" peace and warmth. He didn't want to leave that haven, but moments later he was back in his body, feeling a bit rough around the edges!

One traveler spoke of a schoolmate who was in a coma as a child after having been shot. From then on he was, rather unwillingly, open to other planes. "Dead" people would give him messages for their families. They could prove their identity by using pet names or personal incidents that only their loved ones would know.

Another man was trapped under his boat, drowning. The last thing he remembered was having given up and a feeling of peace. When he came back to his senses, he was lying on the upturned hull. Similarly, children speak of being rescued from drowning by people in white when, indeed, nobody was around.

Sometimes I save an ant from spiraling down the kitchen sink drain and I can just picture it, back at home, telling its friends how it was dying. "Suddenly there was torrential water everywhere and I was being swept away towards this giant cavern. There was no way to escape! And then all of a sudden I was flying through the air, lifted to safety and found myself back on the ground. God saved me man!" Miracles, like magic, are simply what we cannot yet explain.

One evening in the remote highlands of western Turkey, a friend of mine saw at a distance a large creature that appeared to be a bear, moving at around 40kms per hour parallel to his car. All four people in the car then witnessed the creature get up on two legs and run for cover without reducing speed.

An American businessman and his crew, sailing one night, saw a large unidentifiable green glow just below the surface of the dark ocean. A bunch of bewildered Sri Lankan fishermen reported a UFO coming out of the water to a baffled police officer. A catholic priest was perplexed by gentle alien beings contacting him while he was in deep prayer. At this point my "open" box was bursting at the seams!

Road to a New Dawn

NEWTONIAN PHYSICS long tried to understand the world by dividing it into different subjects that could be studied and explained singly. Yet it was unable to find the conclusive core answers because indeed, at the core, all is one. More recently, breakthroughs in science paint a picture of an interconnected universe. We are starting to recognize beyond doubt that we and our world are not merely physical, separate, three-dimensional bodies but that we do have an energetic existence which works "behind the scenes." Science is starting to understand spiritual fields that ancient traditions have long since known of, such as the law of attraction, alternative healing methods and ESP.

The first evidence of the law of attraction I came across decades ago in India. On the road, staying healthy is a primary issue. I soon started to see a blatant correlation between one's feelings and one's health. Over the years I observed that some, those who had trust, could eat anything; whereas others, those who were anxious, would eat very carefully and still get sick. So when I heard early on that debilitating thoughts undermine our health, I could validate that. In a medical science experiment it was found that when people ate a decadent dessert while feeling guilt and shame their immunity dropped. When the same dessert was eaten with joy and relish the immunity strengthened. Regarding the amount of dis-ease in India I would point to their core belief, reinforced by religion, that the body and earthly life is essentially "bad." This causes constant emotional split.

Our body speaks to us. If we are truly happy, in agreement with ourselves on all levels, we do not get sick. As simplistic as it sounds, if bugs of any type get to us we may like to ask ourselves, "Is something else bugging me?" If we are truly at peace, no doubts, no person and no bacteria can affect our resonance.

Sickness indicates an inner conflict. The nature of the sickness, and the part of our body where it occurs, indicate the emotional area of the dis-ease within us. The symptoms thus help us to find the cause and therefore need not be seen as a problem but acknowledged as part of our deeper healing process.

Many western-trained doctors are starting to recognize that the mind and body are not separate entities and now embrace a more holistic approach. Western medicine is the way of the yang, or male mind. "Feeling bad miss? It's not an issue, I can fix it. Take these pills and you'll be fine by tomorrow. Next please!" Holistic medicine is the yin, or female way. It validates the feelings of the body-mind. It allows them to be expressed, through the sickness, and in that way, it tunes into the cause.

To suppress the dis-ease that is felt with drugs, to patch it up and cover it over, is not healing. It stifles the voice of our body. It is just procrastinating. Being sick naturally leads us to a quiet state where we can look deeper. We may deprive ourselves of that quietness, and take pills so we can keep on working in the outside world, not realizing that our inner work is where it's really at. But if our body-mind is not happy with what we are doing, do we then see the folly of taking pills so we can keep on with our activity?

In the same way sickness in our bodies is the red flag, the current symptoms of dis-ease on the planet are glaringly apparent. This is the wake of the turning tide. We are simply being guided to look within. It is certainly helpful to recognize which way the tide is going. It becomes easier to ride the new wave when we know something about it.

UNTIL RECENTLY THE WORLD was going through an outgoing cycle; our history has been one of outer development, action and productivity. We are now moving into an ingoing cycle, regaining centeredness and balance. This new cycle is one of spiritual deepening, of developing intuition and reconnecting to our source wisdom. In the last decade the energy on the planet has been rapidly changing and we have been going through different phases of a new era. Depending on how tuned in and how flexible we are, we experience the current transition more or less smoothly.

It has always been the most sensitive ones who first feel the wind change and start to adapt. We can all recognize that the more open, the more aware of, and the more sensitive to changes we are, the smoother and faster our own expansion happens. Evolution is not really a survival of the strongest but, in the long run, a survival of the most sensitive, the most adaptable. The dinosaurs, actually, died out.

The real history of the planet is the history of evolving consciousness, of awakening. People are blossoming now, not from imposed knowledge but from an inner growth. In one way, it comes about from what we have all gone through, from everything we have felt, within ourselves and within our relationships, from all the efforts we have made and the awareness we have gained. It has to do with our wanting, with our working, and with the strength of our hopes, our desires, our dreams and our prayers. On another level, it has to do with the interactive nature of the universe. For as we open, as we become ready for more and start searching for more, the answers are given. And it has to do, too, with this particular time in human evolution, and with the cycles of the stars and of the ages: a time of awakening that was foreseen thousands of years ago. It is all interrelated.

This flowering is happening now, with us and through us. It is coming through our minds, our bodies and our hearts. We are all reaching a new potential. We don't have to worry about how we will keep up with the stream, we just have to allow the flow to guide us. We are all part of the changing tide, and as we allow it we float with it. Our sensitivity leads the way. Seek silent space and quiet union where you can hear the soft voice of your heart, your intuition: nature, contemplation or meditation, perhaps sport, yoga, spiritual gatherings and sacred ceremony.

Every mystic tradition speaks of this new age. It is no longer the utopian dream of a marginal few. This is a spiritual springtime, a time of spontaneous regeneration. It is nothing less than the awakening of the human race, for which we have each come to partake in and to do our part. Epic changes are on the menu and we are here to embrace them as part of our souls' journey and fulfillment. These are the times we have been waiting and working for, for eons. Let us use them well.

There's no need to feel pressured or to force anything. If we look closely, we can see that we are naturally opening up: we are being encouraged to shed old patterns and expand our understanding and our viewpoints. It is not always a comfortable process but it is wonderful to watch. This is a worldwide phenomenon that is touching everyone's lives.

Through our relationship to ourselves, our inner channels are opening and communication flows more easily through. We thus allow and assimilate new input, whether it comes from an outer source of information or from our own inner wisdom. When all our lines are open, things advance in leaps and bounds.

There is scientific, including astronomical, data that shows we are going through increasingly rapid evolution. We can all feel how things are speeding up, a greater intensity is in the air. We can also feel how life is getting better. Maximum openness is the key to allowing this evolutionary flow through us. All we really need here is our heart.

WHAT I CAME TO APPRECIATE MOST about us humans as I traveled around this globe is the effort we all make, bravely coping day after day with ourselves, others, and a dysfunctional system. Without much understanding of how we got ourselves in this mess, we continuously display the random acts of warmth, playfulness, and kindness that help make the world an enjoyable place to live. It is the indomitable human heart that leads the way.

Life is comparable to hiking in the high mountains. There are some misty zones and some rough terrain, dodgy swinging bridges and wet river crossings, muddy patches and sunny patches, and some enchanting patches. It is a succession of ups and downs, often steep, like a game of "Snakes and Ladders." Yet we always reach there in the end.

Our human journey was a strenuous hike, a bumpy ride, with heartaches and growing pains, but over lifetimes we began to open. And once we started to look in the mirror and to see the reasons for our struggle, we came to trust in the goodness of life and things became a whole lot better.

Like plants that have weathered droughts and storms we are a bit battered now, older but stronger. We may have lost, along the way, some hair or some teeth, some friends and some illusions, some fame or some fortune, but we are becoming more real, more conscious, more aware.

We are a wonderfully ingenious, resilient and adaptive species. We are masterpieces of design, every cell in our bodies a living encyclopedia. Our DNA is an energy pattern that exists throughout the galaxy. And we have, through our heart, a direct lifeline to our source. All we can be absolutely sure of is that we are capable of far more than we yet know.

CHAPTER SEVEN

A Shift of Feeling

*Sometimes the slightest shift in the way you look
at things can alter your life forever.*

~ *Source unknown*

FROM MY YEARS in India I picked up a common expression there: "Everything is possible." This is not to justify blind faith, or to be so open minded that one's brains fall out! It is just to acknowledge that the world is a lot more mysterious than we have yet discovered.

You may well know the story of the blind men and the elephant. Each man is placed by a different part of the animal and describes the whole elephant in accordance to what he has felt. The man who has felt its side says, "An elephant is like a hairy wall," whilst the man who took the trunk contests, "No, it's very similar to a snake." The one who felt a leg reports, "An elephant is rather like a tree trunk," and the one who got the tail end concludes, "Nonsense, it's like a rope."

Funny as this sounds, it describes well how we all project our experiences and own feelings, for we have no other gauge, on the outer world. We all see life from our point of view, which is not wrong, but partial. We see things through the glasses we are wearing; we understand them through the filters of our own feelings. At dinner once a dear elder friend said, "The world situation is hopeless really." One of the new generation, a lovely soft young woman, hit the nail on the head: "Well, you may be hopeless if you like, I'm not."

Even if the men are *not* blind, each will draw a different sketch of the elephant depending from which place they look at it.

Each one is true yet none shows the whole truth of the animal. We are now at a great time in history when we are, metaphorically, starting to walk around the elephant.

Thanks to a broadening of information, intuition and heart, we now see more viewpoints. We are moving beyond a partial understanding that says "this is right so therefore that must be wrong", to a more encompassing approach. We are linking our own view with that of multiple others to gather a more complete picture of our world. Through our connecting we expand our vision.

As we encompass more points of view, we allow ourselves new feelings. Like viewpoints, a wider range of feelings was always available to us but we tended to slip into pre-programmed channels. As we widen our perspective we increase our options in life. We make new, more life-affirming choices, and deep healing takes place. By looking at ourselves, our current situation, and also our past, from a different viewpoint, we are rapidly dropping hurts and fears, changing our feelings towards life, and embracing a fresh, broader, and more holistic outlook.

At some stage I realized that maturing is not really growing higher but wider: expanding. This view frees us from the notion of superiority and paints a more accurate picture. Life leads us to become broader, more inclusive; to encompass more understanding, more feelings and more heart. We are all infinitely wide, we just have to drop our tunnel vision, our walls and our narrow paths, get out on the "high-way," and see just how vast we can become. Note that the essential character of a highway is not that it is high, but that it is wide.

Now, perhaps the term "expanding" sounds to you like middle-age spread, whilst "growing" might make you feel like a pot plant; "learning" could remind you too much of school, and "maturing" probably sounds too much like a cheese. In truth we are just remembering. Whatever words we may prefer, these times are all about change and stretching beyond how we have been. We are on a journey of discovery.

The whole planet is undergoing a monumental change of mind. Just as well I say, because where we were headed didn't look pretty. For eons we have been living on autopilot, following and governed by insecurity and deeply imbedded reaction patterns. Each of us is now helping to dissolve these old behaviors. The old world, the world of belief in opposites, duality, struggle, victimhood and pain is changing fast. Millions of people these days are making the same efforts, sharing the same thoughts and feelings and having the same interests at heart. Millions are expanding daily to greater understanding and greater love. It is a natural development, undeniable and unstoppable. We don't even have to jump aboard, we are aboard! We can just choose to go with the current, and become willing participants in a monumental shift of perspective, or cling to the debris of the old world that is being swept away.

> *The recipients of spiritual development*
> *are not the chosen people, but the choosing people.*
> ~ *Paul Six*

For our individual development we became used to building up attitudes, a personality, and sticking with it. It created and reinforced our sense of identity. Nowadays, as we expand we are pooling our individuality towards a collective uniting. The gift of these days is that old and redundant beliefs drop easily off us. It's a beautiful time to be alive, to witness ourselves growing wider and wiser while making this transition. We will surpass ourselves in ways we cannot now imagine. So don't hang on, because everything we know and are is just a stepping-stone to all we can and will be.

The Call to Awaken

We are the generation of transition. We are opening up to a new paradigm. And it's uncomfortable for us because we have been brought up in the old one. We are disconnecting from old patterns. Changing on a neurological level is like experiencing a nervous breakdown, borderline sanity, because nothing we knew is left to connect to. We are here to develop the sensitivity to see things in new ways and change our patterns. We are giving birth to a new self.

~ *What the Bleep?! ~ Down the Rabbit Hole*

OUR REAL WORK HERE, whatever our social job, is this individual and collective rebirth. We are freeing ourselves so that we, and all of humanity, can regain our conscious state. We are developing self awareness, a sense of detachment from which we can watch the age-old patterns at work without becoming caught up in them time after time. And as we do this they drop off. We are going through this transformative process for our own happiness and our own freedom, as well as for the evolution of our species.

This is the era of our awakening. Everyone is part of this change. Not everyone is aware of this, and not everyone need be. We do not need to know the bigger picture, nor can we, for it is gargantuan. Yet to catch a glimpse of it inspires and encourages us. It allows us to understand, when something feels like it is going pear shaped, that what we go through everyday is part of freeing ourselves and humankind. What may feel like a problem is just a symptom, the beginning of the solution. For the new to come, the old has to change. As a result of our rising consciousness, we are all undergoing a degree of psychological transformation. We are being shaken awake. To find out who we really are, we do have to discard what we are not. This process is not necessarily comfortable. No one enjoys to be woken up! Yet it is highly beneficial.

As we shed the old conditionings, the limiting patterns and beliefs that previously made up our personalities, the persona, the mask, is thinning. We are being led, layer by layer, through an adventure of deeper self discovery. We are becoming closer to our authentic being.

If we are sensitive, open and flexible we can feel the evolutionary impulse of life flowing through us and go with the stream. We are each being coaxed to reveal and release the deeper hurts of humanity. Everything that is not in tune with the rising vibration on Earth becomes noticeably off-key. All our inner doubts, all our unloved shadow parts and all our unaired hurts are being unearthed. Our very identities, our beliefs and our relationships are being, ever more rapidly, both dismantled and expanded. Through a succession of breakdowns, breakups and breakthroughs, we are being set free.

This is all part of our awakening: a worldwide shift in the human psyche. Outmoded mind structures are crumbling fast. Old patterns and grievances may be retriggered for healing. Some old habits may be sticky. If they get you down, pick yourself up, dust yourself off, and be patient with yourself and others. While becoming more open, and hence more sensitive, we are also discovering a sense of deeper calm, detachment and peace of mind. In the midst of these internal renovations we are fast learning to center ourselves, and to release, let go, and trust in the process.

> *The problems of today cannot be solved with*
> *the thinking of yesterday.*
> ~ *Albert Einstein*

The mind loves seeing and solving problems because that guarantees it a job; it can also become our sense of worth. The old mindset is insecure; it focuses on problems and sets about fixing them. The new mindset is one of trust. It recognizes that all is well and focuses on gratitude and appreciation. The old mindset sees the problems that are outside; the new mindset sees the beauty that is inside.

This is indeed a time of healing, but not a time to get caught by prolonged therapies. It is time to clear the past efficiently now and move on. The old mindset is intent on the healing process; the new vision is seeing "it is done."

We can dare to feel now that life is for celebrating. Problem solving keeps us in the realm of problems, whilst celebration affirms our thanks, and our trust in the perfect and loving nature of our world.

> *It is not the mountains ahead that wear you out,*
> *it's the pebble in your shoe.*
> ~ *Proverb*

New information is streaming in. As part of our identity we used to have set opinions, so we could close the file, or put a frame around our picture of the world. These days we are required to constantly re-open the file, take off the frame, throw in some new elements and watch our pictures expand. Very often, the more definite we are, the more we are limiting ourselves ~ because the universe is not definite but infinite. Once our finite picture, our own eggshell, starts cracking at the seams, it is time to let it go graciously.

Novel topics and new areas of life tend to insecure us humans. Some may cover that up by ridiculing them ~ be it new discoveries, new ideas, or the "new age." Our forefathers too mocked new fangled ideas, like cars, jeans, T-shirts or telephones. My friend's grandma was convinced that faxes were a big practical joke everyone was playing on her, until the day she died!

My own soft-spoken dad, bless his soul, was exceedingly obstinate. He wrote: "I had a trait that, if it leads to success, is called determination, and if it leads to failure, is called pigheadedness. Whatever it was, I had plenty of it." Extremely individual he could hardly take advice. To be discerning and wary of manipulation is sensible; to refuse to budge off single-mindedness may be taking it too far.

Resistance is natural when we are in the process of developing individuality. We used it then to find our own way, to protect ourselves, to develop and express our independence. However, in these days, we are being asked to stretch our personality and our borders, to go beyond our traditional comfort zones, in order to become more. So when we see patterns of resistance hanging on in ourselves and others, we can smile warmly at them, understanding the insecurities we are all going through as we learn to let go and flow with the stream.

We are shedding the blocks and the blinders that have limited us on our way to discover who we really are. Recognize the patterns of reluctance that come inherent in our human form. It is what I affectionately nickname my "pet human:" the little part within that is scared of change. It may think if it simply denies it, if it just sticks its head in the sand, it won't happen. So it stubbornly resists, it procrastinates, hangs on to illusions of happiness, and prefers to stick with the devil it knows than to take risks. If we are closed it is because we are fearful. Remember that fear resides in the gap between us and something else: in the unknown ~ whether that is a new neighbor or a foreign country; the topic of death, or perhaps 2012. To familiarize with whatever it is reduces the fear and, in exchange, opens up wondrous new viewpoints and possibilities. The evolutionary flow is now coming faster and stronger. Instead of holding our umbrella up to resist the changing wind, we discover that, when we turn it the other way, it carries us along.

WE HUMANS DERIVE a lot of our sense of security from knowing the view out of our window. If it is suddenly replaced with an awesome full-blown vista of the earth and sky… it's a tad disconcerting, to say the least. And the more hard-earned our view, the more one has sweated and struggled to secure it, the harder it is to let it go. We have part of our identity invested in that view and to have it removed or replaced is taken as a personal affront to our achievements and to our self esteem.

Now, I am not braver than anyone else. My first reaction to sudden change is to get insecure and therefore "stroppy" too. But I have had my view challenged, changed, even rudely removed, countless times, so now I am quick to recognize what is happening. "Oh boy, there goes my rattle again! Okay, I have felt this before, and every time it helped me to broaden, so (sigh…) bring it on, what's the latest?"

As our picture expands, gaps appear in our once well-defined and labeled world. We may quickly paint in the gaps with whatever we think should fit there and stick a larger frame on. But the frame keeps on bursting, the shell keeps cracking, the gaps keep appearing, and our old beliefs, *we*, just don't fit in there anymore.

So what can we do in this case? We can adopt a "beginner's mind:" open and curious, untainted by conceptual knowledge, doubts, and prejudice. As a youngster I used to say: "I'd rather believe in something in the hope of being right, than disbelieve everything out of the fear of being wrong." From there we can sit back, relax and watch it all happen. We can enjoy the gaps and let the right pieces float in from time to time. "Oh look, here comes another one! Now would you ever have though*t that?"*

There is so much we don't know about our world. About what amazing creatures we are. How we got here and what our purpose and potential are. It is all so immensely greater than we have been brought up to believe. And that astounding, bright and beautiful picture is emerging now, blowing holes in the flimsy fabric that is our three dimensional world.

The final idea is not only to increase our knowledge, but to go beyond it, beyond needing to know. The picture becomes fast so big that we cannot see the sides of it. But by then our vision, and trust, will be so big that we no longer need to.

The Rise of Humanity

We are breaking mind patterns that have
dominated human life since eons.
> ~ *Eckhart Tolle*

WE HAVE RECOGNIZED that, by being more aware of our thoughts and feelings, we have each moment the power to change our lives. Each moment we can realize our choices, notice, and congratulate ourselves: "Today I chose a new view. Today I didn't react. Today I slowed down enough to make another choice." Women may have a head start in this area because they have always allowed themselves to be flexible and change their minds as they like!

We are being shown, from myriad sources, how we are physically changing our set-up. When we choose to think brighter thoughts and thus have lighter feelings, *we rewire the thought patterns of our brain and reprogram our body cells.* We literally, physically, "change our minds," one thought at a time. The New York Times reviews *The Brain That Changes Itself* by Norman Dodge, MD: "The power of positive thinking finally gains scientific credibility. Mind-bending, miracle-making, reality-busting stuff… straddles the gap between science and self help."

Science tells us that our body cells have receptors for the chemicals produced by our different emotions. If we often repeat an emotion our new cells will grow *more* receptors for this emotion.

So they will increasingly crave the chemical of this emotion, be it lust, outrage, anger, stress, disappointment, apathy, depression or happiness. By not feeding these receptors, we free our body from its unwanted addictions and renew our cells. We thus change our age-old habitual reaction of feeling hurt, blame and powerlessness into increasing feelings of trust, appreciation and creative energy.

It is *our feelings,* stronger even than our thoughts, that perpetuate our reality. We really create our lives because the world responds to our feelings like a mirror image, or a feedback loop. In the daily task of changing our minds and uplifting our mood, we influence what we attract. Physically and psychically, our joy is our immunity.

The shift we are now experiencing and witnessing around us is largely a shift of feeling. Just as we are changing our minds, one cell at a time, the planet is going through a monumental change of mind, one human "cell" at a time.

We are all healers. We heal every day, every time we work on our insecurities, our emotions or our hurts; every time we choose to expand to more openness, more happiness, and more peace. So whenever the going is rough, and you are dealing with self-doubt, negativity, fears, or loss, remember that each tiny step you do not only changes your own life, but also brings us all forwards. Each task and each person is precious because it is through us that humanity awakens. Through uplifting ourselves out of the old mindset of struggle, strife and suffering we help to turn the tide.

Each small candle lights a corner of the dark.
~ Roger Waters, lyrics

We all chose to be here at this crossroad in Earth's history when things threatened to take a downslide into abuse and destruction due to unconsciousness. We each have the same shadow spaces within us. We each brought, or chose, issues to heal. So let's thank our grievances for showing themselves repeatedly, inside and outside of us, until we finally realized what we came to work on ~ and then, lovingly kiss them goodbye. As with any wound, emotional sores are better not covered up but aired and treated with TLC. We heal by locating our pain, not ignoring it, and treating the area with love but not dwelling on it. We heal when we keep in good spirits and focus, despite our suffering, on the bright future we envision. Through clearing these areas of dis-ease and uplifting ourselves daily we become part of the whole awakening of the human heart and mind that is now happening on the planet.

The struggles we have all experienced are not essentially ours, but part of the "Dark Ages" humanity is now coming out of. We need not identify with our struggles or feel bad about our weaknesses. The fear-based patterns of insufficiency, lack and survival still live in the human psyche. We inherited these patterns. It is our choice to continue to use them or not. We can close the curtains or the pop up and change the scene.

Now, more than ever, we can choose to become part of a planetary change-of-Mind, a shift from victimhood to understanding and from insecurity to trust; from unworthiness to self love and from unconsciousness to light.

This is our "morale" obligation: to change our mind from worrywart to vision holder. It is time to leave the past, to drop all pain and to shift to a bright outlook. Much pioneer work has already been done in this area and awareness is rapidly rising. Wonderful things are now happening because we humans put the effort in. In doing so, not only do we improve *our* lives, we also become part of a contagious healing that is quickly spreading from one cell to the next. Each of us is a tiny cell of the global body and brain. Each of us cells is transforming itself, becoming more conscious, and thus contributes to the global change of Mind.

SO MANY DIFFERENT ROADS we have all traveled, so many different walkabouts. Yet what I see is that people everywhere have largely made the same experiences. We have all gone through similar dramas to reach the same feelings. We are more understanding now, more tolerant, more open, more firm on our own feet and more clear on what we want. And we all want the same. Peace for our families, time for our friends, a fun and friendly world. And we will get that. For there is nothing more powerful than unity of intention.

We have been separated and kept in fear of each other, but

finally we are becoming aware that we are all one people, one mind, one heart. Not everyone is on the same page perhaps but we are all in the same book. *Planet Earth: Why am I here?*

To me, and indeed to many, it feels like we are coming out of the dark ages. It is a blessing to be embodied here at this time. An unstoppable wave of evolutionary energy is embracing the planet. Strictly speaking, consciousness is not evolving, since consciousness is already evolved. It is rather that our physical matter is becoming gradually filled, increasingly imbued, with consciousness.

The light is starting to come through.

We are, in physical reality, "downloading:" bringing the light of our spirit into matter. Anchoring spirit in the material plane, enlightening it. Anchoring consciousness into matter, or rather ~ into the heart of the matter. We often "know" something intellectually, and yet it is a gradual process to fully realize it, apply it, and integrate it into our daily lives until it becomes embedded in our being. This process is the anchoring of awareness in the physical plane.

To "incorporate" is a most descriptive word. "Corpus" is Latin for body. We are, as a matter of fact, in-corp-orating changes: we are bringing them into the body, downloading them into the physical realm, anchoring them in our very cells.

We are the link, the human bridge. Through our work, our openness, our vision and our love, we are all helping to shift our physical world into a lighter, less dense vibration.

Life in a new light

ONE MORNING IN BALI, I awoke in my thatched house amidst the rice fields with a new sense of wonder about life. I wrote an email to my friends:

> *I feel as though I just arrived on the planet. I was told that this body and this Earth is my home. I was warned that I would forget almost everything I know ~ such as who I am and where I came*

from ~ and get caught up in the 'funtasies' of this world. Yet, I was told, every sunrise would be a new promise. Every sunset another chance to return to stillness. And that every night I would reunite with the rest of my being, and be reminded.

I had drawn a rough sketch of what I wanted to do here, and I know that to color in the rest in is now up to me. I was instructed that my heart and my happiness would be my guides. I was assured that I would always be connected to Source, through my breath, and that in stillness I would remember.

So I walk around in awe, looking with new eyes at this beautiful place. I enjoy the many fruits. I marvel at the many life forms which come in all shapes and sizes. And I wonder at the many human inhabitants of this planet, lost in the daydream, so close and yet "mindfolded." At times I get lost too in this Disneyland, especially when a cloud covers the sun. When I realize this, it is through awareness, acceptance and appreciation of what is, that I reconnect to what Is.

There are many of us here, who remember to remember. And through our remembering we start to wake up out of this dream. And through our own stirring we stir others into waking too. And slowly but surely a new paradigm is born.

SINCE WE ARE ALL BECOMING, every day more aware ~ and this awareness is spreading across the planet (through the people, its cells) ~ is it not just logical that in some years (due to the exponential curve), when enough people have woken up enough (to our true nature as eternal, universal, beings) that this enlightening realization then ripples through the Global Mind and awakens the whole body of humanity out of its collective dream: the illusion of existing only in physical reality, in a purely linear time-space dimension?

And that from this revelation the world would be transformed?

Facets of Attraction

Our beliefs ~ the combined energetic power of our imagination and our feelings ~ directly influence the energy field that is the base of our physical existence. Everything that manifests in matter forms first on that inner, underlying plane.

CHAPTER EIGHT

Mirrors and Magnets

I am ~ the two most powerful words in the world,
for whatever we put after them becomes our reality.
~ *Susan Howson*

Living Magnets

NOW THAT WE have peeped ahead just a bit at where we are all headed, you may have caught a glimpse of the value of being grounded in our hearts. Before we take a look at the rewarding process of recouping our self love and hence our wholeness, let's consider some aspects of the law of attraction. For as our feelings shift, so does what we attract.

I first read about conscious "manifesting" on a tiny, all but deserted, island in Fiji. With a lot of accumulated energy and focus due to the utter lack of social distractions, I went and sat under my favorite tree in the forest. Having the well-being of my daughter and a small community place in mind, I made a heartfelt wish for the modest sum of 100,000 Euros to buy a piece of land in the South Pacific. I asked for the news to come by email, and the money to come as a gift, so no-one would have to die for it. It had not escaped my notice that shortly before my father died I had wished for a certain sum, which was, "co-incidentally," exactly what I inherited.

A few weeks later, I met a couple who were looking to buy a property for an eco community retreat. I found the piece of land they wanted in Tonga, but they couldn't afford it. Then one day the guy came bouncing in to our house, all excited with the news: "I just got an email from my dad! He's giving me money so I can buy it. Guess how much…100,000 Euros!"

I thought to myself, "Well done Amber, it was close. Next time you ask the universe for donations, do remember to give your name and account details!"

AS MAGICAL AS IT FEELS sometimes, manifesting is not supernatural. We are simply applying the laws of attraction. We all know how it is when we catch a good wave, we feel great and have a great week. Or when we get up on of the wrong side of our bed and nothing works all day. It has to do with how our energy flows. We are, in fact, living magnets.

It is quite obvious that the "vibe" we exude affects people around us, who we attract and how they relate to us. Indeed, it is scientifically shown that we create our own reality, constantly, through our thoughts and feelings, because these affect our electro-magnetic vibration. Unbeknown to us before, we have been attracting all our lives. The only difference is that now we can do it consciously by watching *which* thoughts and feelings we dwell on.

After my first near hit I tried of course some more manifesting, and sometimes it worked and sometimes it didn't. On my very last day in Tonga, a guy whom I had just met gave me his favorite book: *Excuse Me, Your Life is Waiting* by Lynn Grabhorn. It drove home the importance of our daily feelings for what we attract. As we are often feeling, and focused on, what we *don't* want, we just attract more of what we don't want.

Even wishful affirmations may stem from our view of what we currently don't have, and thus reinforce that position. This is why we want to shift our feelings from the very base by recognizing the wonder of life. Our belief and trust in what is all possible for ourselves is only limited by our imagination, and our feeling of what we are worth. Imagination is the doorway out of our linear thinking; it gets us out of the box.

> *Logic will take you from A to B.*
> *Imagination will take you everywhere.*
> ~ *Albert Einstein*

As we keep dreaming our dreams, we may often look around us and exclaim, "Wow, this is indeed what I dreamt!" We come to recognize that this is not magic. Our beliefs ~ the combined energetic power of our imagination and our feelings ~ directly influence the energy field *that is the base* of our physical existence. Everything that manifests in matter forms first on that inner, underlying plane.

On a deep energetic level we are, our very life force is, creative energy. That is the consciousness that flows through us. Hence, everything we express, be it thoughts, feelings, words or deeds, has tremendous creative power. The more we get out of our own way, the more we clear the blocks to this conscious energy, the stronger and the more instantaneously this power comes through us.

Reaching our dreams depends solely on the clarity and strength of our vision, our focus and our will. We fuel that with the power of our heart's desire, and the enthusiasm, joy and gratitude that naturally arises as we awaken to realize just how remarkable this life really is. Envision and anticipate the end result, with heartfelt gratitude, and watch it all fall into place.

As long as we are fully behind what we wish for, feeling it is believable, and having trust, it will come. Know that you are worthy of it and ready for it, and that life is fair and interactive. Wait, with confidence, quiet expectation and appreciation. Don't concern with *how* it could materialize. The universe will provide. It is in the nature of things, part of our contract. Ask and ye shall receive.

> *It's not your work to make anything happen. It's your work to dream it and let it happen. (...) In your joy, you create something, and then you maintain your vibrational harmony with it, and the Universe must find a way to bring it about. That's the promise of Law of Attraction.*
> ~ *Abraham Hicks*

All we need is clarity and focus on what we want, and enough self love and trust to feel we deserve to receive it. If we don't want, or don't dare to ask for, the best for ourselves, we won't get it. We may be sitting in a restaurant abounding with the most beautiful dishes, but we do have to place an order for the food to come to our table.

> *Now think about the Universal Law. It reflects to you exactly and precisely what you put out. If your thought forms say 'I haven't got a clue about what I want' the Universal Law is going to say "Listen mate, if you haven't got a clue, neither have I.'*
> ~ Stuart Wilde

If our feelings project, "Um, er, sorry universe, but do you think, maybe, possibly, I could just have…a *little bit* money?" then we might find a cent on the pavement.

It is our inner split that weakens our conscious manifesting. If we are not clear or not in agreement with ourselves, our different parts will send out conflicting messages. Therefore we want to recognize and befriend our own smaller side that may be sabotaging our attempts because it doesn't feel quite ready for, or even worthy of, what we wish for.

The strongest backing we have for creating our vision is our integrity, our wholeness. To create what we envision, our intention has to be very clear, and therefore our feeling about it has to be wholehearted. If we are anyhow lukewarm, not quite sure, we disempower ourselves. If we are hardly holding the steering wheel of our life, we cannot wonder that we get pushed off course.

Our lives prompt us to become more clear, more certain and also more careful of what we desire. As we recognize our "don't wants," the "do wants" come clearer into focus. We begin to glimpse and to align with our soul's intent.

LIFE IS INGENIOUS for, in pursuit of the gems we seek, we are brought to notice our responsibility for everything else we attract too! Indeed, there is nothing that can come into our lives that we have not, in some way, invited in. We are, aware of it or not, the co-creators of our daily reality. The law of attraction always responds, automatically, to the vibe we put out. This is why we want to look at which feelings we are projecting.

If it doesn't feel like a warm fuzzy,
either don't say it or change it around.

> ~ Lynn Grabhorn
> EXCUSE ME, YOUR LIFE IS WAITING

This is a vital point to work with. Until we look closely at this we have really no idea how much negativity we are radiating. How often do we voice discontent, discomfort, disappointment, and disapproval? Even our casual expressions teem with what we *don't* want to happen. "I'm sick of this." "What a headache." "It's such a pain." "Give me a break." When we realize the universe reflects what we express, we become more careful what we ask for!

The electro-magnetic energy we emit influences not only the people, but also the world around us, because we are connected to everything through the unified energy field. I am not alone in having observed even electronics and machinery being affected by an adverse feeling. This finally explains why the photo I took in those early days in India was not on the negatives when the elderly sadhu raised his objection.

In *First Light*, Carol O'Biso relates another such story. Once the Maori Tiki statues are all loaded into the truck, on their way to be exhibited in the States, it flatly refuses to start. Her Maori associate understands why. Despite her total disbelief at the time, once he had spoken to the Tiki, reassuring them that they would return to New Zealand soon, the engine burst into life.

I have witnessed similar abnormalities in well functioning vehicles, computers, electrical appliances, and even the electricity supply itself. These can occur from opposing feelings being projected, whether consciously or not. Practice putting the neighbor's lawn mower out of action! I suspect such "co-incidences" to become more apparent. As we free ourselves from our own blocks, becoming more aware of the energy within, the physical world becomes less dense, less resistant. The veil thins, and our co-creations become more instant.

Scientific experiments confirm how our feelings affect the world around us. It has been well verified and documented that we can, through "wishpower," influence the results of a random number generator computer. An emotionally bonded couple, focusing on the same intent, can alter the results six times more powerfully than either of them could individually.[1] Science shows too that the magnetic emissions of the human heart are 5000 times stronger than that of the brain, explaining why it is the power of our feelings that influence and attract, far more than our thoughts. Due to these facts, *our collective feelings and vision have tremendous impact on the world.*

Significant fluctuations in Earth's electro-magnetic field have been recorded when large groups of people are feeling the same way, such as over the death of Princess Diana, and the news of 9/11. Fuelled by the feelings we all share, the power of our human heart is nothing less than *astronomical.*

~

WHEN WE RECOGNIZE just how interconnected and how "magical" our world really is, we realize how much we influence our daily reality and take a look at our deeper feelings. Our core beliefs, our innermost faiths and fears, are affirmations that attract the experience we expect back to ourselves. It is the self-fulfilling prophecy. If we feel, "I'm weak, I'm going to get bullied or sick," guess what happens? From deep within, we may be projecting, "I'm unlovable, nobody loves me," or "This world is unjust, it hurts."

We are all sensitive souls. This seemingly "strugglesome" survival world is the reality we have unknowingly created: the magnified reflection of our stored pain. Inside each of us is a small flame, a flame that would like to blaze but doesn't dare. "I'm too weak, I'm unlovable, this world hurts" are all good excuses not to feed our inner flame; not to trust in ourselves, not to trust in others and not to open too much to the world around us. This mistrust caused us to close up, to act out of separatism and defensiveness. Within ourselves, in our relationships, in our societies, and in our politics. *What we think is what we get.*

---

[1] *CosMos: A Co-creator's Guide to the Whole World,* by Nobel Prize winner Ervin Laszlo and Jude Currivan

Yet now we are discovering that we are not weak; not perfect perhaps but not unlovable; and this world is not unfair. We are not tossed around like a dry leaf by the winds of fate and fortune. We hold the strings, we deal the cards, we create the game.

We have the freewill to vary any outcome by changing the starting point: *our belief.* We don't need to struggle to survive, and we don't need to push or to defend. Life is a gift. We are all good enough, powerful and loveable. We have abundance on this planet. Everyone has a heart. And when we put these thoughts, these beliefs, into practice in our daily lives, we have a very different world around us: One where we do not need walls to protect our seemingly fragile existence from each other. A world where we *can* dare to be trusting and sharing. A world that reflects a united humanity: one that is beyond victimhood and abuse. Where we can, all together, explore the marvels of our human potential.

A new world, if we create it.

THE MORE TRUSTING WE ARE, open to receive, the less armor we have on to protect ourselves, the better incoming information can get through to our conscious mind. Openness enables us to be in the flow.

One really hot day in Ubud, Bali, I was on my way through the rice fields to the pool. As I was about to step into one empty field, an inner hunch warned me. I wondered, "Maybe the mud is still wet?" Then I saw the snake right in front of me in the grass. Shortly later, I passed a new neighbor on his porch and just felt the impulse to say hi and tell him about the pool. From his hammock he exclaimed, "Thanks, I was just wondering a minute ago if there was a pool around here!" We became good friends. This is another aspect of *Ask and ye shall receive* that is well worth becoming aware of, as it enhances our sense of connectivity and awe.

After a time you keep your eyes open for answers. Another day in Bali, where the locals' awareness of the energy within all life contributes to the flow of synchronicities, I was wondering if the dance event that evening would be ethnic music or funk. The next moment a girl passed me by with a bright pink T-shirt that stated: "Funk Party Tonight." So I gave it a miss and confirmed later, it was indeed funk. And just a few days later, while I was pondering if I should really bother to waddle down the street to do some extra photocopies, a guy walked past with a rather uncommon message emblazoned in huge print on his T-shirt. It read: "No More Copies." Now, what are the odds?

Such things happen often, especially when we look out for them. The interconnectedness of this world is beyond our understanding. So we just learn to trust it. You may have noticed when you can't find something, and you give up searching with a frantic, "Where is it?!" that your eyes are often drawn to the very spot. We don't need to become desperate for this to happen, repeatedly and reliably. We just have to be surrendered: open, asking, and quietly "out of our mind."

By loosening up and listening within, after a time you know the phone will ring, that someone is on their way to visit, that there is a snake in the grass or that you should move out from under that coconut tree!

Trust, and keep your eyes and ears open. Working in cooperation with our inner self, we are guided on our way. We really don't have to figure it all out, forge our way alone, or force anything to happen. Following our subtle feelings and impulses can lead us to "prearranged" situations, where we find open doors. Much of our life is mapped out in advance. Our job is to notice, and then follow, the road signs.

The Mirror effect

Each is alone in a hall of mirrors.

BRIGITTE WAS ONE OF MY CLEAR ROAD SIGNS: "Wrong Way." When we first moved out to the Kingdom of Tonga in the South Pacific she was, "by chance," our closest western neighbor. We never got to know her well. She was just a few years older than I and had a lovely feeling about her, however she was physically

worn out, grey, and chain smoking. We talked about natural healing once but I felt as though she had given up.

Shortly later a good-looking, good-energy young couple
rocked up in the harbor in their Wharram catamaran. These boats
are based on Polynesian design and, being home made and funky,
often have interesting owners. I met them one full moon while
camping on an island beach. We felt instantly some connection
and yet, as we were "landlubbers," we had little exchange.

I always look out for the message in such meetings. Then one
day the guy told me that when he had first met Brigitte, just seven
years earlier, she was the most beautiful woman he had ever seen.
She had sailed there across the Pacific with her long term partner,
who had left her shortly after, dismayed. I realized how she was
pining away for him, unable to let go, and was maybe even weakening herself to attract his compassion.

A few mornings later at home, overlooking the beautiful harbor dotted with yachts from around the world, I found myself
singing a Bryan Adams chorus: *Take my life. I would give it all, I'd
sacrifice...Everything I do...I do it for you... Yeah, I'd die for you.*

It was a song I could sing quite well, simply because I enjoyed
the feeling of devotion, of merging, of giving myself up. However,
in the light of Brigitte's story I recognized the words and thought,
"Just wait one minute. What's going on here? No freaking way!" I
realized that I, too, was devotional to the point of self sacrifice. I
was going down the same road, giving away my happiness and
my life energy, for the relationship to which I felt destined.

I remembered how a couple years earlier, in our deepest,
most desperate times in the Australian outback, I had once caught
myself thinking, "Do I need to become seriously ill for him to be
sensitive to me, to learn compassion?" Nuts to that I had concluded! Some have chosen such lives through soul agreement but
it was luckily not my way.

It was some months later that we flew Air Tonga's little 12-
seater to the capital Tongatapu. Brigitte's friends had booked her
on the same flight so we could care for her. She was on her way to
New Zealand for a check up, very quiet, already surrendered. She
was very bright, barely physical anymore, the light of her spirit
shining through. She died there, just one week later, happily in her

partner's arms.

I had noticed how she was my mirror, magnifying a part within me, so I could recognize it. I saw how we had all met at that stage in life, on the great stage of life. Co-actors in the drama we had chosen to play together. Spirit friends, helping each other to see.

〜◯

You don't take what comes, you make what comes.

UNDERSTANDING THE LAW OF ATTRACTION is essential to freeing ourselves from unwanted repetitive occurrences. If our reflections upset us, the only way to change "them" is to change "us."

It was in the South Pacific, buried under all my awareness, goodwill and brilliance that I found the behavior patterns and core beliefs that had repeatedly attracted unpleasant experiences. There is no abuse, mishap, or misfortune that we have not attracted into our lives. Everything that comes to us is a reflection of our deep inner beliefs.

The outer world mirrors our subconscious feelings and expectations. It provides us with numerous experiences that enable us to recognize them and thus get over them. By accepting this full responsibility we begin to consciously write our lives, and even rewrite our pasts by changing our viewpoint. As we shall later see, this frees us of all blame and resentment, which is tremendously healing.

Throughout our lives, we attract events and people that reflect, and thus make us aware of, how we truly feel. A victim attitude attracts fellow victims, as well as abusers to provide the victim experience. The attitude of hurt attracts painful experiences to bring it clearly into view. Self depreciation attracts critics.

Our environment and our relationships echo our core beliefs. Our associates may display, in a magnified way, character traits and habits that are buried within us. For example, they may keep expressing doubt in us, as a test to our own self approval, until we are fully over our own self doubts. Or a condescending attitude until we are over feeling small and sorry for ourselves. We only put up with others putting us down if we hold, deep within, due to our own self judgment, the same misgivings they express towards us. We all mirror each other.

As we release our own patterns, we release others from the need to play a certain role towards us. That is how, by changing ourselves, we change the scenario around us. It is wondrous to observe.

> *It is done unto you as you believe.*
> ~ *Jesus Christ*

Our resonance magnetizes that which is alike or complimentary. We say that our parents and experiences influenced our character, but it is rather that our core feelings attracted them to us in the first place. We may think we have a certain trait because, "I was brought up like this" or, "this happened when I was two years old." But all of it's really due to the law of attraction. Our upbringing, events on the way, and our entire life circumstances come to us because of how *we feel within*. They are *the reflections* that bring those shadow parts of us into the light.

If others have high expectations on us, by referring to the mirror of life we see that they only reflect our own demands on ourselves. Thus critical parents arouse our self judgment and our own suspicions of inadequacy, while absent parents reflect our feelings of rejection and abandonment. They do not, essentially, give us that pain; they highlight the pain that is already in us. I came to see that we have really "chosen" the environment that brings out most effectively the inner traits we are here to recognize. It thus awakens our latent talents and strengths, our greatest potential, and our power as healers.

Take Bob Marley as a good example. He even says of himself, "I was born Rasta." He slotted into, or chose, downtown Jamaica because that fitted with his picture of social oppression and his desire to express his freedom-fighter spirit; the musical trend of Jamaica gave him that possibility. Our upbringing and environment is not the cause of our character; it is our background, our canvas, on which we develop and express *that which we already are*.

This is great news for parents, because it frees us from responsibility for how our kids "turn out," and also frees us from blaming our own parents. We slotted into, or chose, a certain family and place because that is where we fitted. We appear to have inherited traits from our parents, but in fact we just came together because we shared that mind-set. We also inherit their physical features and "genetic conditions," yet the bottom line is that we are similar because our bodies are *formed* by our emotional character. Life exists first in the energy realm and then it materializes here.

We are creators in training, learning to refine our creations. If we don't like what we have created, we can adjust something within ourselves. Becoming aware of this power we are given, we get over the feeling that life is unfair and we are hapless victims of fate. We begin to glimpse the truly amazing set up behind the scenes. We both accept and feel gratitude for the reflection in the mirror. And as we grow in appreciation and love, our reflection becomes more loving.

The Changing Face of Relationships

If you accept that the relationship is here to make you conscious instead of happy then the relationship will offer you salvation.
~ Eckhart Tolle,
PRACTISING THE POWER OF NOW

THE TOPIC OF ATTRACTION brings us, of course, to everyone's favourite subject. Our relationships have been the source of much bewilderment, misunderstanding, and invested effort. We finally come to see that they all depend on one thing, and the partners and friends we attract are all signposts, clearly pointing us towards it: our own inner relationship. In one way or another, everyone assists us, as we work and play together, on our priceless journey of self discovery and expansion.

Years ago in Canary Islands, a long camaraderie I had with a male friend was heading towards a spectacular finish. We had always felt a strong attraction for each other but were as opposite as could be. A girlfriend gave me *The Celestine Prophecy* by James Redfield, and when I reached the bit on "control dramas" it all made perfect sense. This is truly the stuff that should be taught in primary school!

It described how, through the need to receive attention, support, and approval, in response to our parents' patterns, we develop in early childhood unconscious "control dramas:" ways of pulling energy towards us. These are the basic household patterns that have held us on either side of victimhood. They magnetize, in turn, partners with the opposite, matching dramas and the tug of war for energy, "pushing each others buttons," continues.

In brief, the four interactive control dramas are: the forceful intimidator who draws energy from others' anxiety, the interrogator whose criticism pushes others to justify themselves, the distant aloof who calls for concern and interest, and the "poor me" who pulls for sympathy.

As we have just seen, our parents really only highlight the already existing tendencies within us. Knowing that our relationships are designed to reflect and trigger our inner patterns explains why we keep attracting the same type of partners. We can then better understand others' roles towards us and drop all blame. Freeing ourselves from our own unconscious dramas makes it possible for our partners to be different towards us. Or at least, failing that, enables us to attract different partners! Once we have recognized the main patterns, we continue to spot and to shed the more subtle behaviorisms that kept us in the loop. By realizing that energy and love is not limited, we open ourselves to receive it in other ways, starting with our own self approval.

MY GIRLFRIEND'S MOTHER happened to be a great example of the "poor me" syndrome: she was always threatening to kick the bucket. While I was visiting one day, my friend called her mum to invite her over for Christmas dinner, to which the mother typically moaned, "But I may not be alive at Christmas!" "Don't worry," my friend dryly reassured her, "I'll buy a small turkey, just in case."

꙳

The oak and the cypress grow not in each others shadow.
                    ~ Kahlil Gibran

As we shed our old patterns, as our old personalities are being dismantled and thus expanded, so are our relationships. The fact that many partnerships have experienced stress at the seams, that many couples choose to separate, and that many individuals prefer now to stay single, is a good sign. You may laugh, *"Seriously?"*

It shows that people are growing into more self awareness, self reliance, and self love. Seeking more peace of mind and fulfilment within, rather than relying on partners to love them and "make them happy." Many individuals are now feeling more content, balanced, and comfortable in themselves.

Not seeking our own fulfilment outside of us enables us to accept others just as they are. As they no longer have to satisfy what we have not found in ourselves, we don't have to improve on them. All over the world the face of relationships is changing, not only between couples, but also family members, friends and associates. It is a part of the upgrading we are experiencing, part of the whole change of mind and heart that is now sweeping the planet. It is part of the age of ethics and integrity we are in, part of the impulse of evolution. It comes naturally that as we expand we seek new ways of relating.

> *Don't walk in front of me, I may not follow;*
> *don't walk behind me, I may not lead.*
> *Just walk beside me and be my friend.*
> ~ *Albert Camus*

AS WE FIND GREATER PEACE within ourselves our outer relationships become more harmonious. As we become more whole, balancing the masculine and feminine energies that are within each of us, we less need the opposite sex to complement and fulfil us. This doesn't mean they do not continue to inspire us! Rather that, by growing in self approval and emotional self sufficiency, we are moving beyond dependency and possessiveness, and beyond the roles we have all been playing together. We then relate with greater sensitivity and respect, not as spouses, or parents, or advisers, but from one individual to another. Many couples are separating now simply because they have accomplished their work together, helped each other to where they are now, and are each ready for the next step.

We do want to go easy on each other in these times of transition, as we are all experiencing inner transformation and paving the new road as we go. It is a process of self discovery, maturing and expansion so we stand stronger in our self love and hence on our own two feet. If we find we are not supported by others, perhaps we are meant to find *our own* approval first.

Where we are headed is a new way of relating, a way of cooperation that respects both our independence and our inherent oneness. The time is calling us now to clear the energy dynamics in *all* our relationships so we can move on with greater love. In a critical environment our vitality shrinks, whilst in a supportive one, it thrives. And as we uplift and encourage those around us to open and bloom, we raise the whole vibration we live in.

Our faith in ourselves, in one another, and in the inherent goodness of humankind, is a most powerful affirmation. Neither limit yourself nor others, for there is so much more within us ~ a sacred element ~ that is rarely perceived. The Hindi word for "Hello," which is *Namaste*, expresses this reverence. It means: *I greet and honor the place in you that is the same in me.* We bring out the fulfilled being within each of us by acknowledging its presence, rather than maintaining the feeling that we all still have to get there. Recognizing another's qualities inspires them to shine and your faith empowers them.

> *A true friend knows your weaknesses but shows you your strengths; feels your fears but fortifies your faith; sees your anxieties but frees your spirit; recognizes your disabilities but emphasizes your possibilities.*
> ~ *William Arthur Ward*

We may feel that we need, out of care, to point out others' shortcomings. But think again: this may actually be weakening their self esteem. And by putting them in survival mode, they close up. It is only in the warmth of love that we can fully open, only with the light of love that we can dare to seek whatever is within us, and only with the power of love that we have strength.

Whatever we put our focus on grows. It is like creating a garden. We can either nurture the flowers and watch them bloom, or worry about the weeds. In making others okay with who they are we affirm, honor and support the beauty within them. And we find that they *are* beautiful and that they blossom.

Inspire each other to be, to the fullest, whoever *they* are. Our daughter was brought up with no notion of wrongdoing and no fear of punishment, so she felt no need to hide. With no split within her, little social mask, and no imposed cultural identity, she remained open, genuine and radiating a natural zest for life. You see it in those kids who have not been put down, and in those who have bounced up again. In our wholeness, the fullness of the spirit shines through.

The future seems daunting for many of our youth. Bear that in mind when relating to them. It is not surprising: on one side they may feel pushed by the demands of society, on another they strongly feel the changing of the tide. It may split them to try to fit into the old system while their soul calls for a new dawn. The best preparation for life ahead is a degree in openness, awareness and self love. We may well find that our children are further down that track than we are.

IN THE LAST DECADE we have all been pushed to greater integrity, within ourselves and therefore towards each other. We are now building new relationships with more openness and more free-dom, less resistance and less distance; that honor, uplift, and encourage each other's individuality. It is a space in which we all thrive. I figured it all out once, when I was bird-sitting a parrot. Parrots succeed in having life-long relationships because they have found the ultimate trick: they never disagree, they just repeat what the other one says!

Among the old patterns that are now falling away are infringement, pressure, judgment and various other control mechanisms. These all stem from our own insecurities. We can trust that life itself gives everyone the opportunities and guidance they need, and can dare to feel that, indeed, everyone does already the best they can. Through acceptance, approval, and trust in ourselves we notice and release these patterns from within us. It changes the world around us.

CHAPTER NINE

The Good News

For most folks no news is good news;
for the press, good news is not news.

~ Gloria Borger

WHEN WE FIRST went to Australia we parked on a quiet little street in front of our friend's house. We made the traffic warden's day and got two fines: one for being parked "the wrong way around," and one for being parked in the same spot longer than 24 hours! We went to discuss these trivialities at the station, coming, as we were, from India, where you could park an elephant in the middle of the street all day and no-one would bat an eyelid. In a country of a billion people, parking fines just didn't exist. The officer friendly-wise explained to us that the Aussies are a wild bunch, descendants of deportees, and have to be kept under tight rein or they run amok. Now in my experience, if you let the Australians loose, they'll just pack the icebox and go fishing! We thanked him for letting us off the fines, which confirmed to us the age-old rule, "it's easier to apologize than to ask permission," and laughed all the way home about the "wild Aussies". Anyone who has been there knows that these guys are about as normal as it gets. In fact, all over the world, the people are just that: normal. They want friends, free time for fun, and peace for their families.

If you read the news, however, you could be led to believe that people are generally an uncouth and unruly bunch.

We can't quite decide if the world is growing worse,
or if the reporters are just working harder.

~ The Houghton Line, 1965

Although we are still a primitive species, the true history of humankind is one of ever-increasing exchange, awareness, and cooperation. The daily "news" would have us believe otherwise. Imagine the accurate headlines: "6,890,882,537 People Acted Normally Today, as Usual!" It just wouldn't sell.

~

IN NEW ZEALAND WE HIKED through lush rainforest and fresh clean air to a beautiful waterfall. We sat on moss-covered boulders, enjoying the mystical feeling of an untouched world around us. Nearby we overheard a small group of Americans. One said, "Did you hear the news today?"

Another replied, "I don't want to."

Eager to spill the beans, the first guy continued, "It was in the headlines today about this guy who…" His pal cut him short in his slow American drawl, "I'm sorry, but which part of '*I don't want to*' did you not understand?"

To share bad news is for many still almost a compulsion. Our pain body feeds off it and one part inside us is looking for reassurance. We want to get it off our chest. Perhaps, don't put it there in the first place? We may think we can read all that stuff, sort it, stay objective and not get affected. Well, would we tell it to a small child? How is our small part going to feel about the news… shocked, scared, horrified? Do we really want to add to our own worries an event that may have happened a million miles from our home, and then increase the negative effect by broadcasting it to others? Of course we don't, it's just a habit. Actually, all we want is to share the pain in our own heart.

In some cases we may feel it is responsible to share the information. It's worth thinking about, or rather *feeling* about, that one. Reading the article, what does it do to our own mouth angles, our feeling, and our energetic vibration? It brings them all down and thus affects what we attract. We are free; we can simply switch off the TV. [1]

---

[1]*Uplifting* news and papers *can* be found, just google: good news websites

Some people do have the most unenviable job of digging up all the shit, and to bring the darkness into the light is part of dissolving it. It is strengthening to face the shit, the dark, to accept it and to go through it. One doesn't want to wallow in it though! All outer news distracts us from our own lives, our own reality. Yet it also points us, if we wish, to focus on ourselves, for whatever we identify with on the outside, be it poverty, war, manipulation, abuse… is a reflection of our inner feelings. So the bad news is not only bad. It helps us to find the source within, to resume our own responsibility, and to take action. Thus such information, and the fear and pain it triggers, has its place and purpose in our healing.

THE SHARING OF OUR INNER PAIN is the source of much news on conspiracy "theories." The alternative population, those who are actually changing the mindset of humanity, are of course a popular target. A lot of bad "news" is fired in their direction, often revealing threatening "hidden" agendas aimed at making us feel powerless. We may, in turn, feel to prod or shock others, feeling that people need to wake up, so as not to be caught in a slumber-land of cozy beliefs. This may well be true, but it may not be necessary. We may ourselves be intellectually capable of understanding a lot, yet be heedless of our small part struggling to process the fear. Not everyone has the emotional strength to handle the shit without getting bogged down by it. Nor do all of us need all that information, for simply the power of our hearts, however it is awakened, is enough to change the world.

⁓

OCCASIONALLY, WE'D TAKE A BREAK from the tropics and go visit the folks "at home." Everyone who travels a lot does this with a small dose of apprehension and a dash of dread.

The family starts off with a cheery, "Well, *how was it?*" And within two minutes, five if your photos are really good, they start to tell you about the local events: the dog had puppies, the school football team won a match, *and,* not to forget… there's a new hairdresser on the corner. Now I'm not belittling the good ol' folks at home. They love you and feed you and sometimes let slip, "There's a nice place in the village you might like to settle down..." Their heartfelt advice is to lay your dreams aside. "Forget about all that running around the globe, it's much safer here. You just don't know what's happening in the world today."

Of course, how could you? You don't watch the evening news.

When you decline to join them in this daily ritual they say you are not facing reality, you are shirking responsibility. You *should* read the news, you should settle down, you should get married, get a job...

And finally they ask: "What is it you are running away from?"

BAD NEWS SELLS, and, intentional or not, keeps us in fear. Once we turn off the TV and stop reading the news, within a short time we feel the world is a kinder place. Likely there were no bombs in your neighborhood, no shootings disturbed your sleep. You didn't get mugged, run over or struck by lightning on your way to work. And nor did your family members, friends, colleagues, or perhaps come to think of it, anyone you ever met.

As one trots around the globe and gathers news from other travelers, one comes to see that our world is really a safe and friendly place. We often found ourselves in so called "trouble zones," amidst warnings of unrest and epidemic. We would be living it up in some beautiful peaceful location and friends would call and ask, "Are you guys okay? Are you safe? Are you sick?" And just because there was one event, on one day, in one place, the whole country would be on the "travel warning list" for a year or two.

Newspapers are unable, seemingly, to discriminate between a bicycle accident and the collapse of civilization.
~ *George Bernard Shaw*

Being in the country itself, you see that the facts and figures reported are wildly exaggerated, and you see the anxiety and panic caused by the media. You see there is really no epidemic, nor is there antagonism between the people in the street. Not between the Fijians and the Indians, nor the Hindus and the Muslims, nor even the Israelis and Palestinians. And you begin to wonder.

The truth will set you free. But first it will piss you off.
~ *Gloria Steinem*

My partner, being a historian, and I did hundreds of hours of research into the truth, and the lies, of the shadow government, using our common sense logic, discernment, and experience. In those times I often fell asleep holding my inner child by the hand. If you are not ready to have the carpet pulled away beneath your feet, it's wiser to just put "conspiracy theories" in an "open box" until more evidence comes along, than to strike off all such thinkers as "idiots" out of one's own insecurity. After all, they could be right, and what would that make you?

If you think there is no control or manipulation going on, you'll be surprised one day to find out the extent... However, if you believe there is one central organized force behind the scenes against which we have no chance, then think again too. There is a lot of exaggeration and "leaked out" disinformation that would have us believe exactly that. Yet there is a great deal of dissention within those circles, inner turmoil, resistance and dropouts. It was already foreseeable that, due to their own lack of integrity and internal power struggles, they would not be able hold the fort forever. And then, through the change of the ages that we shall look into later , they lost all support.

So consider, just for once, that things are not as they seem. What if, indeed, things were *better?* Global warming: a natural event throughout our whole solar system which NASA has already documented; terrorism: a fabrication to increase control; wars: not due to enemyship but a long used method: "Divide them to rule them." Poverty, "evil" and upheavals: the collective shadow of our own internal split.

We all get jarred when the truth is not what we want to hear. But only by facing our illusions and going through the darkness of our own insecurities do we end up firmly on our own two feet. Once we have done that, we feel not *more* scared but *less* scared. Because we know that the wars are fabricated, the "attacks" are laid on, the enemies are not real, the sicknesses are invented, the economy is manipulated and we are just being controlled through our own fear.

This may look like a rather sorry state of affairs! Yet we know too that 99.9% of the world population are fine people and that awareness is rapidly growing. That global warming is due to increased light energy in our solar system (see chapter 35), that the aliens are not hostile, that we are masters of our own destiny, and that we *can* all live in peace.

The good news about the bad news is it gets us over it. Eventually everyone has heard more than enough. We do not want to feed the victim consciousness, our pain bodies, anymore. We are ready to find, support, and nurture the healing and empowering aspects of life. We recognize that we, and only we, have the power to direct our attention, our creative energy, *towards whatever we want our lives to be.* And once we shift our focus, we find there is good news on every corner and in every bookshop. Looking to ourselves, our families and our communities with new eyes, we can recognize indeed that life is good and getting better. We acknowledge, and thus contribute to, the shift that is already happening, a powerful shift of human values that is taking place around the globe. The change that is occurring on our planet is coming not from the outside but from within: on the level where the power really lies. It is not a change of government or a change of doctrine ~ it is a change of heart.

The Shiny Side of the Coin

> *You don't get rich by holding onto your money*
> *like you don't live forever by holding your breath.*
> ~ *Popular wisdom*

IF YOU LOOK ON THE BRIGHT SIDE, the need to make money is a wonderful institution. The working life gives one numerous opportunities to become enlightened, such as practicing unconditional love on the boss, and extreme acceptance while sitting in traffic jams. It pushes us to be imaginative and creative, for necessity is the mother of ingenuity; even if it's just inventing reasons why we can't go to work today. It stretches us to new areas, obliging us to go out and exchange with people we maybe wouldn't choose as friends. It puts us through countless situations we really don't like, and so steers us to find out what we would rather prefer. It helps us to learn gratitude ~ for every minute of free time we have with our friends and family. It adds hugely to the suffering of humanity and, since people can only take so much, helps us faster out of the box. Unpleasant as the process is, it thus benefits our growth as everything does. There is no stopping evolution.

Working, slaving away, producing in a world that is already overbuilt, overdressed, overstressed and oversupplied, obliges us to see the blatant senselessness of the system. We use Earth's precious resources, and our precious lives, to make a hell of a lot of stuff that really isn't needed. We then use our hard-earned cash to add to the consumer cycle of more and more rubbish, which then needs to be, somehow, somewhere, disposed of; thus adding to the pollution that was created by producing all that nonsense in the first place. Thanks planet, for putting up with us. One reason economies are sliding is because we don't seem to know when to stop.

~

AFTER MY PARTNER AND I watched the Disclosure Project Press Conference in 2001, we wondered how the world could just keep on going about its daily busyness when such extraordinary things are taking place on our planet. (We will get to this in due course, in chapter 30.) Shortly afterwards, we came across a small article about the Mayan Calendar. It resonated with our feelings that there are natural cycles in life and that things on Earth could not continue as they were going at the time. At that point, submerged in work, we felt that one either had time or money, and suddenly the first seemed a whole lot more important!

> *You have to decide whether you want to make money or make sense, because the two are mutually exclusive.*
> ~ *Buckminster Fuller*

So on that gut feeling we stopped working, except on our inner homework and sharing our findings with whoever wanted to hear them... or not. We were helped in our decision by a "random" meeting when we went to Japan to visit friends.

After the overcrowded, rattling Indian buses, we were enjoying the luxury of the spacious, comfortable airport coach into

Tokyo. There was only one other passenger. He sees this young couple with their baby and, being Indian, comes and sits right next to us. We had lived long enough in India not to find that unusual, so he poured out the essence of his life story. Unused to such directness, one could have felt that as an infringement, but we took it as a message, delivered as it was, clear and out of the blue. He said, "When I was young I wanted five 'Lakh' (100,000 rupees). When I had that I wanted 20 Lakh. It still didn't feel like enough, by then I wanted 50. That didn't satisfy me either. Now I have successful businesses in Tokyo, Hong Kong and Singapore. My sons are going to the best schools there. And I am still not a happy man. It is the nature of the human mind to be discontent. Rarely are we satisfied with whatever we have achieved."

This confirmed a little sign we read, ironically, of all places, at the check out counter of Kathmandu's first supermarket:

> *Money can buy you:*
> *A bed but not sleep,*
> *Food but not appetite,*
> *Medicine but not health,*
> *Books but not wisdom,*
> *A watch but not time,*
> *Company but not friendship,*
> *Amusement but not happiness.*

We took the cosmic hint and his experience on board. We realized that we, too, were no longer that happy with what we were doing and that it could be much more rewarding to attend to other areas of our life. We were also encouraged by the many westerners we had met traveling who lived quite freely with very little money indeed. They were life's artists, living for the moment, neither much worried nor planning ahead. None of them ever starved.

We saw it took us a considerable amount of money, and of course all our time and energy, to keep in the money-earning cycle. There were many places in the world where we could spare ourselves that pressure and live off our savings, having a far more natural and relaxed lifestyle. We had limited funds, no house, and no income, but lots of faith.

Soon enough we noticed an interesting paradox: while we were working for money we always felt like we didn't have enough, but once we had stopped, after a time of not being involved in making money, we started to have the feeling that we must be indeed well off. Simply because we were no longer caught in the machinery, and mentally engrossed with *the lack* of cash. We had little and spent little, but we were very grateful for what we had and what it gave us. We basked in our free time while far wealthier friends, comfortably set up with houses or boats, were working nine to five. Selling that security could have given them the same freedom, but not everyone has the same way. So although our account balance was going down, our self esteem was actually going up. We felt the support and easiness of life, and so, over the years, life responded by giving us more.

The laws of the universe are not that mysterious, just a simple energetic principle. We learned to trust in life rather than force it. Like all matter, money is a materialized form of energy. Hence it is not bad, and it is abundant. Its flow is representative of how our energy is running. It shows us the exchange of energy that is happening between people: when we are just freely giving our energy away, when we are in balance, or when we are hoarding and blocking energy rather than letting it flow.

Everything becomes easier when we make the life-affirming choices that serve our own, and therefore our global, evolution. We open ourselves to channel life's creative energy and to feel its continuous support.

CHAPTER TEN

Your Guiding Star

We are born at a given moment, in a given place and,
like vintage years of wine, we have the qualities of the year
and of the season of which we are born.
~ *Carl Gustav Jung*

MANY, MANY MOONS AGO, on "Om Beach" in Southern India, I was fortunate to be shown a book on "moon nodes." I have in turn shared this fundamental information with many others and its accuracy can be quite disconcerting. It's a simple and fascinating study that can be rather helpful. By giving us greater clarity about our personality, our life's journey and our soul's intent, it assists us to align with our soul's evolution. It's also a very useful tool for understanding and respecting others who we are either close to or have to be close to. (See details in Appendix I.)

Some may have, understandably, discarded astrology, due perhaps to the horoscopes in tabloid papers, as a hyped-up fairy-tale for wishful housewives. However, a good chart reading leaves everyone wondrous at its accuracy and the apparent influence and imprint of the cosmic constellations upon us.

In the science of astrology, the moon nodes are a key factor as they describe our major life theme. They explain the basic track we are on in this life: where we are coming from and where we are going to. They describe the fundamental traits of our personality and the course of our growth from one sign, one area of life, to another. Our south node details where we start from: our foundation, our familiar ground, the areas we are comfortable in, and our deeply ingrained behaviors. Our north node sign is the symbol of our future: what we aspire for. It gives us a sense of direction, like a guiding North Star. It describes the uncompleted, unfulfilled areas of our soul that we have not yet experienced or expressed. Going towards there is both insecuring and extremely rewarding. It is the one aspect of life we have the most apprehension about, yet it has a curious magnetic allure. Thus it pulls us from our comfort zone to the uncharted territory where our happiness lies, where fulfillment awaits. *That is why life can feel like such a stretch.*

Our north node does not promise a future point that will make us happy once we reach there ~ it is rather that every choice we make in that direction gives us greater fulfillment. Reading my own nodes made it clear to me why I had strong feelings for community and brotherhood and yet was brought up in relative isolation. Why life never encouraged me to merge in communal activity or relax in emotionally supportive relationships, and why, instead, I kept finding myself rather alone, placed in situations that made me build strength, individuality, and focus. Seeing the reasons behind this, my soul's agenda, I could stop feeling that life was an obstacle course, and I was missing out. I understood how solitude benefited me and could better embrace my current path and stop trying to go the other way ~ backwards. At this point I realized that if we are in agreement with our destiny we do make our lives easier! It could be said that our destiny is our own freewill. We still have the choice to accept it or to resist it.

We are required to move beyond any limiting patterns of our south node aspect and to develop the qualities of our north node, which nurture us. However, our south sign also holds our strengths and talents that may be the foundation for this life's achievements. It is once we reach our north node potential that we become complete and can truly use the qualities of our southern base for our and everyone's benefit.

Seen from the linear viewpoint of reincarnation, the south sign symbolizes our past: the unfinished areas or unresolved matters of previous lives that have brought us back here. Your childhood may have been happily immersed in your southern origins, or, if you felt you needed to press on, like I did, could have been right away the challenging stage for your north node character to evolve.

The wider our scope, the more holistic we become, the more we are able to stretch to our north node while retaining the qualities of our southern origin. Because we are no longer limited to one way, one aspect rather than another, we can now embrace both sides, the whole spectrum.

> *It is to be noted that as one's mind and emotions rise above polarized thinking, the two opposite signs become a dynamic equilibrium rather than an 'either-or.'*
>
> ~ *Mary Orser*

A FEW LAST WORDS ON ASTROLOGY. Moon nodes are just the base. On top of that is our sun, or zodiac birth sign, the positions of our planets, and the "houses" they are in. A personal chart reading can see our strengths and our weaknesses, the areas we want to be wary of, and those where we will find happiness by fulfilling our potential. It can point out our fields of interest and our specific talents; it gives us confirmation, pointers and encouragement as well as tips on where to put our focus.

The demands of our society can cloud our vision, so sometimes in life we may like to be reminded of what it is we really wanted to do here ~ by tuning into our innermost dreams or looking for guidance. Hence astrology is having a renaissance in "human design," which is becoming increasingly popular. Described as a "personality assessment tool," this is a fusion of world astrology and other traditional systems that conveys detailed and deep understanding of one's individual qualities and path.

Our astrological set-up is not, on a profound level, our essential soul nature. It is the personality, the character we are currently playing. To know our part, and the potential of our character, helps us to both better play and, eventually, to transcend the role.

The moon nodes and the zodiac show us that everyone is part of the collective human journey, working out different stages of the cycle. We are all doing different jobs and may understand each other's challenges and talents better if we know what their role is and see things from their standpoint. What is easy for you may be fully new territory for someone else, and vice-versa. As my French teacher once said to my math teacher: "Don't think what is obvious to you is obvious to another."

Some of us are here to develop the individual ego, while others embody the step of sharing; some are learning to serve, and others to surrender. None is better or more worthy than another; we are all playing a part in humanity's experience and expansion.

We contribute best to the orchestra of life when we know which instrument we are. If we are a drum, we best not spend half our lives trying to sound like a flute. Nor can we be a great lead guitar if we lay low like a bass.

There is a funny story that illustrates this. Some well-meaning intellectuals decide it would be better if all animals had the same chances and learned the same skills. So they opened a school. They tried to teach the rabbits to swim, the snakes to jump, the birds to slither and the fish to fly. The poor critters did the best they could in the classroom, but were miserable and "failed" miserably.

Play your own tune, follow your own star, remember your own dream.

> *Your only obligation in any lifetime*
> *is to be true to yourself.*
> ~ *Richard Bach,* ILLUSIONS

Return to Wholeness

We are a bridge: it is through our fundamental inner relationship, through our daily work and presence, that we each facilitate the light of consciousness, the light of love, to become increasingly anchored in our world.

CHAPTER ELEVEN

The Befriending

A chain is only as strong as its weakest link.
~ *Proverb*

AS INDIVIDUALS, and as a race, we may be very advanced in
some areas while still taking our baby steps in others. We may be
intellectually or technically brilliant, yet when it comes down to
the most fundamental and necessary ingredient in life, the heart of
the matter is: we are all here to develop our capacity to love. It is
very simple. So while some topics may feel basic to us, this lack of
base is, precisely, what weakens us. As tempting as it is to race
ahead, we do well to build our lower rungs strong, for we are
climbing a ladder to the stars.

> *It's more hazardous to race up a shaky ladder than to struggle on
> the lower rungs while making them secure.*
> ~ *Source unknown*

In our desire to get further faster, we tend to skip some steps.
This leaves us rather ungrounded and is the cause of much emotional instability, lack of self appreciation and other issues in our
modern culture. We have largely become separated from ourselves, from our sacred inner connection, and from our sense of
gratitude and reverence towards life.

We are now reconnecting. Our relationship to ourselves is the
key factor. We are a bridge: it is through our fundamental inner
relationship, through our daily work and presence, that we each

facilitate the light of consciousness, the light of love, to become increasingly anchored in our world.

This lifetime is not about getting higher, to transcend, to escape the physical plane. We are en-light-ening *this* dimension. The only way beyond it is *through* it. Hence life repeatedly brings us down to the ground, to our base, until we embrace it. It is thus, through the ups and downs of life, that we build our internal ladder. Linking and integrating *all* our parts we open our inner lines for wisdom to flow. We become the living channels through which the love of our inner self, our spirit, is downloaded into the very depths of matter.

~

YOU ARE THE ONLY PERSON you will be with your entire life. The most worthwhile, personally rewarding thing anyone can do is to work on that inner relationship. It is a lifetime journey of opening and discovery, of increasing acceptance and love. Through it all strength and wisdom comes. At the base of all mistrust is our mistrust of ourselves. Either that we won't do things right, are insufficient, or that we will judge ourselves harshly for failing to match up to *our own* expectations. By befriending ourselves we befriend life and the world. Mostly we quite like ourselves, on the surface; but look a bit deeper and oh no, what are those odd bits hiding in there? Suppressed, because we are scared we are not good enough. For whom may I ask? We only have to be good enough for ourselves.

There is so much we do because we don't feel quite adequate. We work to get more, push to be more, use discipline and force to "achieve" more. Whatever we do on the outside is never quite enough. I found myself once attending a workshop on building power and psychic protection that, much to my surprise, included a number of taxing physical exercises. Wondering, "Why am I doing this?" I realized it came from a sense of insufficiency, thinking I wasn't strong enough. Then I saw the little girl in me, who came into life feeling vulnerable and powerless amidst an insensitive world. I saw how we first undermine ourselves with doubts, and then we spend energy over-compensating for our "shortcomings" when, really, little was wrong in the first place. We are only short of trust and self approval and nothing we can do on the outside is going to make up for that.

As if to prove the point, the workshop teacher asked us what had come up for us. So without further consideration, I told him. This bright and lovely guy had been studying this traditional method of self empowerment for 20 years and was, as the living proof of its efficiency, strong and confident. And yet, noticeably shaken in his self esteem, he at first became defensive. He soon got over it and graciously acknowledged the point. To be comfy with our weaknesses allows us to be relaxed with ourselves and others. Our biggest contribution in life is not to adopt a certain style, a certain image, but to become at peace, in harmony with ourselves.

It is very understandable to want to be steady on one's feet, especially in a challenging society and changing times. Yet what this exchange most showed to me is this: the point is not to put on confidence from the outside, but to look within. Before we start tapping into cosmic energies as our power point, we do well to start on the ground. To address the cause, not the symptom; that which is keeping us vulnerable: our mistrust, our fear of hurt, our doubt in ourselves and hence in the world.

The tendency is often to override the sensitivities of our small part to become "stronger" or to fly higher. Actually, we weaken ourselves through this repression and this split of our wholeness. A strong facade simply covers up our vulnerability. It cuts off the feelings that are our true guide. Do we really need to become *better*...or just more trusting, more in touch with our own loving base, more at ease with our sensitive and softer side?

The wish to protect that insecure part is fair enough, but the remedy lies not in a tougher skin. That is just armor, a surface solution. It does not heal the underlying hurt we feel. What is it that really makes us strong? A solid foundation. *Unshakeable strength lies in understanding, in acceptance, and in trust: in ourselves, the world, and the process of Life.*

～

THE ANSWER LIES WITHIN. By checking out our core beliefs we find what it is inside ourselves that keeps attracting what we don't want. What comes to us in life is not random fate, it is a reflection of our innermost feelings and our often unconscious focus. It is our unacknowledged parts that sabotage us and knock us off balance, repeatedly raising our emotions or sending us to the bottle, the fridge, the doctor or the box of tissues. We want to be in full agreement with ourselves; this integrity is our protection and our core strength. Once we look into our own shadows and love whatever we find within, we become steady. We embrace our weaknesses and detach from disempowering thought patterns. We constantly undermine our own power, our potential, and our progress with self depreciation and doubts. It is by recognizing our self judgment that we discover the healer: compassion. It is, finally, our return to innocence.

It is through compassionate self appreciation of all we are, that we express, and thus benefit from, the strongest power in the world: Love. Through love we come to know that we are already okay, perfect with our imperfections. And once we feel this, we can relax. Growing is not about pushing ourselves to become someone, but opening to love who we are. For as long as we are striving to be *better,* rather than just enjoying to expand, we are affirming that we are not yet good enough. So the great news is you don't have to be the first to climb Everest in the nude. The only way to be more is to love more. Our assignment here is simply to love ourselves. Make it your pet project.

Through really loving ourselves we drop force, the old mindset that humanity has been in: "no pain, no gain." (And we *wonder* why life hurts!) We find that when we are easy on ourselves, life is easy on us. For we are the ones who are directing our lives. Everything comes without force, if we allow it to. To do so, we need trust.

Recognize that we are already whole, perfect, and that the route of the least resistance is the way water flows. Doing something against the grain, because we feel we ought to, may not be benefiting us. If things feel desperate, go jump in the pool! At play we are closest to our true nature. Right brain activities like playing, singing, dancing, contemplation and sharing love are natural ways to regain balance and reconnect to our inner being.

My life has shown me again and again to stay in touch with my smaller side. It is the measure of our self love. When that part is relaxed and happy we are more open, and thus work better, hand in hand with our higher selves. We avail ourselves of tremendous guidance, support, and creativity by recognizing that we do not need to push anything to happen all by our little selves. When we are in tune, everything flows with ease and grace. I am weary and wary of too much discipline. We often try too hard and block ourselves, whereas when we trust and are at ease the expression of our beautiful inner self flows naturally.

It is when we go on holiday or into deep relaxation, when we let go of the worries and the tensions, that our fullness, the pure joy of our being, shines through. Unburdened and open once again we feel reborn ~ and reminded: This is who I really am.

At the risk of sounding like a skipping CD, I will keep repeating: Be kind to yourself, befriend yourself. The tired face we sometimes catch in the mirror is struggling not only with outer conditions but with its own mindset. So give yourself some loving. We can't get it all right all the time, but we can appreciate ourselves for what we do well and not mind ourselves for what we don't. Whenever you feel inadequate, just remember... you were once, out of millions, the quickest sperm! We can relax, we got here. We already won.

~

WE EACH HAVE THE TWO YEAR OLD and the thousand year old within us and, of course, everything in between. In fact each of us is a bridge between the human plane and the divine. No wonder life feels like a stretch! The relationship within us, between these parts, is the key to all other relationships; personal, social and cosmic. It is the ladder we are building to the stars.

We mostly take refuge in our stronger parts and repress the smaller ones until they burst out, and we break down. Yet it is when we feel those aspects of ourselves that we actually approach our purpose. Our smaller being has the hardest job here. It carries all the fears, feels all the hurt, and gets judged as not good enough. It gets ignored, silenced, forgotten, hidden, blamed and locked away!

Recognizing this weakest part is the key to our expansion. For it embodies the very aspects of the human psyche we came here to integrate, to uplift and to en-lighten. That is why our shadow traits are the opposite of our brightest side, and by ac-knowledging them we unleash our creative energy. It is why "we teach best what we most need to learn."

It appears some very bright spirits have chosen extremely dense matter: fear, anger, hate, or addiction. They have delved the deepest, taken on the most resistant patterns, so as to download the light and warmth of love into the deepest depths of the unconscious.

Our spirited part holds the vision, the courage, and the light. Our personal part carries the feeling, the softness and the sensi-tivity. So let's listen to the little one with empathy. It is the part we are here to merge with. Whether we see it as our inner child, our little sister or brother, our shadow or our "pet human"… it is time to reopen the dialogue. Tune into, and trust, our highest part too, for it is here to help us through our insecurities to another world. Through this openness we bridge the gap and we re-establish a loving relationship within ourselves. We become whole again.

OUR JOURNEY HERE is one of reunion: Rekindling the bond. In-deed, we are still "hu-man becomings." Through the merging of the human being and the spirit being that we are, we are destined to become a "HU-man" in the true, literal sense of the word, a "god-person."

CHAPTER TWELVE

Ode to the Ego

There is nothing in a caterpillar
that tells you it is going to be a butterfly.
~ *Richard Buckminster Fuller*

WHILE WE ARE ON THE TOPIC of befriending ourselves, let's tackle a tricky part: our ego. Being the smallest one, the poor little ego gets all the blame. Between religions condemning it as the root of all evil, and priests, professors, parents, peers and partners all highlighting our self doubts, the maligned ego really takes a battering. No wonder then that everywhere one goes on this planet, most people have, whatever their status, one thing in common: not enough self worth. Hence the tremendous need for approval that we seek from others. Whose approval are we really missing? Our own.

Now there is no critique in this; you, Bob, and I are all in the same boat. And we know, from the mirror effect, that this feeling of insufficiency is not really given to us by others, but an innate trait we brought to heal with love.

So, what is our ego, where is it valuable, why is it put down, and how does it feel to be without it? Don't get me wrong here! One afternoon tea at an ashram in India, I remember a smug American who, on seeing someone reading a book on how to overcome one's ego, ostentatiously remarked, "I still remember how it felt when I lost mine." Yeah right...we all know that the spiritual ego is a common pitfall! But equally damaging is the religious trap of condemning the ego, to ensure that the spiritual seekers on the planet don't have a foot to stand on.

What most institutions aim at, is to forcibly diminish the ego through uniformity and conformity. Religions tend to crush the ego, with the concept of sin, and with ascetic practices. Devotees hope that through meekness they may reach a state of ego-less bliss. Hence the notorious bed of nails! If diminishing the ego by force was an effective method, we'd all be enlightened by now! A master may well be someone who sits cross-legged, doesn't eat pizza, and wears orange. However this is his end result, not how he got there. We won't become masters by sitting cross-legged, not eating pizza, and wearing orange.

I have to say here a "big thanks" to my mum, whose graduation thesis was: "Methods Used to Control the Masses," for having the guts to tell our primary school headmistress, "My children will not wear uniforms." So in all the class photographs, amidst the grey and white shirts and blazers, my sister and I are conspicuous with our ginger hair and our colorful flower dresses. Interestingly, this difference never made me feel split from my school mates. Diversity, I found, is not contrary to togetherness.

There has been a huge effort made in human history to hold down, cramp, repress, crush, stifle, squelch and even stamp out our individuality. Recognize that it not only enables our personal power, it is also *the* doorway to our uniting and our collective human evolution.

WE HAVE BEEN TOLD THE EGO is "at fault." This is like saying a child is at fault for being childish. The ego is not a culprit; it is just a natural stage of development. Our ego ~ our personality, our character ~ is like a cloak we wear: it is what gives us an individual identity. This coat insulates us from the whole, enclosing us in the capsule of our own separate identity. It thus enables us to relate to others, but, due to feeling separate from "them," also causes us a degree of insecurity.

Stripping off this layer we instantly experience a sense of oneness and, therefore, such peace and love. We can sense this whenever we let our borders fully down. If we are fortunate, we may at some point have experienced a "gap" that took us deeper. This can happen through meditation, or spontaneously, through shock, silence, or surprise...whatever brings our attention to the present moment, into "the Now." In the case of brain scientist Jill Bolte Taylor, it occurred through a stroke. She explains in her book how the left side of the brain is the seat of our ego personality:

> *The left brain organizes, describes, judges and critically analyses everything. Through constant brain chatter it manifests my identity: I become an individual entity separate from the whole.*

So how does it feel to let go of our ego identity? When Jill's left brain shut down during the stroke, her separatist identity dissolved and she became aware of our right brain character, which is always there in the background.

> *The right brain realizes that the essence of my being has eternal life, is part of the cosmic flow. It knows we are laced together, life is good and we are all beautiful just the way we are. It is my intuition and higher consciousness. The character at the core of my right brain is completely committed to the expression of peace, love, joy and compassion. . . . Wasn't it interesting that although I could not walk or talk or understand language, speak or even roll over, I knew that I was okay? I was aware that I was the miraculous power of life, a being of light radiating power into the world.*

Considering the contrasting views of these two sides, it is not surprising that we are often in two minds about things!

> *My left mind thinks of me as a fragile individual capable of losing my life.*

Our right brain personality, always present at a deeper level of our being, is largely blanketed by the separatist identity of our left brain character. It is where a child resides before it learns language. It is the part that connects us to the eternal element of our being, and thus to our intrinsic unity.

I didn't want to lose my connection to the universe, to experience myself as a solid separate from everything. I didn't want my mind to spin so fast that I was no longer in touch with my authentic self. I didn't want to give up Nirvana.

Our left brain identity is the source of our feeling separate from oneness. When we venture beyond our insecure, separatist left brain ~ our ego character ~ the reward is the discovery of our blissful being as part of the whole. It is indeed a pity for us that the insecurity inherent in the ego enhances our separation and therefore we cannot experience the "onederful" sense of oneness. But it is not a defect; it is simply part of the design. The actual "problem" that stems from the ego is really *the insecurity* it experiences due to this state of separation. For one, we feel we are alone in the world and, worse still, we feel surrounded by "others."

Would it be possible for me to recover my perception of self, where I exist as a single, solid, separate from the whole, without recovering the cells associated with my egotism, desire to be argumentative, need to be right, or fear of separation and death? Could I regain my personal power in the world, play the game of hierarchy and yet not lose my sense of compassion or perception of equality among all people?
~ Jill Bolte Taylor

Our natural insecurity of, and therefore our comparison towards, the "others" has been amplified by our societies and politicians. It has been easy to prey on our basic survival instincts, ensnaring us in fear of insufficiency and scarcity, and therefore in greed and competition, to keep us working and consuming. Western society would have us believe that our worth, what we *are*, depends on what we *have*. So we may well feel lacking in ourselves: not clever enough, rich enough, or pretty enough; or fear the shortage of jobs, fuel, water, land, power, or money. We may even be led to believe we have to fight for these.

Insecurity causes us to put on armor: a hard outer shell to protect our tenderness. And in this insensitive world a bit of armor can feel protective, insulating. But it is also isolating. It protects us, not only from the hurt but also from the love. It separates us, so we do not feel that we are connected to all others, and supported by the whole, but a fragile being that needs to defend itself and fend for itself. Alone, against all others. So we may push and pull, hide and hoard, maneuver and manipulate.

Society encourages us to compete for survival ~ in a world that has enough of everything! An abundance of fresh air, water, food, money, energy… and, oh yes, people. Yet every man, woman and child on this planet, given one quarter acre each, would still *all* fit into Australia. An amazing statistic. Then, honestly, people say to me, "But most of Australia is desert so they couldn't live there." Duh! Australian Immigration will not need to toughen its laws any further. "No worries mate," the idea is not to move the entire world population into your outback! It simply illustrates that our planet is not overpopulated. It is just mismanaged.

IF OUR EGO, our separate identity, is too strong, our borders are tightly closed, and we become cut off. If however it is not strong enough, and we are aware of others' feelings and needs more than our own, then we don't affirm our personal borders and are easily abused. A well-balanced ego enables us to appreciate and to nurture our own personality and talents, and to pool them for the benefit of a communal purpose while retaining our own integrity. This is a really essential ingredient in our daily lives and in our expansion. Humanity is starting to embrace an advanced, united consciousness that requires our distinct individuality. Otherwise group consciousness, a "united" humanity, simply means to be absorbed by the group. In some societies, the group mind can be seen to suppress individual growth and expression, encouraging obedience, self sacrifice, and a docile mentality that is easily manipulated. Hence a clear sense of self, a certain degree of "selfishness," is actually vital.

> *The trick is to be yourself in a world that wants you*
> *to be like everybody else.*
> ~ *Source unknown*

A good healthy ego is like a good healthy appetite. It sustains us; it shows our gratitude and love for life, and for all that has been bestowed upon us. Through self appreciation we acknowledge the gift of life. If our ego gets too big however, just like our appetite, we become overweight and inflated. Undernourished egos are faint, hesitant, with hardly enough sense of own identity or self value to dare to express their inner power and play their part to the full. Dedicating oneself to the whole is best achieved when one has developed a fully individual and self-loving character to dedicate.

Self doubt holds us back. Our degree of self esteem determines how much support we are open to receive, and hence how much energy we have to contribute: our gift to the world. The self-obsessed ego, which is a calamity to itself and those around it, has long since been lamented. We all know the havoc it causes. However, the overt lack of self worth ~ and therefore lack of trust in ourselves, in our world, and in life itself ~ is equally destructive. It limits our receptivity, undermines our strength, keeps us small, and is the source of many of our wacky behaviors: energy-pulling patterns and other addictions, power games, criticism and control. It is even the source of the bloated ego. So however imperfect we may feel, by accepting and loving ourselves ~ insecurities, ego and all ~ we treat the root cause rather than battling with the symptoms.

To condemn our personal ego as being opposite from spiritual is, from our perspective, condemning ourselves. By making it the enemy, we censor and split ourselves. We find self acceptance and balance, and grow beyond the confines of the ego, when we recognize it for what it is. Our ego personality feels separate and, therefore, that it has to manage all by its little self. This causes it undue effort. Unaware of how connected we always are, it tends to become focused on its security and consequent achievements. Not recognizing that all we are and receive is really a gift, it may then even feel it has been successful, "all by itself," and become big-headed.

Concerned for its own identity that it associates with its survival, the ego tends to wrap us up in "the little story of me." This is not bad ~ it certainly has its place in our development ~ but it becomes limiting. When engrossed and submerged in our own small dramas we miss the beauty, diversity and enormity of life. Our insecure ego prevents us from seeing the bigger picture, including how much more we too are, and how we are always supported. Simply turning the ego's volume down, lowering the walls of our separatist identity, naturally allows us to expand towards our right brain character ~ at one, at peace with the world.

HAVING AN EGO IDENTITY does not prevent us from feeling with others. Mine enables me to know my feelings, my borders, my priorities and my space, and therefore to respect others' too. Yet it risks infringing on those it is fond of out of insecurity: when it fears that they may miss something vital to their well-being. It used to be a constant source of dismay to me that everyone is here to learn from their own experiences. I would personally far prefer to take a shortcut, sparing myself all that unnecessary struggle. However, the shortcut is not always obvious at the time!

> *It is smart to learn from ones mistakes.*
> *It is genius to learn from the mistakes of others.*
> ~ *Popular wisdom*

That my loved ones couldn't just pick up my experience from the tail end frustrated me. If others insisted on learning the hard way, okay, but why my own daughter?! Obstinate and independent from the start, she really taught me to let go. I eventually learned to respect that everyone has their own way, their own path to tread, in their own timing. I came to understand about the role and place of resistance, and the role of suffering. I came to appreciate our long journeys and to see the value of personal experience ~ each and every experience ~ for our own growth as individuals. And I came to recognize the importance of separation to develop our individuality. To form our ego, to focus on developing ourselves and our self love, is the first natural step of human creativity.

> *Life is not about finding yourself.*
> *Life is about creating yourself.*
> ~ *George Bernard Shaw*

You can see it clearly with a child. They have to be allowed to grow naturally. They have to be brought up, not brought down. Preventing a child's ego from forming is like nipping it in the bud. At home, school, or church we all go through some process of socialization that criticizes how and who we are. Researchers tell us that during its upbringing a child hears 25,000hrs of parental instruction, which may be mostly negative. In its first few years it is told, "no," "don't" and, "don't want" some 60,000 times. Little surprise then that we tend to feel powerless.

We hold ourselves down by not allowing our natural instincts and our expression to flow freely. We are constantly doubting and censoring ourselves, especially those on the "spiritual" path. To hold the core belief that there is something inherently wrong with us does not support our self esteem! Without self worth we cannot be, express, or trust ourselves. Without a solid sense of self approval, a healthy ego, where will we find the strength to face our own shadows? It is our personal work, and reward, to discover who we really are, and to retrieve our true self worth. We are here to explore and express our inner beauty as openly as we dare.

If our ego is not allowed to blossom, we cut off our own life force. Our ego is our tool to express our creativity: the artist's brush, the singer's voice, the dancer's body. Through us the creative life force flows. We are the way through which consciousness lives and blooms in matter. It is our offering to express this life force as fully, and diversely, as we can.

Enclosed in our ego personality, insulated from our oneness, we are here to focus, first and foremost, on our own evolution: to develop our relationship to ourselves and our creative potential. We thus grow in individuality, love and freedom, and the seed for our ~ and humanity's ~ flowering is formed.

In the same way that a child has to separate from its parents to find its own identity, self worth, and expression, our being isolated from the whole enables our self discovery, our growth in self love. It is then that a child can return and relate to its parents as a fulfilled individual and enrich them with its specific personality and talents. It is then, through our individual fulfillment and uniqueness, that we can serve the community, and the whole. It is by everyone playing different instruments, melodies and harmonies, that we make music together.

OUR COLLECTIVE FLOWERING is a gradual process, yet once the basic steps are done links happen rapidly, and sudden, spontaneous evolution can occur extremely fast. Picture yourself as a seed. A seed, like a baby, starts off soft and unprotected. As it grows, the shell hardens to safely shelter the maturing which is taking place within. The seed is developing the specific DNA information that it alone carries to full strength. The child, too, forms a shell to protect itself from outer intrusion while its own unique personality and potential are being formed. When the seed is ready, the outer casing breaks open and a shoot, a sapling, a tree, bursts forth. We take this transformation for granted. *Yet it is one of the wonders of nature that the information for a gigantic oak is contained in a tiny acorn.* A seed is programmed to be mature at a certain season. For the seed to open, the time and the conditions must be right; it has a certain window of opportunity. At the first signs of spring a few seeds will shed their coats, and then a few more, and then many more, increasingly rapidly, until multitudes burst open simultaneously.

It is like a symphony, first one violin starts, then a cello joins in, a piano, and pretty soon all the instruments are in harmony. Each individual plays their part with gusto, and the blend of notes and melodies creates a giant cosmic symphony.

CHAPTER THIRTEEN

Surrender Now

﹏〜⤸

Life is about learning to dance in the rain,
not waiting for the storm to pass.

~ *Vivian Greene*

WHEN OUR DAUGHTER was one and a half we flew from Japan to Norway, a most beautiful, magical country. North of the polar circle, we spent the midsummer nights watching the midnight sun dip almost into the sea and then rise again. They have long, slow cycles up there, from 24 hours of daylight in the height of summer to 24 hours of darkness in midwinter. We could feel a tremendous difference of speed between our globetrotting child and the local kids. When she was two, we estimated she had taken a dozen intercontinental flights and had slept in 200 different places. We decided to slow down for a bit and moved, by boat, to the Canary Islands.

By the time she was eight, we counted she still hadn't lived more than three months in one place. So we chose to spend the whole winter season at a quiet beach in South India which attracted young multi-cultural families and musicians. One could count on it not to rain for those six months, so we slept outdoors, under the shooting stars, in a garden right behind the beach. Our home was a rustic coconut leaf hut which took the locals an entire day to build. The eco toilet was a deep hole under a convenient tree whose branches reached, considerately, almost to the ground.

One early morning, fresh out of bed, there I was, squatting mindlessly under the "bathroom's" green canopy. After a brief moment my attention was drawn to a patch of sunlight on the leaves just a couple feet away. Therein sat the local cobra. Let's just say, it was not a moment I could easily move; nor did I want to shock the poor snake from its morning reverie. There was little else to do but surrender. Snakes seem to do that to one. So we looked at each other, the snake and I. Time held its breath. Quietness engulfed us. The air went still and the sound of the waves seemed another world away. Every leaf stood out clear and crisp. The snake's scaly body was pulsating in slow motion. I sent it silent compliments: "nice snake," "sweet snake," "pretty snake." After some time, leisurely, it went on its way. The bubble burst. Time started running again. The waves crashed on the beach.

This slight shift reminded me of a similar occurrence, 10 years prior. When I was nineteen, I wrote off the family car. This minor incident left me unscathed, but wiser. It also granted me another glimpse through the thin layer of veneer we call reality. I remember standing next to the wreck, in a space of peace-filled stillness, watching the morning traffic speeding along the highway on the way to work. I had just stepped out of that mad race and was in another world. It had a very different quality about it, and I was aware that this was the real world, the reality when all else stops. It was quiet in that world. My breath hung in the cold winter air and I felt deep peace. After what seemed like ages, someone stopped to offer me assistance. My mind started up again. The sound of the traffic flooded in. I was back.

Surrender is a portal. It stops us in our tracks, enabling us to recognize the silent screen, the backdrop of our life's movie.

The Power of Yes

MANY YEARS AGO IT WAS ALREADY foreseeable that waves of "refugees" would move out of the States in search of what they would feel they had lost at home. While I was living in the South Pacific, numerous Americans would turn up looking for new lands to settle, as they do all over the globe. They bring with them the diluted spirit of their ancestors, the pioneers, as well as many opinions on how things should or should not be done. Time away from home benefits them greatly.

Enter John and Bob. These two Texans had come to Tonga to scout it out. The Kingdom of Tonga is a group of tiny isles utterly removed from the rest of the world. I had joked them on arrival that the only way to make it out on the islands was to "surrender now." Most people just couldn't adjust to the lack of pace out there and the way that things *weren't* done. A few buildings had recently burned down on the main street and the rubble was piled high on the pavement. "When are they going to clean up the debris?" Bob asked.

Raising my eyebrows I jokingly reminded him, "Surrender now."

"Well, yes, but maybe just the sharp bits?"

I laughingly shook my head, "Surrender now, Bob!" He did, bless him, at least surrender to the understanding that he couldn't live out there.

Westerners often want to help the people of the "third world" countries who are, in many cases, happier than we are! The Peace Corps is one of America's many attempts to charitably sway the rest of the world to their way of thinking and doing things. So I met numerous unsuspecting volunteers who were trained and sent out to improve the relaxed lifestyle of the South Pacific islanders. Tonga is poetically advertised as "The land where time begins." It is, even more accurately, the land where time stands still. I would arm the over-eager volunteers with the following prayer:

> *Grant me the serenity to accept the things I cannot change,*
> *the courage to change the things I can,*
> *and* [above all] *the wisdom to know the difference.*
> ~ *Reinhold Niebuhr*

Being industrious is *not* one of the local's priorities. A Peace Corps girl voiced her desperation: Most unbelievably, the local supermarket had stopped ordering a popular tourist item because they had to restock the shelf too often! Of course, after two years of mission work nothing had changed on the islands at all, except for the brave volunteers themselves, who matured tremendously.

Life on the road certainly puts one through plenty of unpredictable tests. Imagine you board the late night train, to find that your berths for the 50 hour journey ahead have been double-booked. When you finally arrive at your destination, the hotel has lost your reservation and is full. You have to wake up at 3am for a flight, only to discover, when you reach the airport, that it has been cancelled... Our choices are to accept the circumstances, change them, or leave. And firstly, we do well to stay cool and assess our plight. If that is the situation, right now, we might as well accept it! Uttered with a sigh, a shrug, or a smile, "It is as it is" became our motto.

We repeatedly cause ourselves unhappiness by not accepting what is. By focusing on what we *don't* like, we put ourselves in resistance mode and block our own flow. Kinesiology is a well proven method of muscle testing diagnosis that taps into our cellular wisdom and reads the energetic flow in our bodies. Our muscles test strong if we say, "yes" or hold a good feeling. Our muscles cannot hold strong with a "no" or a disempowering thought. Our life energy, simply, is not flowing through.

So by first accepting a situation we really open to our own creative power. *Then,* if we can't live with it, we can change it. If we can't change it, we can leave. Now this may explain why I kept on traveling! We do well to first consider any situation as if we had chosen it, because on some intricate level, behind the scenes, we have. In this way we work with our own movie script, not against it. Life becomes our friend, not our enemy. Often, in its reflective way, through utterly subtle hints, it is trying to show us something. Resistance holds our eyes, ears and hearts closed. It shuts our own valve and cuts us off from the flow. Accept, agree, acknowledge, allow, approve and appreciate! The world becomes a far friendlier place.

> *When I loved myself enough I quit wishing my life looked some other way and began to see that, as it is, my life serves my evolution.*
>
> ~ *Kim McMillen*

After a stroke, Ram Das, inspirational author of *Be Here Now*, had to be driven around in his own car. He expressed: "I can either be a frustrated driver or someone who is content to be chauffeured." We may like to remember this choice for the road ahead.

~

AS I ROAM AROUND OUR COLORFUL PLANET, I often find that people in "developing" nations cope rather well with unexpected events. They don't take things so personally, like it's all against them. They haven't got the "bratitude" that kicks up a stink because it can't get its own way. This, in turn breeds a more gracious environment for all around: "So the girl can't figure out the cash register? It's alright, I'll wait." They then use such an opportunity to chat with the stranger behind them.

Resistance does have its survival-based purpose in our individual development. It starts with a simple evaluation of what is good for us or not, but we easily become exclusive. There's no question that individuality is great, but overdone it rather becomes resistance to what is: our dislike of this, our disagreement with that, our disapproval of the other. It becomes a part of our special identity and our daily outlook: I don't eat this, I don't like that, I don't believe it... Because we attract what we focus on, it is very helpful to notice that whenever we don't feel good, we are focusing on something we don't like.

So, next time you're at the drive-through or waiting in line, silently taking out your impatience on the innocent person at the counter or in front of you, thus causing yourself to become more irritated each half minute longer they take... why prolong the agony? Surrender now! Use those few minutes instead to relax and enjoy the moment. Every moment is precious.

We have been taught it shows intelligence to be critical. Now, to be discerning: Yes. Critical? No. For by being exclusive, we actually exclude ourselves. We miss to partake in the variety, the abundance, and the wonder that the world offers us every day. The likes of poets, philanthropists and philosophers feel the mystery and the humaneness of life. Gardeners, photographers and artists notice the details in nature, lighting and form. Their world has more beauty and, in turn, they give our world more beauty. As we choose gratitude over "bratitude," we open our own valve to life. By becoming aware of the abundance around us, we open the door to our own inner abundance.

The key to this door is a generous, approving, inclusive and embracing outlook. One funny, holistic life exercise always makes me smile. Going to sleep, waking up, and anytime in the day you happen to feel closed, repeat: "Yes, yes, yes, yes, yes." This instantly opens our flow.

At some stage I noticed that "no" was my default setting, my first reaction. It felt safer. I still remember my mother warning me, her own fears enhancing mine, "If a handsome stranger in a Jag offers you a lift, say No." Yeah right! As we *become aware* of our own holding back we can start to make other choices. By opening to life, seeing the world as fully cooperative rather than inherently hostile, we enable ourselves to recognize our options and opportunities and to receive the support that is always there for us. We see the wonder of the world, the gift of life, and we feel immense gratitude. This gratitude opens all doors.

Once we embrace life, we begin to live in a space of trust ~ a "yes" philosophy. This is the right key to sing in. Life is "amping up," which inspires us to be more spontaneous. The time will come when multiple events unfold instantaneously, so we will not choose with our minds but straight from our hearts. The universe will bear us gifts and we would like to be, *instinctively,* open to them!

As we are now becoming more accepting of ourselves and others, we refrain less, oppose less, criticize less and control less; we find ourselves becoming more at peace. The more we nurture ourselves, the more we say "yes" to life and thus open to receive, the more life gives us. The more we appreciate, the more we are given to appreciate. It's an interactive game. And as we start to recognize the astonishing degree of connectivity, we enter a zone of easiness and flow. Synchronicities abound. Life begins to feel like a game of "Join the Dots" rather than the usual ups and downs of "Snakes and Ladders." We recognize that life certainly works in mysterious ways but it is, always, our helper.

Admittedly, this is not always obvious at first sight. It may indeed seem at times that life does not have our best interests at heart, but what do we know? Sometimes not getting what we want can be a great stroke of "luck." How often has an apparent mishap turned out to be beneficial to us, leading us to develop new contacts or unexplored areas! By noticing this we regain our trust, and we no longer *force* things to go our way. It's only when we stop pushing outwards that things can flow towards us. Quite obviously, we cannot swim against the current and float with it at the same time.

> *Everything you desire is downstream.*
> ~ *Abraham Hicks*

Our resistance came only from the feeling of having to fend for ourselves and manage all alone. Once we recognize the interactive, interconnected nature of our supportive, loving world, we can relax. Life becomes indeed simple, guided, and flowing. Letting go of how we are always brings us closer to our dreams. And downstream is where our dreams await. As my good old friend from Sirius says:

> *Resistance puts us on the local train to our destiny.*
> *If you understand your role and co-operate with life,*
> *you get put on the 1st class express because you are*
> *part of the solution, not part of the problem.*
> ~ *Paul Six*

The river of our collective destiny is leading us from separation to union, from resistance to cooperation, from hurt to gratitude. Everything that is not in line with this stage of our evolution feels increasingly dysfunctional. Hence, we can no longer find fulfillment or success in separatist ventures that are not in sync with our greater purpose, and do not acknowledge our community, our collective being. We don't sacrifice our individuality when we dedicate it to the service of the whole. We put the current of life behind us, and it empowers us. Rather than playing our single tunes separately, we become attentive to the composer's guidance and discover how to harmonize together. We are the screenwriter, the director and the actor of this movie. It is our play, the song of humanity.

*If you can learn the simple act of gratitude,
  your evolution will happen of its own accord.*
                                        ~ Osho

THESE DAYS ARE CALLING FOR OUR UNITING. Used to being the king of the road, the poor little ego part may feel threatened, scared of losing its borders and its hard won individuality and independence. Yet what was previously part of our integrity, for our protection, may become our bondage. At first, for the separatist ego, to surrender feels like psychological suicide. The fear of losing oneself can cause one to kick and scream and create drama: it is how the separatist ego part feels, and reinforces, its identity, the borders between itself and "the others." Yet as we keep choosing love in the face of a contrary reaction pattern, we find this is not self sacrifice but an expansion beyond the line we had drawn for ourselves: *this* is who I am.

Going through these internal renovations can feel like losing one's identity, losing one's mind. For indeed, what our left mind has limited us to being, is slipping away. It is not by condemning the ego's reactions but by understanding and allowing the insecurity of this part that we can reassure it, and enable it to gradually relinquish its hold. If we don't muster the love to open bit by bit, we can always "do an Eckhart" ~ an overnight transformation ~ for intense anguish is the default setting that pushes us through.

Realizing that we are indeed not separate but an interdependent part of a larger story enables us to willingly align with it. It is not a sacrifice, it is a collaboration that leads to our expansion. All our paths are part of humanity's journey. And once we recognize our connectivity, and the grace of life, it is simply out of gratitude that we wish to serve.

Our separatism keeps us isolated from the whole, and hence keeps us small. We miss to benefit from life's flow. It is through our individual expansion, through truly maximizing ourselves ~ not through self aggrandizement but through increasing cooperation ~ that we each become a channel, each in our own unique way enabling the inner life-force that unites us all to blossom on Earth.

THE HAPPINESS WE ALL SEEK, in so many inventive ways, really lies in our own approval. Having found that the striving, shopping, and socializing doesn't quite do it, we slow down. We refine our search, we reduce, we redefine the essential. Ultimately, our joy can only be found within. We discover the lasting peace of mind that comes with approval: "The world is okay as it is," "my mother is okay as she is," and first and foremost, at the base of all other evaluation: "I am okay as I am."

Some 20 years ago, when my brother was at the impressionable age of 22, he was flying for a family reunion from Fiji Islands to Canary Islands, on the other side of the blue planet. His flight included a 24 hour stopover in San Francisco and our mother recommended he go down to Fisherman's Wharf. He did, and was approached by a couple of girls, with the great pick up line of, "You look like a lonely traveler who is seeking a purpose in life, to do something good for the world, with a great team of like-minded people." He landed in the arms of a very powerful religious sect. Our mum's worst fear had come true. He never took his onward flight and disappeared from our lives.

Now, I am one of those people who tends to work too hard. Yet once I have done my best to no avail, I finally, graciously, give up and let go. This was one of those many lessons in life. After numerous letters, pleading him to retain his free spirit, I surrendered to the circumstances. I consoled myself that worse things have happened to better people. If my brother, my mother, or even my child has a different path, so be it. We can trust that everyone's life is perfectly designed to benefit their, and our, opening.

Thoroughly appreciate your life and this world. It is such a blessing. Latest when we are getting ready to leave, and hopefully long before, we will understand how good it was to us, even when it "wasn't." We will probably wish we had taken it all less seriously, enjoyed it more, and eaten more chocolate! I joke that "God" may pat some of us on the head and say, "You were very eager, you did very well, but did you get the point of the game? It was to have fun!" The best way to show our appreciation for all we have been given is to enjoy it! Suddenly life blooms.

ACCEPTANCE IS A PORTAL. This explains why there were times in India I'd be walking down a filthy, smelly back lane full of rubbish, not minding it at all, and out of the blue, I'd be feeling euphoric. Or resigned to sitting on a crowded bumpy bus with an intoxicated driver and the speakers blaring out distorted Hindi pop music…and for no apparent reason, I'd be feeling high as a kite.

We cannot transcend what we condemn or deny. Acceptance bears the gift of transcendence. It turns the key to our personal fulfillment and the key to the end of suffering. We are here to approve of ourselves and the world; to recognize that all is right as it is, that the set-up is perfect. That allowance, in itself, is a change of mindset, which in turn manifests a new reality.

Hence it serves our own evolution to see our "less than ideal" past as being perfect towards us becoming who we are now: wiser and warmer beings. If our past is stored in a memory file labeled "bad," we won't get far off that point. By changing our feelings towards the past we invite a different vibration, a different future, into our lives.

Similarly, the paradox is to acknowledge that our world is as it is now for the very best of reasons ~ while knowing it to be in the process of evolving, of transformation. Everything, including ourselves, is in a state of constant and ever-escalating change. This is the only inevitable fact for us to accept in life; not "death," and certainly not taxes. Therefore we don't find happiness by clinging to, or insisting on, what we have ~ we find it in going with the flow. Don't hold yourself back by saying, "This is good enough for me." Or even, "It doesn't get much better than this." Believe me, it does.

CHAPTER FOURTEEN

Embracing our Shadow

~~~~~⌐

Be what you is, coz if you be what you ain't,
then you ain't what you is.

~ *Unknown epitaph*

OUR SELF APPROVAL is the cornerstone of our being. I met
many people around the globe, often with high status, who had a
confident outgoing manner that covered an insecure, rather unsure of themselves, inner feeling. It was in trying to figure out this
polarity, that I came across the "shadow" concept. I didn't realize
then the extent of the phenomenon and what a decisive role it
plays in our daily lives and in turning the tide of human history.

It caught up with me by surprise some years later in Bali at a
friend's place. A few of us, not suspecting what would be on the
menu, were watching an interactive movie, "The Shadow Effect."
Pen in hand we each wrote our answers as Debbie Ford led us
through a series of questions designed to reveal the viewer's main
shadow. I enjoyed watching how the answers came together on
my page, how it all linked up. I understood myself better, my family members, why I attracted certain types of friends, and what
they were mirroring in me.

The traits that most bother us in others are those we don't
like in ourselves. Otherwise it wouldn't bug us so. Of course, it
takes one to know one, does it not? We all have these traits that
we were told, or felt, were "bad" when we were young ~ so we
learned to hide them, not just from others, but also from ourselves.

Let's be very clear here: our shadow part is not the problem.

The problem came from labeling it "bad," as society had trained us to. This split us. Only when we accept and love these parts, do we become whole again. It boils down to knowing and approving of our whole selves, so we can be more relaxed with who and how we truly are. Then we don't need to be *better* than we are, we can just be at peace with *who* we are. We become more confident and more genuine.

ENCOURAGED BY OUR OWN DRIVE, our parents, and our education to excel, we have been all our lives busy enhancing and applauding our best and brightest sides. That's all cool, except that the other parts, the less liked ones, have been ignored. Pushed into the shadows of our subconscious, they became our shadow. Unknown to us, our shadow determines our daily life, affecting our relationships to ourselves and to others. For just as one can't hold a balloon underwater, what we resist will persist, often bursting out at inappropriate times. Not only do we use excessive energy to keep it down, we also deprive ourselves of the energy held within those areas. Like an ignored child or a task put off, it will continuously bug us.

It is vital for us to know our shadow parts so that we harbor no inner conflict, and therefore no dis-ease. So that one part of us is not condemning another part for not being smart enough, strong enough, or good enough. And so that our "acknowledged" part does not overpower, override, or overcompensate for our "unacknowledged" part.

What are our shadows likely to be? Often a part that feels not good enough, incapable, hopeless, or depressed; or a part that is superior, mean, manipulative, or greedy; or one that controls, intimidates, or freaks out. Now let's look where that originates from. Imagine a small human being, who has to cope, without an instruction manual, basically alone in an insensitive, competitive, seemingly struggle-some world. A world that may feel at times shocking, hard, and unjust. Of course the little thing doesn't feel up to it! Pretty normal I'd say. It may feel under pressure and threatened. To avoid hurt it develops survival tactics: defensive, aggressive, or escapist. And yet, what we resist will not only persist but magnify.

It is one thing to identify our shadow, another to accept it, another still to love it.

Commonly we express confidence to keep our low feelings at bay. However, when alone, our lack of confidence, our self doubts and fears surface. Not wanting to accept or deal with these feelings, we may tend to avoid quietness and time alone by keeping socially or mentally busy. We may push for happiness to avoid depression, insist on an attitude of fun to cover up survival fears, or express superiority to squelch our own feelings of inadequacy.

Rather than being purposefully hidden by us, our shadow feelings are often just repressed, usually through fear of not being socially accepted. Having taken on that judgment and rejected part of us as not good enough, *we* start to feel rejected and not good enough ourselves. Yet once again, little was wrong in the first place. Many perfectly normal traits are considered "bad." Sensitive is called weak. Want is seen to be greedy. Honesty is impolite, expressive is disturbing, quiet is unsociable, and relaxed is considered lazy.

By accepting those parts we become more centered. We stop the swinging from one extreme to the other. Our shadow side has been yelling for our attention. By approving of it, we stop running to the other side, and so it stops pulling us back. Accepting the "dark" doesn't mean we have to wallow in it. Simply allowing it to be there, it stops bugging us. When you pick the child up, it stops tugging at your sleeve. We retrieve our balance on the tightrope of life. We become at ease with our undercurrents, we stop avoiding them and they stop ruling us.

We overcome our enemies when we make them our friends.
~ Dalai Lama

These unacknowledged traits are continually brought to our attention through the people and events we attract. Once we do acknowledge these parts within ourselves, we magnetize them less, because now we no longer need to have it put in our face. By welcoming our shadow parts, we better understand and accept ourselves, others and life; we gain great peace of mind.

We have been told that if we look within we will have to face the dark and terrible parts of our subconscious, our biggest demons, a monster, our deepest fear... Well guess what? All you will find is that you are human. Big deal, join the rest of the world. Our shadows are not evil but from our stored fear and pain. A bit embarrassing perhaps, but really not so bad. Most likely a hurt soul, a lost child, maybe a bit of natural jealousy, the antics of a big spoilt kid or the revenge of a wounded ego. Nothing we'll go to hell for. *Unless we condemn ourselves.*

No one expects you to be perfect, except you. This is being a wee bit tough on yourself, for there is always going to be the 3 year old within us, and we have to understand it and love it, even if we don't let it run amok. By not listening to our inner child we lose touch with our true feelings, our greatest ally.

Contrary to our social education, as we allow ourselves to show more of that part, we are actually more liked, more accepted. By showing our soft spots we are more real, others can identify with us, and suddenly we are not so alone. We become more open, less isolated, and strive less for outer appreciation.

One pioneer in self healing, Louise Hay, helped open a lot of minds and hearts to the existence of our inner child and the deep healing that occurs through developing that relationship.

When I loved myself enough I began to recognize a
community within me; we hold team meetings.
~ Kim McMillen

EVERY TIME SOMETHING BUGS YOU in another, do an internal search. By continually seeking our shadows, we start to include all the parts of ourselves that we so far deemed foreign to us. Our personality becomes less defined, broader, and more inclusive.

It can be hard to recognize our whole self because it has been buried for so long. It's time to dig it up and dust it off. Welcome it; give it some loving to make up for it having been locked away. You are re-uniting. Throw a homecoming party! "I'm back! Partly! More to come, once I've got them all out of the closet."

The good news is that we are not just the facade we had so far limited ourselves to; we are, already, much more than we realize. Expanding our personality is like increasing our wardrobe, adding more styles and more colors. Why limit the rainbow of our personality? We are here to love all our parts: the bright, the strong, the soft, the sad and the vulnerable. It increases our scope. What we deem as our weaknesses are often our strengths, such as sensitivity and affection. It is therein that we can feel and access our true spiritual selves. When we see our own "weaknesses" as gifts we can see that in others too. Those who are not ashamed to display their shadow side may be further down the road than we think.

We hear a lot about the sensationalized "dark" side of ourselves that we have to welcome back. Let's not forget our sunny parts too! All the expressive, strongly spirited, fun-loving and cheeky parts that we may have held back to be approved of, to fit in, to be respectable in our society. And wonder, and trust, our relaxed part and our carefree part, because through a sense of responsibility and all the struggles of life, we stopped believing in them.

Why do small kids have so much magic, so much energy, so much power? Because they are whole. They haven't yet condemned, split themselves. Our creative power, our very life energy, our own flow, is blocked by holding ourselves down. Remember the balloon in the swimming pool. That is why to discover the shadow empowers us: we become true to ourselves.

Our less preferred traits have also been part of our growth: stimulating us to overcome them, to develop our brightest qualities, and to climb high towards our vision. And with that strength we are able to return to the lower rungs and to acknowledge, love, and thus integrate our weakest links. It comes back to widening: from the identity we had become limited to, to the multi-personality we really are. We are spreading our wings. One wing is the "lowly" parts we were ashamed of, the other wing is the high parts we are scared of. Between the two we stand, and with the two outstretched, we soar.

The Shadow in the Mirror

As the sun sets on the old world
the shadows loom big in the evening light.
~ Step JurJahn

THE SHADOW PHENOMENON has long been apparent, in psychology studies, ancient mythology, and between the lines of our human history. These times can look dark and troubled, but remember: the brighter the light, the darker the shadows. It is because we have already done the first steps in self love, that embracing the shadow is simply the next thing on the list.

You have been taught to hate and fear the dark. It is just
a trick so that you don't find your way out. In time you'll
process that "darkness" within you, by loving and accepting it.
Then nothing can touch you.
~ Stuart Wilde

If we are not split from within, if none of our parts remain hidden or kept in the dark, then there is no underground resistance, no opposition "sabotaging" us, and we are not holding our own power back. Openness is the way to reconciliation and to wholeness, within us and within our societies.

Our collective shadow is projected large across the planet. Our own separatism, our energy games, our control tactics and our power trips are reflected glaringly back at us. They are magnified in the restrictions and the manipulation we see in the power structures around us. These represent the insecure part of us, resisting change, clinging to old behaviors of mistrust and exclusion.

When we focus on, criticize and blame that which is outside of us, little ever changes. But as we look within, we become aware of our own unconscious patterns that really rule us. And as we discover these within us, understand them and accept them, they lose their grip on us. Parallel to this, the outer shadow is also exposed and loses its power over us. On all levels we take back control over our own lives.

By finding more balance and harmony within ourselves, we help to create the same in the outer world. The state of the planet mirrors our own internal imbalance, our own split, and our own belief in struggle, our own stored pain. It is our own disempowering behaviors and victim stance that attract rulers and abusers. We just cannot expect the world to change without us changing. That is why we have to *become* the change we want to see in the world.

The unconscious can only exist without the light of awareness. Once we do our own shadow work we are no longer controlled by our unconscious parts. Now, equate that to the world picture. We have been shadow boxing. Like my old philosophy teacher: we have all been scared of our own shadows, projected larger than life on the movie screen of Earth.

THE BIGGEST TOOL the "dark" has and uses, seemingly "against" us, is fear. But in facing us with it, "they" actually help us to recognize our own fears. To become aware of, to face and thus go through, our survival fears is very empowering indeed. By labeling them as something "bad" or "dark" we give them power over us, we give our own power away. By simply recognizing them as a normal aspect of physical life, caused by the feeling of separation, we thus accept, re-integrate, and finally en-lighten those areas, both within us and "outside" of us.

That is why it is the darkest before the dawn. The dark is not the enemy; it is just the unconscious part of us, the last and deepest residues of humanity's stored pain, that is calling for healing.

Our shadow character embodies the very traits we took on to integrate. It is by discovering and nurturing our inner relationship that we take on our own evolution. It is the part we came to do here at this epic time. That is why it keeps bugging us until we do. This inner reconciliation is nothing less than our personal contribution to the uniting of humanity.

CHAPTER FIFTEEN

Healing of the Human Heart

*All judgment reveals itself to be self judgment in the end,
and when this is understood, a larger comprehension
of the nature of life takes its place.*

~ *David R. Hawkins*, POWER VERSUS FORCE

SINCE WE LANDED on this planet, most of us have been
whacked, silenced, pressured, scrutinized, intimidated, pushed
around, yelled at…and lied to. Are we all that surprised that we
have some odd bits inside us? Even though we don't have the luxury anymore to blame "the others," we can reckon that different
treatment would have brought out other qualities. It seems it has
really been well designed, and we can trust it has been, to bring
out the worst in us. It always struck me that if our education nur-
tured our *best* qualities, then the "leaders" wouldn't have to be
afraid of the masses. And yet it's all part of the far greater set-up,
enabling us to see these unacknowledged bits within us that we
are here to befriend, and without which we cannot move on. If we
doubt, criticize and belittle ourselves, is it a wonder that our reflections do the same?

In varying degrees of subtlety, everyone, at every social level,
is the same: we humans simply do not value ourselves enough.
Our insecure left brain, in its obsession for our survival, constantly
points out what may not be alright with us or with our actions!
This original need to evaluate turns into self judgment that splits
and undermines us. It weakens our trust in ourselves and, hence,
our trust in the world. Making judgment too early, before the heart
has become compassionate, we are simply too hard on ourselves
and of course, due to that, on others.

We all put a lot of pressure on ourselves to get everything right and cope in this world. On one hand our ego has been repressed so we can hardly feel good enough, on the other hand we are required to maintain a social image and pretend that we are superman! This has split people considerably. Even among "new age" spiritualists can be some expectation to be saintly. We are all socially conditioned as to what we *believe* we should and should not express. We have mostly suppressed our natural instincts, lost our childlike spontaneity and become too diplomatic for our own good. Repressing what we truly feel doesn't make us non judgmental. What does take us beyond judgment is full acceptance of who *we* are. Only through approval and love of who we are, can we truly accept others as they are.

With a full dose of self acceptance we can toss out any imposed manners that make us stiff. We can be our genuine selves and not be ashamed of expressing all that we feel. We can be natural, allow our kids to be kids and our own inner child to bloom. We want to love our inner child, not to censor it. We don't have to be saints before our time.

Acknowledging the small child within us ~ its sensitivity and fragility, its disappointments and its efforts ~ actually enables us to love ourselves more. And when we feel how hard it is trying to get it right, all we *can* do is to love it. Imagine we all didn't worry if we are good enough, how we can be faster and smarter, how we can prove ourselves and be somebody. All that energy becomes released to nourish ourselves and others; to play together rather than against each other; and to focus on the more interesting topics in life: "Who am I really, what's going on, and what the bleep am I supposed to be doing here?"

> *Every being is unique. But man goes on living in imitation. You can only be yourself, there is no other possibility. But we are all trying to be someone else. That is the whole story of our failure. My work consists in helping you to respect yourself, love yourself, accept yourself and be yourself. I am not giving you a certain character, or a certain lifestyle, but only an insight, an awareness, so that you can choose your lifestyle, so that you can live in your own light.*
>
> ~ *Osho*

As visitors in the countries we lived in, we were always on the fringe of society and therefore not imposed on by it. It was not until our vibrant daughter was in her mid-teens that she really encountered social judgment and peer pressure. She then underwent the process of socialization which split her, as it does all of us, latest when we go to school. Made to feel that she was wrong for being different, teased for being outstanding, she went through a period of self doubt, self denial and low self esteem. We didn't know when we went to Australia, enjoying the relaxed façade, that it is notorious in this respect. Being strategically told they are the descendants of convicts, and not only "down," but also "under," does of course little to boost anyone's self esteem!

This illustrates too the importance of our growth as individuals, knowing our own self worth, before we enter group consciousness. Yet the "others" who criticize us in fact mirror our own inner doubts and judgment patterns, until we accept them, transcend them, and no longer attract that reflection. We all have these traits within us, and the outer circumstances, systematically, contribute to make it more obvious to us. They are simply part of the human psyche, due to the separation we experience in this reality. So once we're easy with that, we become easy on ourselves and can get on with the great job of loving ourselves for who we are.

We can only outgrow these areas if we don't judge, refuse and suppress them. Many people live, not only in closed boxes side by side, but like closed boxes side by side. It's socially not accepted to show any emotions that are not comfortable for anyone else. They may feel embarrassed, we may feel shy. So we tend to bottle things up; and then the distance between us, and within us, grows.

It's not so much the things we say that bring us closer together but the things we don't say that keep us apart.
~ *Alyne Keller*

Eventually the isolation obliges us to face our inner relationship. As we establish the connection within us, the part of us that constantly criticizes and condemns our apparent imperfections, becomes aware of the split, the disempowerment, and the hurt this causes within. Judgment turns to compassion. Separation to reunion.

As we dare to open, and become more accepting of ourselves, so does our outer reflection. Others are already far more charitable than we are towards whatever weaknesses we may deem "bad" in ourselves. We are our toughest judge. And indeed, when we consider the world as our mirror, we are our *only* judge. Because of our own disapproval it can take courage to face all we are; through compassion we open our hearts to love ourselves unconditionally. This is far more important than any outer accomplishment.

> *I think everybody should get rich and famous and do everything*
> *they ever dreamed of so they can see that it's not the answer.*
> ~ Jim Carrey

The answer lies within. It does not matter what else we achieve here ~ for the greatest benefit to ourselves, to humanity, and to the planetary vibration, is to accept and love ourselves. Now, as we are, with all we have and have not done. When we can feel, despite social pressures and our egos' desire for glory, content with ourselves, then we have truly arrived. We cannot reach peace of mind through outer achievement, unless we first find the peace within.

To do this groundwork within ourselves is most empowering. Anyway, there's not much point hiding *anything* from oneself because deep down one knows it's there. The more we know ourselves the better. So take a look at it. If you don't like what you see look deeper, dig for the origin, the root cause. We only lie because we are scared of punishment. If we have bullied others, either we must have been bullied, or felt we had to defend or prove ourselves. If we have hurt others, somewhere we must have felt hurt. We manipulate because we lack trust; we cheat because we feel cheated; we take because we feel deprived. We act tough because we feel vulnerable; we become stroppy because we feel insecure; our outbursts stem from desperation. We are mean to others because we feel we have been put down, made to feel not good enough. We criticize others because we reject ourselves. We only feel insufficient because we judge ourselves.

Be honest and be loving and then, whatever you dig up, whatever you unearth, it will not hurt to find it, it can be accepted, it can be forgiven. And once we approve of ourselves lovingly, as we are, there is no more conflict. We can still grow further, but now there's no more fight within us between the "good" and the "bad." Now there is just the choice between what is good and what is better. Between the doubts and the reactive patterns that we can now accept as okay, and the better choices we still aspire to make. As we start to feel we are perfect, in this moment, with our imperfections, we can see the world in the same way: perfect in the moment, evolving as it is, towards our greater vision.

Recognize that we all do the best we can with the cards we were dealt. If we feel bad about anything, the fastest way out is: change it! When we focus on what we like in ourselves, and do things we can feel good about, our other concerns become the mere detail they really are. Don't beat yourself up when you feel you have goofed again. We are not here to be perfect. We are here to love.

> *When I loved myself enough I forgave myself all the times I*
> *thought I wasn't good enough.*
> ~ *Kim Mc Millen*

WHEN WE LOVE OURSELVES ENOUGH we choose a new view. How often have we kicked ourselves for what we did "wrong," only to find out after that it was fine? You always did your best, out of your own heart, to stay afloat. Approving of ourselves affects not only our own resonance and those around us, but also the collective field. Recognize that the depths we go through in life not only bear us the gift of surrender, they also become our personal contribution to transforming the mindset of humanity.

When we are happy with ourselves, everything else falls into place. We become our own best friend rather than our own worst enemy. Is there really anyone else you'd rather be? It's only a matter of fine-tuning.

When we feel we are alright, imperfectly perfect and perfectly imperfect, then we realize that everything else is alright too. All we undertake is really geared towards our personal discovery. All the trials we go through are not because life is being beastly to us, but to bring out our own disempowering patterns and core beliefs. Once we recognize them we can expand. Whatever our social profession, our real daily work and life's purpose is nurturing our peace of mind, inner beauty and love. And anything we would like to be ~ a movie star, a pop idol, a corporate tycoon, a president ~ is nothing compared to what we truly, and already, are: an awesome, eternal, individual part of the human soul. The way to become closer to the power and splendor of that Being is through our heart.

Our Labor of Love

> Beyond a wholesome discipline, be gentle with yourself. You a child of the universe, no less than the trees and the stars; you have a right to be here. And whether or not it is clear to you, no doubt the universe is unfolding as it should. Therefore be at peace with God, whatever you conceive Him to be. And whatever your labors and aspirations, in the noisy confusion of life, keep peace in your soul. With all its sham and drudgery, and broken dreams, it is still a beautiful world. Be cheerful. Strive to be happy.
> ~ Desiderata

As WE BECOME AT PEACE WITH OURSELVES, we become allowing of others on the same rattling human journey. In my younger years I was very perceptive, with a clear view on others' blocks and potential. Frank and forthright, I didn't waste too much wrapping paper or ribbon in presenting them. Without compassion for other's weaker parts, not having found my own inner child, my observations obviously felt both invasive and critical. My voluminous writings would start off with something small on my heart I felt I had to say, and end when I ran either out of breath or out of ink. They were deep and insightful, and this would usually guarantee that I didn't get a reply! Seeing the latent potential in others made it hard at times to recognize that everyone always does their best even if it seems that they sometimes don't. It's all part of our widening process, discovering the art of compassion and learning to look in the mirror! In the same way that love without wisdom can seem blind, wisdom without heart can seem unkind.

It is a bit embarrassing to have been concerned with the human problem all one's life and find at the end that one has no more to offer by way of advice than "Try to be a little kinder."

~ Aldous Huxley

Let us not overlook the obvious and be fooled by the apparent simplicity of this message. All the great souls who have graced this Earth, and all those who still walk among us, all those who have seen far and wide, come to the same conclusion. For compassion is a key force that leads us out of separation, guides our hearts out of pain, and reveals our unity with all that is.

Compassion is not pity, not a superior feeling, and not charity. "Com-passion" means "with-feel." It is empathy. You feel-with your own "pet human," from its standpoint, and you accept that as okay. You feel-with other people and you become aware of, and sensitive to, all our insecurities. And as you do so, you reach yourself a hand: you open your own door. For everyone on your path is an aspect of yourself.

EACH REFLECTION benefits our own journey to wholeness. For we are here to care for our own evolution, not to infringe on our sisters' and brothers'. We can never really know where people are in life or what step they came here to do. What may appear small to us may be all they need to accomplish.

I remember a tough Austrian mother in India whose child everyone felt sorry for. One beautiful star-studded night we all slept on the roof. The mother slept curled up and sucking her thumb. I then realized where she was coming from and that she, too, was doing the best she could. Back in my beloved school days, a teacher once gave a friend of mine the same grade she gave me and, because I knew that her paper was not quite as good as mine, I asked the teacher why. I have always appreciated her answer: "Because for you it was easy, while your friend had to work so much harder to write hers."

If you think someone looks really tight or suffered, just count your lucky stars and wish them well on their journey. You haven't walked a mile in their shoes! You likely wouldn't want their past or their patterns, or what they are going through. Consider that those who seem to be entrenched in disempowering habits may have just, and willingly, taken on more difficult aspects of the human psyche to work with and uplift. Those who seem abusive are victims too, acting out of their own insecurities and feelings of insufficiency. Having chosen the hardest tasks in self love, their contribution is huge. Finally, it is those with the deepest hurts that are among the greatest healers.

Life brought me to recognize that we all have different talents and roles to play out which, although seemingly disconnected, are all essential, in their colorful diversity, to the expressing and experiencing of the human soul. So now, if someone likes to walk around with a green monster tattooed on his bald head, I think that's simply wonderful. It takes many types to make the world go around, like it takes many notes to make music.

Feel reverence, for everyone has their place and their purpose. Have no illusions, for how we consider and treat others is a direct reflection of how we evaluate ourselves. What we think of another really says much more about us than it does about them! Superiority comes from comparison, from the need to feel good about ourselves, which suggests that somewhere, deep down, we don't.

Of course there are many wonderful, beautiful, powerful, fulfilled, successful, and aware people on this planet. Whatever features you admire in others, don't let their strengths make you feel insufficient. Use your own progress and self love as a measuring stick. Each of us is a journey unto himself.

Twenty-three years ago, faced with a beautiful abstract design I said to a friend, "I can't compete with that!"

"Life," she sighed, "is not a competition."

I wrote:

Life is not a competition. It is inspiration.
We are all here to inspire each other:
To laugh more and worry less, to like more and judge less
To live more and work less, to feel more and fight less
To trust more and fear less, to love more and more and more...

Delight in others' talents and achievements, for we are all aspects of each other. We are the body of humanity, all working together as a team, each developing different facets of our human soul potential.

COMPARISON CLIPS OUR WINGS. We are often taught in modern societies that intellect is superior to manual work. This causes separation. There is simply no comparison to be made. Sometimes we use our mind, at others we enjoy our body, and there are times ahead when we will live only from our heart. Where would we brain-orientated people be without support; without, say, the skills of the plumbers and the builders? What would we eat without the farmers, the people of the land? We wouldn't want to be without our base. All over the globe it is among the simple people, those the least obstructed by mental concepts, that we find the most heart. We may be well surprised in which fields our fellow companions excel.

Whatever we may have in life, there is no reason to feel either superior or guilty. For everything we are and own is because we have been given it, or the talents to acquire it. So feel gratitude, and pray that we can be up to it. By being our best we honor our gifts.

I have repeatedly seen that whatever credit we give to others, we give to ourselves too: *we open our own door.* Whatever we do out of our hearts for others, we reap the benefits too. It was out of compassion for my cheery Spanish teacher, faced with a most unresponsive class, that I first dared to open my mouth, and actually learnt the language. It was through empathy for some rhythmic "buskers" encircled by a stiff crowd that I first overcame my own shyness and allowed my body to dance. It is through feeling with others that we stretch ourselves to new areas. Out of love for others we overcome our attitudes and limits and thus reach greater tolerance, understanding and approval. It is by accepting others "shortcomings" that we grow to accept our own. Through sensitivity for our kids we honor our own inner child. Through empathy for them we forgive ourselves the same weaknesses.

Make a gift of your life and lift up all mankind by being kind, considerate, forgiving, and compassionate at all times, in all places, and under all conditions, with everyone as well as yourself. This is the greatest gift anyone can give.
~ David R. Hawkins

Everyone has had enough of struggling ~ with themselves, with each other, with their demons. It is time to give everyone more loving, including ourselves. Break the trend today: approve of yourself unconditionally, say a cheery good morning to the neighbor, be *honestly* friendly to the boss, and beam at likely looking strangers. In some parts of our globe, the latter is considered perfectly normal. So, depending on where you live, you will generate many smiles or, at least, perhaps one nod. In colder climes it's usually best to practice this on the weekend, and once you've become really good at it, test out your skills on a wet Monday morning!

We can't put love on, but we can let it out. We can look long and hard enough, at ourselves or another, until we muster compassion for the tiny, loveable part within which, out of its own insecurities, does all that nonsense. Try it on your boss or partner. One day you may watch him ranting and raving and you will laugh "It's true, seen from that perspective, he is actually quite cute!"

Be compassionate. Everyone you meet
is fighting a great battle.
~ Plato

With compassion, we neither punish ourselves nor do we push others. Have trust. Our trying to improve things for our loved ones is likely only coming from our own insecurity. If it's truly and purely out of love, then our expression, too, will be loving. Remember that everyone, and that includes us, judges themselves too hard already.

If I am not for myself, who will be for me?
If I am not for others, what am I? And if not now, when?
~ Rabbi Hillel

We free our hearts from hurt and blame when we recognize that everyone on our path is an aspect of our self: our mirror, our guide ~ reflecting bright or dark shadows, stirring sensitivity, inspiring dreams. We are all assisting each other's evolution. And who are we to judge, for do we know why people choose the lives they do? The call girl can arouse compassion in the heart of the very guys who use her: "Why's a nice girl like you doing a job like this?" A soldier may find his compassion through remorse for those he has killed. Every human heart is awakening ~ including our own ~ in its own sweet time.

Sometimes we forget to see
Everything we're given for free
The sunlit days, the silent nights
The changing colors of the light
The earth below and the stars above
The magic of beauty and love

Sometimes we forget to feel
Everything that is for real
The ease of flowing with the stream
The awesome power of our dreams
The wonder seen in children's eyes
We let the child within us die...

It's always there if you look
Remember the time you never took
For your child before it grew
For your neighbor that you never knew
To smile at a stranger in the street
Perhaps a friend you'll never meet...

'Cause in our busy lives we close
Our eyes, our mind, our heart, our soul

Just rise above this hurt and fear
Open to love, it's always there
Open your heart and you will see
It's waiting for you to be free

Sometimes we forget to see
Everything we're given for free
The sunlit days, the silent nights
The quiet feeling of twilight
The earth below and the stars above
The magic of beauty and love.

CHAPTER SIXTEEN

Love is in the Air

Love is not something you do,
it is something you are.
~ *Osho*

FIFTEEN YEARS AGO I had a very uplifting experience which lasted about three weeks. I made a most uncharacteristic move for a devoted mother and faithful partner: I left "home." The atmosphere, between my hard-headed child and her short-fused father, was starting to take its toll on this lover of peace and harmony! So I headed off to the next island, arranging for them to follow in a fortnight. Already on the boat I felt such a release from that space of tension and effort. I dropped all my concerns and all my defenses; it was a complete let-go. Love fell in.

I went sky high; I found everyone beautiful just as they are. Radiating love, I was in bliss. I wasn't the source of the beaming love that I felt for everyone, it was rather coming through me because nothing was in the way, none of my walls were up, and many people, including strangers, felt it. It wasn't that I was in love *with* anyone, or even that *I* was in love. Love was just what was, the music all around me, I was its instrument, and it was playing through me. This lasted for a few weeks and gradually faded out.

I understood much later that this euphoric experience came simply as a result of my being wide open. Literally, *love is in the air.* It is always here for us, and whenever we give it space it enters. That is why you can easily feel love when you see cute kittens or pups or babes, watch children at play or a beautiful woman. You open up at the endearing sight, and love slips in. The baby cries, the kids scrap, the woman's boyfriend turns up, and you clam up. The love is gone. In truth it neither came nor left. You were either open to feel its presence, or not.

It is not even that you really love the cute kittens or the pretty woman; after all, you hardly know her. It is just that you are receptive towards them because you have no defenses against them. They give you an opportunity to open up and receive. The target of your love could be a stone, it only matters whether *you* are open.

We can only love what we trust. Hence our self love too is rooted in our self acceptance. This is why we want so much to face and befriend ourselves, and embrace what we find with compassion. Full self love arises when we are in wholehearted agreement with ourselves, when we approve of ourselves as we already are. Love happens to us when we allow it to.

Obviously doubt or worry, any insecurity or negative emotion, closes our valve. Sex is a valve opener: we are in the moment, open, trusting, merging. Our thoughts drop off, love drops in. That's why it is called "making love."

How can it be that when we let all else go, love is what we feel? Because that is what we are. We are touching base with our essence, our life energy; it is the base of our existence. Making love is the search for unity, to reunite with, to experience our oneness, our essence: the energy of love.

So the good news is: love is not something we have to generate in our hearts; nor do we depend on the perfect partner, or on anyone else, to give it to us. It is simply everywhere. It permeates the fabric of existence, the very air that we breathe. It is the fundamental energy of all life; the underlying energy field, omnipresent, all-pervasive. And all we have to do to access it is open up to feel the love. Now, could you ask for anything better than that?

You can let love in with a fond memory, an open smile or a burst of song. You can feel it singing with others, or watching a sunrise, or alone in the woods: a feeling of warmth, of blessing, of bliss; a sense of connectedness, of sacredness, of union. Your heart is a portal: your own link to the divine. Through your heart, through you, Love flows.

You may worry that in the state of love we are vulnerable. It has happened before, we have been abused. That is because we were open hearted, yes, but not strong enough yet in self love to know our borders. Before we can properly merge with others we need to have fully developed our individuality. Self love is rooted in our feeling of self worth. Only then can we expand, dedicating ourselves in service to "the highest good of all," while being sure that this "all" includes us too! It is a minor but essential detail that the loving people of the earth had often forgotten in their sense of caring for others! If we don't care for ourselves no one else will, and we then end up disillusioned that the world is selfish.

> *I suggest we learn to love ourselves before it is made illegal.*
> ~ *Incubus, lyrics*

DON'T BE SCARED OF THE WORD "LOVE." Like "god," it has been wildly misused. We are not talking relationship ~ with its expectations and therefore disappointments ~ we are just talking love. You do not need another person to fulfill you, for you are whole within yourself. You do not need another person to love you, for within you, you are love.

> *Love is a state of Being. Your love is not outside; it is deep within you. You can never lose it, and it cannot leave you.*
> ~ *Eckhart Tolle*

Real love is not dependant on, or directed to, another person. It is neither sacrificial nor possessive. It unites us to the creative life-force, making us feel boundless, connected but free. We cannot expect to receive love from another. It is a gift from the divine within.

> *I beheld love as the most powerful force in the Universe. Not a personal sentiment, a romantic feeling, or even tender emotion. It is a force that moves effortlessly through us when we allow ourselves to be open channels for its expression. In viewing love from the other side, I know it to be a power.*
> ~ *Dannion Brinkley*

Love is an infinite stream that does not originate in our heart, but flows through it. Our heart is a portal, transmitting from another space. Love is our life energy, which is why we want to align with it. We can facilitate it through opening; through appreciation, surrender, and reverence. We can tune in. A sense of devotion and immense gratitude arises when we realize that all we are is due to the loving life force that flows through us.

Allow yourself to feel more of that love. It is such a healer. Alone, let it overwhelm you. Practice flowing it to a tree; flood appreciation into your cat; pour your gratitude to the stars. It comes through our devotion, our passion, our joy. Give it to yourself, to your family, to someone who really isn't suspecting it at all. You are strengthening your heart.

Whatever your circumstances are now, open yourself through appreciation to love them. Firstly, because they are the result of your own choices! And secondly, whatever is around us is a reflection of something within ourselves. Approve of yourself as you are, for criticizing your weaknesses will close off the loving flow that helps us to expand. As we become warmer so does our reflection and we find a loving circle around us.

INSECURITY CLOSES US UP. Hence we can understand how our usual love is not total: because we are possessive, scared to lose, not sure if we are good enough. If our valve is closed with too much thought, doubt, or argumentativeness we cannot feel love for others, nor feel their love for us. It's finally more interesting to have the same feelings as others than to have different concepts. If we feel we are more aware than another, then it is up to *us* to warm up the situation with our understanding and compassion.

Worry bogs us down. To worry for others, out of love, actually closes off the love until only the worry remains. We lose our own power source. To just give love and lightness to the situation is often more helpful and healing then trying to solve the issue. So stay out of the grip of anxiety. It is when the insecurities and judgments of our left brain stop that we rediscover our right brain character: at peace, at one, in love. Return again and again to that space of trust. Let go, come back to love. I was jotting this down on a bus in Nepal when we stopped next to a truck with these words painted on the door: "Love is the secret language." Without any words, love can say and do more than a lecture.

Although I enjoy understanding things because it helps me immensely, I came to see it is not really more knowledge that we need but more love. Knowledge enables us to see why the dysfunction, but we can't heal with answers unless we love. We can be shown patterns in ourselves but without self love we just feel bad about them. It's the love that heals. Love is our intrinsic intelligence, the creative force, the transformer. In a space of tough judgment you can understand yourself, but without love nothing ever changes. People can tell us many weird and wonderful things but only we can turn the key to our own heart.

I believe ...
...that our care for ourselves reflects our love for ourselves.
That even if we seem to feel good about ourselves
sometimes deep inside we do not.
That if we do not love ourselves enough it is because
we judge ourselves to be unlovable...
...and that whoever we are and whatever we do,
if we cared to understand ourselves
and accept our insecurities
we could love ourselves fully.
And this love I believe to be the greatest healer of all.

Feel the Love

The first lesson is to love yourself as you are. That does not mean you have to remain the same forever. In fact this is the first step of transformation: if you love yourself you will be able to grow quicker, faster. And you will be able to truly love others. Love yourself because it is only through love that you will

become harmonious, that you will become one. Don't condemn
yourself. You have been given an amazing body. You have been
given a beautiful mechanism called mind. If you use it rightly
it is of tremendous importance; if it becomes the master then
it is dangerous. And you have been given a soul ~ a piece
of existence. One cannot ask for more."

~ *Osho*

LOW SELF ESTEEM IS PERHAPS THE GREATEST SHACKLE of the
human race. We have not been brought up to believe in our own
power, to know that we are all beautiful, unique, and eternal spirits. Imagine we had all been encouraged to bloom, instead of
molded to fit into a mechanical working structure? However, now
is not time to lament but to reclaim our true identity. Each one of
us is a unique personality, rich in experience, able to share warmth
and understanding. Each one of us is a star-child, able to transmit
the love and light we experience from the divine. We are here to
learn to love ourselves, and therefore each other. Because when
we do, life flows.

Through loving ourselves we partake of, and express, the sacred energy that is within. We open our own door. Tuning into,
being in, that vibration enables us to feel the love that surrounds
us. It is there at all times, yet we are often too preoccupied to notice. We can feel on a daily level that the qualities of our heart carry
us to another space: a space of joy, ease and flow. Our heart is, in
fact, a natural stargate.

We are, as self-aware life-forms, with the ability to co-create
our reality, the pinnacle of this creation. If we don't feel good about
ourselves, what is the Mother of our galaxy going to say to the
next one? "I was doing well with Earth, I got 99% right, but it
seems I goofed somewhere on the humans. I was rather chuffed
with the result myself, I think they are pretty cool, but it so happens they don't even like themselves." Every mother wants their
kids to love themselves and each other.

The cosmic game is good. We can only love others when we
trust them. Now figure: humankind is split into two sexes, and
further divided into different colors: whites and blacks, reds and

yellows and browns. We have multiple diverse body types, tastes and opinions. There are 5 races, 39 main religions, 196 nations, 1000 tribes, and over 2000 written (and over 6000 spoken) languages. We have been further separated into different social classes, and diverse political groups.

And now we have to realize we are all one?

Our hearts are being stretched. Can we still trust, can we still love, through all this apparent separation? It's by including "others" that our hearts grow and we thereby learn to love our own multifaceted nature. Perhaps only within the multicolored diversity of humanity could we expand our own hearts enough to bear unconditional love.

ONE ORDINARY AFTERNOON in Tonga, I was sitting on the porch in our little wooden house above the harbor reading *The Power of Now.* I reached the part where Eckhart gives techniques for being in the now: portals into the present moment. Just reading those lines, allowing that feeling in, brought my mind to pause. This triggered an extraordinary happening. It felt like a huge space opened up around me, like a lid was lifted off, and I was in a timeless zone of utter peace. From that quiet spaciousness I looked over at my partner, with whom I was going through an extremely difficult period, and I felt an amazing other-worldly love.

This love that we access in the gap transcends that which we normally experience. It has another quality. It is far beyond the intense love we may have in a crush, the deep love we may feel for a soul mate, or even the devotional love we feel for our own children. This is not to belittle whatever we have felt so far, but just to say there is more to come.

Then one line was planted in the stillness. A very clear voice from within me said, "You don't have to stay with him."

It could have told me the meaning of life, or hinted at a winning lottery ticket, but that was all it said. I found it was a most interesting statement to receive in that moment of utter love. It enabled me to recognize that I was free to leave, not out of personal resentment but simply because I had another path to tread. We were faithfully bound together out of a feeling of destiny. To realize that I had another choice, out of such an extreme loving space, was quite a revelation.

I understood too, from the way this opening had occurred, that it was my mind coming to a standstill that had provoked all the previous surreal moments in my life. These gaps had allowed me to enter into the timeless zone: the backdrop of our physical existence.

And within that zone, just behind the scenes, is the state of peace and love we can recall from long ago. It is always there, obscured by the constant activity of our thoughts, silently waiting for our minds to pause.

CHAPTER SEVENTEEN

Return to Softness

Real strength is not to act big.
Real courage is not to be scared of our softness.

~ *Popular wisdom*

IN OUR STRIVING for outer achievement we forget there are natural cycles in life. There is a time for power and a time for material growth and then, like the dusk falls, like the winter comes, there is the time for a return to softness.

We can all plainly see that the current rate of development is unsustainable for the environment and that it's time for a more sensitive approach. Perhaps after all is said and done, after all the push and productivity, there will be a return to a more holistic lifestyle: more grounded, organic, and spiritually earthen.

Like a young person, humanity has been evolving through outer experiences and growth. Yet at some point in everyone's life comes the time for a shift of focus; a change of direction, facing inwards. Our society had pushed so far outwards that it became unbalanced through neglecting inner space. And yet this too was part of the natural cycles, leading up to the turnaround which is written in the stars.

Mayan astronomy describes huge cycles that influence the development of our identity and our relationship with the source of our being. During the expansion phase of our universe, the outwards moving cycle, our consciousness becomes increasingly individual, or masculine. Through physical endeavor we express our spiritual growth by manifesting it into matter. We are just now reaching the turning point, a still point; and as we are preparing to

move back inwards, towards our center, our consciousness becomes feminine again, more unified and less separate. We are already shifting towards a more direct, intuitive understanding.
Increasingly, we gain our knowledge no longer from conceptual
information but directly from our intuition, our inner guidance,
our source of all-knowing, our own inner light. This eventually
culminates in an enlightening revelation of full inner understanding, of complete consciousness.

When we recognize the size of these cosmic tides, we realize
there is no other way to go. The rules of the game are being
changed on us and it may feel like the carpet is being pulled from
under our feet. It is no longer about separate self achievement, it
is about aligning with our collective soul journey, about our surrender to the whole. Our life circumstances are currently realign-
ing us with the return to the feminine principle, our new road to
travel. The yin way is more sensitive, more intuitive, more devotional, more reverent and brings us closer again to the essence of
our being.

It is particularly in competitive, western society that has now
spread to much, but by no means all, of the world, that we have
been conditioned to associate self worth with outer achievement,
drive with success, softness with weakness, and toughness with
strength. In the German language for example, the word for "lazy"
is the same word as "rotten." This does not inspire the population
to have a chilled out attitude! In fact it is the mark of an advanced
soul that it can disengage from our social conditioning and allow
itself to relax. There are natural cycles of outgoing and ingoing energy in life and the universe. Ingoing cycles, like the night, winter
or monsoon, and even illness, are opportunities for deepening and
inner growth: times of reconnection, integration and regeneration.

ALREADY IN PRIMARY SCHOOL I felt sorry for the boys because of
the pressure put on them to play big, compete, and achieve. This
forced them not to show their sensitive side, which became isolated within while they put on a pretended air of confidence and
machismo. It distanced men from their true feelings, from each
other, and from the women they were so hard trying to impress.

Women too have been strengthening their male side, particularly from the pioneer days, the industrial age, and the "women's lib" era. The so-called "feminist movement" is really misnamed as it did little or nothing to enhance femininity. It rather gave women a chance to develop their masculine side, so much so that many now have to reclaim their natural softness as much as men do.

Some years ago I watched my beautiful 17 year old daughter, helplessly, as many mothers do, heading for a crash. After a lifetime in foreign cultures, she wanted to belong somewhere and, always a chameleon, she quickly adapted to the teenage Australian society. To fit in with the lads she adopted a bit of a coarse, tough, strong and sporty image. One day while visiting us in Tonga, her friends tied a rope to the top of a coconut palm with a wooden bar on the end. They then took turns leaping off the upstairs porch and, holding the bar, would swing around the tree. She was scared but wanted to be up to it. So she grabbed the bar, pursed her lips, and launched herself off the second story veranda… and, to her boyfriend's yell of "Oh shit!" smashed right into the tree.

I tried to explain the obvious, but she wasn't quite finished with making her own experiences. Some months later, the big crash happened.

On Christmas morning I woke up in our coconut leaf bungalow. Pen and paper in hand I stepped out onto the beach, lay in the fine white sand and wrote:

Christmas Presence.

Our Christmas present this year is waking up on a small South Pacific island which we are caretaking for the off season. It's warm and tranquil, and this morning the sea is a calm turquoise mirror. Christmas evening we watched a full yellow moon rise out of the quiet dark ocean into a clear sky. The high tide was lapping on the shore just meters away from our coconut thatched holiday hut. Luck? No, rather choice. Following our dreams.

For all of us our Christmas present is really just waking up at all. Waking up, breathing in, and being alive now in this beautiful world. This place, this endless life, is so deeply amazing that the

more we see into it the less we can grasp it. So many layers of
mystery to explore, enjoy, play with…
So feel blessed to be alive, because we are.

Some days later my daughter wrote about her late Christmas evening car crash: "I woke up feeling so fortunate to be alive. So appreciative…." It dawned on me, with an awesome chill, that I had picked that message up from her.

The crash was the beginning of her return to softness.

～

GUYS, LET'S GET THIS STRAIGHT for once and for all. I am not saying that male energy, yang, is bad and female energy, yin, is better. It is all a matter of being in balance, first of all within ourselves. Each of us has a masculine and a feminine side, a left and right brain. The left is structure and stability: it enables us to organize and stay on a path. The right is inspiration, creativity, and intuition which enable us to be flexible enough to welcome change. When the two sides work together, within us and between the sexes, there is harmony and it is beautiful.

Male energy is good for mountain climbing. However, too much yang is pushing for the summit late in the season when the weather is changing. Many have tried. There is a time we have to be content to come down, to acknowledge: this is bigger than me, I have done well enough, I give way to the greater force. We are now being called to find the yin within us: acceptance, care and contentment. We are human *beings*, not human *doings*. Agree to mellow out. We age slower and grow faster. The state of let go is a state of trust.

The male cycle has empowered us all to go outwards: exploring, conquering our world, and developing the ego. It is up to us womenfolk now not to push the guys to achieve more but to guide them, while we are on our own journey of rediscovery, to embrace the feminine aspect of life. Not only is tussle and struggle undignified, it is also strenuous. The drive for prestige and approval is behind much of our excessive activity. When we move beyond struggling, with ourselves, in our relationships, and with life, we see how effortless and flowing our lives become. We retrieve balance.

VISITORS HAD GIVEN ME THE ROMANTIC notion that the South Pacific is a place where the feminine energy still survives. Although this wasn't obvious to me at first sight, in a way, it is. Pacific means peaceful and it was there, in the spirit of the islands, that my own return to softness began.

The hefty, smiley, afro-haired women of Fiji didn't exactly look like your archetypal nymph; nor did the Polynesian Samoans, Tongans or Cook islanders. The men too are cubic, with biceps that make a weightlifter look puny. Even brawny westerners would find themselves standing next to these Pacific hulks with a look of, "oh boy, I hope he likes me."

Yet these gentle giants speak in the softest of tones, expressing an inner sweetness that we have lost or at least buried. When you are that grounded, quiet in yourself and trusting, you have no need to put on big macho airs. In a society where being your genuine self is enough, you have no reason to pretend to be any more than who you are. They are one of many indigenous cultures that revere the feminine principle: remaining aware of their feelings and the presence of energy in their everyday life.

The inner sensitivity of these people can be astounding. They pick up on the slightest of your feelings and respect them. They are non-infringing and non confrontational. If you should ever confront them with a "why?" as in, "Why did you not come to work for the last week?" they will tell you that the tree fell down, the moon was full, or the grandmother died...once again.

Never lie to a Tongan though, as they evolved in an environment extremely conducive to intuitive, right brain activity. They have not overdeveloped their left brain, which includes the sense of separatism, or built up defensive walls. Therefore they will pick up and respond to what you really feel, rather than what you say, and may well answer questions you have not yet asked!

Many such cultures are used to far less mental and verbal exchange than we are in the West. They can comfortably sit together just sharing silent space. Exchange is always more about feeling good together and laughing than comparing ideas and opinions. In these societies family and community is first. There are two words that simply do not fit in their vocabulary or lifestyle: one is "work," the other is "fast."

When we are not at ease, we keep on running from our pain, our shadow. We don't dare to slow down to the speed where we could actually feel what's really going on. We cover it up with activity, distractions and escapism. We miss the subtle hints. We don't notice until a breakdown, an economic regression, a sickness, or an accident happens, that something was wrong. We were simply not tuned in.

When we are slow, when we are quiet, we are sensitive. We are humble and open, on the lookout for guidance. For we don't receive by luck, we receive by being open to it. Then we see things coming, we sidestep in time. We choose to slow down before we have to slam the brakes on. We no longer just run blindly down our track and say in retrospect, "well how could we have known?" It's really not so hard. When we listen to and follow our own feelings, our fellow humans, our bodies, our Earth… then we don't need a breakdown or a blow up, a shock or a crash to wake us up. Obviously, the more we are out of tune, off key, the further off our own line of integrity, evolution, and destiny, the harder we are shoved back onto it. Life evolves. We can either let it kick us in the butt or allow it to lead us by the hand. Either way we get there. The choice is always ours.

WE MAY BE SCARED OF SILENCE, scared of losing our borders, scared of the feeling of merging. Allow slowness, quietness, stillness, to enter your life. This is where the reunion happens; with yourself, with others, with our essence, with the source.

Once again the feminine principle is our guide to surrender. We no longer need to forge our own way. The path is already cleared before us and all we have to do is to recognize it and step onto it. Trust, open up, and listen within. A woman expresses love in yielding, giving of herself. Dare to express your beauty, your softness, your devotion, your warmth; it is part of our offering to this world. Strength and softness are not opposites. In fact, our softness is our strength.

If you feel that toughness is your protection, then the idea of a return to softness is very scary indeed. Let's look again at a seed. From the early stages of vulnerable, naked softness, it develops a hard outer shell to protect its inner growth. It has to be resistant to outer influences. Once it has matured within, the shell softens again ~ as the seed expands ~ and bursts open to enable the seed's fruition, its fulfillment, its very purpose. If the protective shell remains hard, the seed cannot open, grow and bloom.

I propose that the season is right. The time is now. I propose you are the seed and you are ready. You are all you need to be.

ONE MORNING I woke up with a new song in my head.

We are a seed soon to burst open,
We are a bud that's soon to bloom,
We are the fern soon to unfurl,
The butterfly still in cocoon.

We are the children, children of the sun,
Our dreams are dreamt, our songs are sung,
Love light our path, you guide us thru...
We're on our journey home, home to you...

Hold our hands, hold our hearts
May our dreams guide our path
Hold our hands, hold our hearts
May your love light our paths

The Tide Turns

When I say we may be over suffering, that we may not need it anymore as a tool for growth, people look at me as though I was trying to change the laws of the universe. Well, life is in constant change, is it not? It evolves. Because of the density of matter, a certain amount of resistance is intrinsic to the physical world. So downloading the light into matter has indeed required a certain amount of overcoming, a certain amount of working against resistance. Yet soon enough, consciousness will become fully merged with matter, and the very source of our struggles will cease to be.

CHAPTER EIGHTEEN

Brothers and Sisters
of the Road

*People think a soul mate is your perfect fit, and that's what every-
one wants. But a true soul mate is a mirror, the person who shows
you everything that is holding you back, the person who brings you
to your own attention so you can change your life.*

~ *Elizabeth Gilbert, EAT, PRAY, LOVE*

AFTER 20 YEARS on the road, 10 years in Mother India, and everything I had been through, I thought I knew a lot. I was well informed, spiritually orientated, and happy natured. Life happened
and I coped, but looking back... yikes, was I living unconsciously!

Having concluded early on that life is a struggle, the
Hindu teachings of withdrawing from the world naturally ap-
pealed to me. Certainly the philosophy of "Do less, Be more" balanced my overactive western mind tremendously. It shifted my
focus from outer activity to inner expansion. But finally, one cannot complete the journey here while burdened with an attitude of
hurt and regret. We cannot take the future in our hands *until we
stop carrying the past.*

Eventually, I ran away from the world to my childhood
dream, and it was there, under the open skies of the South Pacific, that I *really* started to wake up. Indeed, we are all waking
up now. We are remembering. For a time we had quite forgotten, but when we became aware of that embarrassing fact, it
made us only more humble.

In the South Pacific islands I met a number of soul mates who were the catalyst for my turnaround. It's always exciting to meet people we instantly click with ~ although the benefits we take from such encounters are not necessarily what we first expect! One of these kindred spirits was Rob. He was a realtor, at the time one of my least liked professions. Yet in spite of my prejudice, we connected like long lost friends. We were on the same wavelength. We talked for hours about what's all going on behind the veil, be it the shadow government, extraterrestrials, "death," or the meaning of life. Brought up with conscious manifesting he had often witnessed the power of thought and beliefs. Puzzle pieces were flying in. On one level, he saw Earth as the Disneyland we all chose to play the game of life together, just for fun. This became our ongoing debate.

"Playful is good," I would write him, "and our spirits have a great sense of humor. But with all due respect... I have to wonder why boundless, peace-loving spirits in an intimate, understanding and caring spirit world would come to such an unruly planet just for FUN?? Enlighten me there please..."

He could never fully convince me. Still, fun was indeed something I had quite forgotten in the exigencies of life and I most gladly added it to my shopping cart!

Deep within though, Rob was also a hurt soul. His gentle manner reminded me of my youth, surrounded by quiet, cultivated British family members. They were always extremely polite, would bottle up their feelings and develop bowel cancer. *Noblesse oblige.* I had moved from this extreme to the other, choosing ~ if that's the right word! ~ a partner with little social façade: direct and expressive. He was as impulsive as I was cautious and as self-indulgent as I was overly modest. Charismatic, dramatic, and problematic, he provided me with a lengthy and engrossing mission. Having the feminine tendency of wanting to improve on those I love, our relationship most conveniently postponed my having to face the even more daunting task of my own creative power and potential.

When I first visited my in-laws I was aghast. There I was, back in Europe after three years in Asia, baby and all, in a house where only German was spoken, and usually at top volume. This was certainly uncharted territory! I eventually learned that they were not *always* arguing but that such loud discourse was considered perfectly acceptable in their neck of the woods. Discussion was kept lively, interesting, and extremely lengthy by categorically opposing what the other one said.

For my partner this pattern was very normal, and gave him a chance to vent the anger and anguish he carried deep inside. Needless to say, and much to my dismay, a large part of his torrential outbursts was aimed in my direction. Before that, I had always thought it took two to make an argument! I didn't realize that my self-protective justifications were just adding fuel to his fire.

It took me all of ten years to be able to shout back. At first it felt good to be able to express my hurt and draw my borders. I had indeed become stronger, developing a certain toughness that matched the barren Australian outback, our home at the time. But after some years of this survival tactic, I disliked how tough I had become. I had never been sugar sweet, yet I was sad for the bit I used to have and had lost somewhere along the dusty road.

I had noticed over the years that different countries and places have very distinct energies, which affect and reflect diverse aspects of our human soul. So we sold our camper, and followed my childhood dream to go to the South Pacific, with visions of pristine beaches and gentle tribal people. My mother had been brought up on a ranch in the desert, and had followed *her* childhood imagination to live near cultivated Paris. Us children, having been dragged around museums and art galleries from an early age, soon had our fill of culture and stiff environments and yearned for a more natural lifestyle. For me the beach was the epitome of a place where nothing could build up, a place that is always washed clean by the ocean tide: pure, trouble-free, and unspoiled. I remember once basking in a warm, turquoise, pacific lagoon and thinking, "Now, how cool is this, we have yachts anchored in our swimming pool!" At times it was so dream-like that I hoped I wouldn't wake up one day and find myself back in Scotland.

On my second day in Vava'u in the Kingdom of Tonga, I asked a local family from one of the even smaller islands if there was somewhere I could stay over there. They invited me to overnight with them. I didn't know at the time that this meant sharing mattresses on the floor with the whole family and one million mosquitoes! We chugged slowly in their small boat to a long beach lined with trees. The garden of their little home extended right onto the sand. The grandfather was scaling fish. A pretty daughter in a torn dress greeted us with open smiles. It was a peaceful and idyllic setting. I sat on a mat by the shore surrounded by the cutest bunch of kids, piglets, pups, and chicks ~ and glared at the smoked octopus in coconut cream they had cooked for me. Ever since watching a Jacques Cousteau film, "Poor Little Octopus," it was one thing I refused to eat. However, in this situation I felt that my hosts' feelings were more important than mine, or even the poor octopus' at this point. It was the first of many attitudes I was to lose in the strong years ahead.

For beneath the gentle façade, this stunning and remote island group is a very powerful, raw place. It always looks to investors like it is about to boom and become a new Hawaii. But the energy is distinctly different. This is obvious in the way the locals *don't* do business and anything taking off gets brought back to ground level. I commented to a friend who had lived there a couple of years, "This place is very strengthening."

He laughed. "Yeah, right, as in what doesn't kill you makes you stronger!"

Tonga was like a rite of passage: An initiation through fire. It was a very humbling place, and in these times I am grateful for its lessons.

My own experience there was, eventually, very empowering. It was a time of deep introspection and quiet grounding, through tough outer circumstances. After four years of relative isolation, lack of distractions, and constant earth tremors, which all combined to shake off my attitudes, opinions, and beliefs, I hit base. I was, indeed, on the ground. Finally. And it had taken me only 45 years to get there!

> *I realized that to build someone into a very smooth, clear personality, you have to strip down the old framework. Rather than replace it with dogma and mumbo-jumbo, you replace it*

with nothing, leaving the person almost bare, in a free zone
of uncluttered energy.

~ *Stuart Wilde*

This describes my stripping experience on the outer South Pacific islands ~ specks that they are in the open sea, standing alone in a free zone of uncluttered energy. These days we may well feel that we are all going through this continual process of shedding limitations and freeing our old identities. It enables us to expand towards embracing the entirety of who we really are.

The dark night of the soul

I WILL DO MY BEST to make this next phase of our human journey sound more cheery than it felt to me at the time! It was only later, when I watched a presentation on the Mayan calendar[1] that everything, to my surprise, fell into place. It revealed how the changing energy dynamics of the world had affected ~ and continue to affect ~ everybody's lives: our relationships, our corporations and our economies. I dare to say the worst is over, but that depends on us. It really helps to have smooth sailing if we know which way the wind is blowing.

Those days I didn't, so I had a bit of a rough ride. My own story illustrates perfectly what was going on at the time, and perhaps your life had similar aspects and you can relate. The year was 2008. A lot of issues were coming up in the world, and they largely centered around integrity in relationships.

The expat community of Vava'u, Tonga was all of a hundred strong, which isn't huge if one is looking for like-mindedness. All very alternative and acutely individual characters, they didn't really merge that well. The beauty and seclusion of that island group attracted yachties, would-be kings, hard-headed businessmen, and dreamers. This was a most intriguing cast of karmically entan-

---

[1] "The Evolution Continues," based on Dr. Carl Calleman's book,
  The Mayan Calendar and the Transformation of Consciousness

gled characters and promised to be a rather interesting play! Most suffered from "small island syndrome" and the squabbling foreigners were a never-ending source of bewilderment and amusement to the pacific locals. The tourist season was both short and lean, and there were just a few western couples running small cafes out on this tiny rock in the middle of the Pacific Ocean, planet Earth. You'd think they'd feel a lot in common, but, in fact, they would generally refuse to talk or work together at all. A bit strange if you ask me, but nobody did.

Survival was the mindset and the name of the game. In clear contrast to the locals who had a strong sense of solidarity, the expats approached everything from an attitude of "every man for himself." But once the illusions wore off, the isolation set in. Attitudes were crushed, shaken off, or just slowly crumbled, yielding to the forces of time. The self-centered and even manipulative foreigners were coerced to develop a more communal approach, while the more sharing types, the locals and others like me, were pushed and prodded to greater self awareness. Uncomfortable as it felt at the time, it was the perfect exchange, and a scenario I was to observe worldwide. Everyone was being turned to face their own inner relationship. Those with very strong egos, through the emotional isolation they found themselves in, started to soften and appreciate others; and those with weaker egos, who had withdrawn into their own space to avoid further abuse, thus developed stronger individuality. Both this sensitivity and this self strength are essential for any healthy relationship, as well as for our moving forth to a unified, harmonious, group consciousness.

So we were on the right road, but that was not the only area where our own integrity was more than just a little bit shaky. The next one was a biggie, but therefore it was also the huge last drop that brought me to the end of victimhood. A realization so beautiful, so liberating, that I hope you will journey with me through the rest of this chapter.

As if the social life in the South Pacific wasn't minimal enough, my partner and I played Robinson Crusoe for some months ~ caretaking a god-forsaken resort on its own tiny tropical island. I had

asked the universe for a beautiful beach location for the summertime and, shortly after, the owner of said resort had called from
Mexico: there was an emergency situation out there and could we
possibly jump in? We did, with both eyes shut. The setting was
idyllic, but it was to be by no means the honeymoon period I was
naively looking forward to. Not only was it monsoon season, and
the thatched coconut huts faced the oncoming storms from the
north, it was also the 5th night of the Mayan calendar: the deepest
phase of the current age, "the dark night of the soul."

I will keep the story of our own turmoil mercifully short. Suf-
fice to say our survival was not limited to coping with isolation
and leaky roofs, the seldom working radio that was supposed to
give us hurricane warnings and the hordes of hungry mosquitoes.
In tune with the climate, my partner was stormily working on
deep issues he had inherited from the collective psyche of his
Russian-Polish forefathers. I was working on how to keep both
my sanity and our relationship alive. Together we were working
on finding enough to eat in the garden while we sat out three
weeks of rough weather without any food deliveries. The only
book on the island that wasn't on Polynesian sailboats was, what
a coincidence, *Men are from Mars, Women are from Venus* by Dr. John
Gray. This puzzle piece came in, as they often do, in the 11th hour.
It described our different ways of giving and recognizing love, and
hence our misunderstandings and why we were losing appreciation and respect for each other. It also showed me that there was
no one to blame for not having got it all right. Still, unfortunately
for me, it didn't clarify the more complex issues of the Russian-
Polish psyche!

Coming out of the Dark Ages

WE WEREN'T THE ONLY ONES who were going through a zone of
turmoil back then and it brought people closer together in a very
genuine way. My friendship with Rob reminded me of a different
way of relating. In stark contrast to the usual feeling that I was

struggling to survive in my relationship, I blossomed through his trust, encouragement and support. With this approval, I believed I deserved more and that I could receive more. And whatever his ulterior motives, it worked for me. Despite a chauvinistic streak he set a standard of softness and respect for any further exchange. It is not by chance that we live in a world of great variety, for it teaches us about choice. He was of course reflecting my own acute readiness for a more sensitive, loving space, a wish that had actually been strengthened by my previous "hardships." As we appreciate ourselves more, we receive more respect; as we grow in self love, others become more kind; as we become willing to take on more, doors open.

I finally put my foot down with my short-fused partner, who was equally unhappy with his own explosiveness. The energy dynamics that our relationship had been built on were no longer possible to maintain. I realized that in trying to help him out of depression all those years I had actually been feeding the pattern, thus prolonging his misery as well as mine. Through isolation and inner work he had also reached a new doorway; it was high time for new beginnings.

My own turnaround was triggered by a book a friend loaned me. It reminded me that we have all planned this lifetime, and chosen our partners, for our benefit, even if it doesn't seem so at the time! It wasn't that this told me anything new, but in a time of desperation when I was really open for clues, I totally *accepted* the fact and *applied* it to my life. This perspective enabled me to drop not only all the hurt I had carried from our 20 year relationship but also, while I was at it, my whole attitude of victimhood. Once the puzzle pieces of our past are brought together, such a change of heart can really happen overnight.

After one evening of inner turmoil, I was lying out on the veranda in the balmy night air looking over the tranquil moonlit bay. The porch crowned a flight of 50 stairs, and it was eerily reminiscent of being on top of a Mayan pyramid.

Music was playing in my head:

Listen as the wind blows from across the great divide,
voices trapped in yearning, memories trapped in time,
the night is my companion and solitude my guide,
would I spend forever here and not be satisfied?
                                    ~ Sarah McLachlan, lyrics

With a fully accepting, surrendered feeling, yet earnestly asking, *"Why* this relationship?" I slipped spontaneously into a deep
trance state, which I was familiar with from a previous hypnotherapy session: dropping within myself to access a subconscious
level. I saw a close up scene of my partner and myself as gladia-
tors, two brothers, dueling. I was the younger of the two and he
had me between a rock and a hard place. I asked him: *"Why* do
you do this to me?"
    He replied: "Because I can."
    "And what's in it for me?" I protested.
    He replied, "It makes you stronger."
    I had a sudden awakening, an enormous "ah-ha, of course!"
We receive mistreatment because *we allow it,* we support it. *Nothing*
can affect us that we have not in some way invited. It is due to the ab-
sence of self love that we attract abuse to us. We think we are loving
and caring and what can be wrong with that? But we have, by missing self worth, allowed ourselves to be used. There is no blame, just
understanding. We are indeed not opponents, but brothers in arms.
    I wrote to my close friends:

This magic moment was sparked by a series of timely coincidences.
The biggest of which is our huge buddy Pluto, the planet of trans-
formation, who gave me a hand, as it ended a 248 year cycle and
began a new one. This doesn't happen every day, nor indeed every
lifetime. It is setting a powerful time now for change, for the
dropping of old habits, and for new beginnings.

*   Indeed I feel like a slate wiped clean. When I realized how my*
partner actually helped me to this point in life, where I was strong
enough to say 'No more,' the feeling of hurt instantly dropped

away. And with it, lo and behold, I saw the very next morning that a tiny expression of hurt that I carried since so many years was gone from my face. I could have imagined that, for no-one else even knew it was there. But the following day my partner surprised me, 'You look good, there is not that hurt look you had before.'

So we can heal our hurts and our hearts. If I can, you can. And all we have to do is to change our minds. Surely, we can't ask for easier than that!

Thanks to everyone . . . for their hugs, nudges, kicks in the butt, and the odd pinch along the way!

After this powerful revelation I woke up every day in total bliss. Evenings I would lie in bed deeply feeling the beauty and wonder of life. I felt so liberated, I felt it wouldn't matter if I died now, I had arrived. I still enjoy recalling that feeling and basking in that deep gratitude for life. Many experience a more gradual shedding, but once out of victimhood, having moved to a different viewpoint, our world takes on a new dimension. We neither feel nor attract hurt in the same way. As we make this shift we step into a lighter level of existence.

Many sources confirm that the most essential step for each of us, and for our human race as a whole, is to shed the shackle of victimhood. This is our freeing and our destiny. It is our launching pad to a new world.

CHAPTER NINETEEN

Evolution in Progress

You are led through your lifetime by the inner learning creature, the playful spiritual being that is your inner self. Don't turn away from possible futures before you are certain you don't have anything to learn from them. You are always free to change your mind and choose a different future or a different past.

~ *Richard Bach,* ILLUSIONS

THE EVENTS of our past may be objective. But our relationship with the past, the feeling we hold towards it, is not. Our past is really only memories, perhaps many of them bad! Yet it is only the emotions we carry on that bind us to these memories.

Everything that happened, the good, the bad and the ugly, was part of our growth. It brought us to the state of awareness we have now, to be the person we are now. Seeing it in the light of that acceptance, we can feel grateful for it, or at least be ok with it. And then we have a new feeling towards our life. We awaken as out of a dream. It may take some time to fade away, but it will.

We are now reconciling, regaining inner balance. Our female, sensitive quality acknowledges our true feelings, and has the depth and the courage to go into them. Our male quality has a sense of adventure, fun and the drive to move on. The key is to use them both in balance so we are in touch with our deeper feelings ~ not overriding them ~ yet do not become entrenched in them. These two sides within us work together, for only when we have really felt something can we transcend it. We can't turn the page until we have read the page. But once we have read it, it's time to move on, our life is still ahead.

The inglorious conclusion is: we humans are often too insecure to change. Despite all the dramas, we may well feel it's safer to cling to what we know than to face the new. We hang on and don't let go till it hurts. Pain gets us over being content with compromise.

I felt reminded: "Marriage is when two people become as one. The trouble starts when they try to decide which one."

In retrospect I saw the co-dependency and the infringement in our traditional relationships, all in the name of love. But hey, we live and learn, and eventually we learn: *we are not the doormat!*

My partner and I had done this journey towards the end of victimhood together and since the further purpose of our relationship was still not clear to us, but we nonetheless seemed to be on the same bus, we continued to stay together as friends. I had always felt that we had a deep connection and had trusted it was right, and in the long run it had proven to be so.

While I was doing my internal spring cleaning I cleared up other areas of my past. I saw how the many teenage years of rift with my sister, my brother joining the sect, my dad dying, my mum disowning me, and my partner not supporting me emotionally, had all made damn sure I would realize that I had only my own two feet to stand on! Each and every relationship in our life has its value, time and place in our journey. Once our exchange is complete we may be ready for other co-actors with whom to uncover new areas. Understanding this enables us to let go graciously, *and separation can be a celebration of a step well accomplished.*

I had ripened greatly through my experiences. And I could see, in all honesty, that it was not my one and only predestined path in life, but the long and winding road that I took. I never realized how much choice we have in life and how by taking the driver's seat, slowing down, and reading the map right, we can save a lot of struggles and a lot of years. It woke me up to choice. I won't say the tough way was bad for me ~ but next life I sure know which road to choose! There are no wrong paths, no wrong decisions. All roads inevitably lead us ~ just more or less smoothly, more or less swiftly ~ to the same destination. The choice of which way to go is ours.

THE WORLD SIMPLY MIRRORS OUR BELIEFS. If I hadn't felt that life is hard and hurtful, I would have attracted a different relationship.

As actors, we don't hate our co-actors who have to play their role "against" us. We have arranged beforehand to play these roles ~ and always out of caring for each other! We often take on partners and projects that push us to overcome deeply ingrained patterns and offer us the biggest stretch to new areas of life. Once we see this, we may stop playing opposition games. Or else choose to no longer act in the same play! Competition, struggle, and hurt are all part of the old belief system, the old script. Now we see behind the scenes: We are all helping each other.

If you feel anyhow hurt, resentful or misunderstood, just ask yourself: how did I *grow* through these parents, this relationship, and these experiences? What has it helped me to see within myself and therefore to overcome? Which feelings and intentions did it strengthen that empower me now?

In a relationship where, for example, the guy is abusive to the woman, what looks and feels like a battle for survival is in fact "evolution in progress." The man's emotional isolation and regret eventually leads him to greater compassion. The woman is steered to become stronger in her self love, and with this quality she can guide him back to softness. All attempts of control and manipulation finally work in our favor. Once we have seen that in our neighbors or ourselves, we can extend this change of view to the world situation. The would-be oppressors, those who try to abuse or control are simply, unconsciously, motivating the weaker ones to evolve to greater self worth. By pushing their "victims" to realize what they definitely do not want, they urge them to develop their individuality and to strengthen their vision. There are no victims and no abusers. We are all collaborators.

This is often confirmed by people's Near Death Experiences such as this one from *The Experiential Guide to the Celestine Prophesy:*

> *I was filled with gratitude because I still existed and yet I knew perfectly well that I had died... I remember I knew that everything, everywhere in the universe was ok, that the plan was perfect, that whatever was happening in the world, wars, famine, whatever ~ was ok.*

This change of perspective, this change of feeling, transforms our lives.

CHAPTER TWENTY

Shift Happens

~~~

Don't be afraid your life will end,
be afraid it may never begin.

~ *Grace Hansen*

WE LIVED IN various small remote islands in the South Pacific, for four long years of near solitary confinement! As someone pointedly asked me later, "What were you hiding from?" Indeed, wherever we go, however far and fast we run, the same issues keep coming up. Eventually we find that all roads lead us back to our own front door.

At the time though, I didn't realize just how connected everything is. It seemed that going to the South Pacific was simply following my childhood dream, looking for those virgin beaches without a care in the world. Since 9/11, we had looked deeply into conspiracy "theories," so it also seemed, like it did to many others out there, a sensible choice. The world situation at the time appeared to be declining into the state of control long since planned and predicted. We hadn't yet noticed that the tides had turned.

The gift that lies for us within our dreams is often not quite what we had in mind. By the time I left the Pacific, I understood how my own survival issues, in my relationship and otherwise, had brought me to the perfect place. We see our patterns reflected in the outside world so we have to deal with them; and in doing so, rather than repressing our human traits, we accept and integrate them.

One night on a distant isle I curled up on the sofa, watching the gale force winds pushing the pelting rain across the lonely bay. Pen and paper at hand, as usual, I wrote a verse for my latest song:

So I seek my inner child, she is hiding with her joy
Tucked away in a corner where she keeps her special toys
She cries this world is too hard, I seek shelter from the storm
May I rest here on your shores awhile until I feel the dawn…

THERE IS A SURVIVALIST STREAK in many of the expats that move out to these remote places. Aware of, and away from, political and economic changes, they are preparing for the worst. The worst is not really the worst, as living off the land is a very grounding experience: as the word suggests, it brings us down to earth. It puts us back in touch with the basics of life: the Earth, the elements, and the natural rhythms. It thus makes us humble, appreciative and caring.

Self sufficiency is also a mindstate, an exercise in self reliance, as we wean ourselves from the society that both protects and controls us. Such survivalist attitude among westerners may seem laughable to you… however these guys are often getting more than they bargained for. To face and go through the depths of our instinctive survival fears is most grounding and empowering.

Many expats move out there with high-flying ambitions and aspirations, and the islands have an uncanny knack of bringing everyone back to the ground with a painful bump. With its white sandy beaches and turquoise sea the place may look, from Google Earth, like your picture book paradise; and yet, as many westerners have said, it is the most humbling place I know.

From generations of living on these tiny isolated islands, blown by strong winds in the midst of the open ocean, the Pacific people are, as their cubic stature suggests, rock steady. Contrary to the emotional westerners, nothing fazes them. Hurricanes can come and go, they quietly pick up the pieces and carry on. They have learnt the art of acceptance. They could live cut off from the outside world and nothing much would change out there. In this day and age there are still many villagers around the planet who do not depend on money. Some hardly use the stuff. Talk about different realities! Imagine that.

I have felt fortunate throughout my life to have always had good "working" conditions. I lived the largest part of my life in beautiful quiet places, without supermarkets or traffic lights, often not using a vehicle for weeks or even months. Much of the time I wouldn't know what day it was. The sun rises… and does it matter if we give this day a name or a number? And the sun sets… on another day in paradise.

When we were not busy processing the turning tides of the ages within ourselves, we would look out over the vast ocean under the vast sky. The mind dissolves out there, with nothing to grasp onto, and it was easy to zone out into the state of "no mind," the state before thought began. It is a quiet, content, but uncreative feeling that encompasses the islands. It surely has its place holding a certain energy field on the planet, and we joke that if Earth should enter a phase of no-mind the islanders won't even notice!

Over half the population of Tonga lives now in western countries. It was a clear case of "those who had the get-up-and-go, got up and went." Finally the day came, when we too had to reclaim the shreds of our identity from the vast quietness of the endless ocean, wind and sky. We had by then also had our share of being brought to ground level. I felt I had lived basic enough for long enough and if a return to bare survival was all the future had to offer then I wasn't playing Eartheyland anymore!

I felt that the world was abundant. It was 2009 and there I was, living the whole off-season on an exciting diet of papayas, bananas, coconuts, and the only three types of vegetables the market had to offer during those six months. And sometimes, when we were lucky, there were carrots…courtesy of New Zealand and the weekly supply boat. My partner did his best to present this wide range of gastronomical delicacies in different forms. I was adamant. The minimal food selection paralleled the social state of affairs and I was getting off that ride!

I was aware that wonderful happenings were taking place all over the world, flourishing through the rise of consciousness, and I wanted to be part of that expansion. I yearned to share and contribute to that side of life rather than dwell on the anxiety of survivalism that friends and newcomers expressed.

If you do not change direction,
you may end up where you are heading.
~ Lao-Tzu

As much as I could see their logic and the benefits that way would give them I just could not bring myself to invest my energy in that direction. It seemed to me that in setting up for a survival scenario, not only could one be attracting it ~ for if anywhere gets cut off, it's those distant islands ~ one would already be living in that reality.

We can either fear that human culture is falling apart, or we can hold the Vision that we are awakening. Either way, our expectation is a prayer that goes out as a force that tends to bring about the end we envision. Each of us must consciously choose between these two futures.

What the end-times seers were receiving was an intuition that in our time, two distinctive futures would be opening before us. We could either choose to languish in the Fear, believing that the world is moving into a Big Brother style of automation and social decay and destruction....or we could follow the other path and consider ourselves the believers who can overcome this nihilism, and open to the higher vibrations of love, where we are spared the apocalypse and can enter a new dimension in which we invite the spirit, through us, to create just the utopia the scriptural prophets envisioned.

~ James Redfield, The Tenth Insight

My final liberating push, the last drop, was a powerful book I read, written by a man of great integrity. Once again I took it on board, accepting its message and applying it to my life. It faced me with the possibility of impending disaster and the feeling that "it could be too late." What bugged me most was that I felt I had not contributed enough. I briefly hit rock bottom, allowing my deepest desperation and fears, and thus going through them. Powerful action arises out of such surrender, out of having faced the facts. I was no longer denying, no longer resisting, no longer upholding hopes and no longer holding back. When we relinquish our own individual survival and existential issues, we connect to the larger picture and allow tremendous power to flow through us. Fear becomes a gateway to a new life.

As you begin to work through the fear that is holding you back,
you will usually discover a fuller understanding of who you are,
and what your current life is about. Most important is to look
deep enough to remember what you want to do with your life.
                                   ~ James Redfield, THE TENTH INSIGHT

I couldn't quite remember yet, but I had emerged greatly strengthened in my creative energy and vision. I wrote: "I know one thing,
I am ready to thrive not just survive." I had been shocked out of
my inertia and into life. The sleepy seclusion of the islands no
longer reflected or matched my mood. It was time to leave.
Nonetheless, I was still questioning my choice to give up this relative pacific paradise, where one would awaken every morning
to the timeless tranquility of the turquoise bay. The next book I
was loaned contained this line:

Now we can imagine ourselves either striving to survive
in an age of unpredictability, or we can imagine ourselves
thriving in an era of triumph.
                      ~ Dannion and Kathryn Brinkley, SECRETS OF THE LIGHT

I thanked it for the confirmation.
      Once I know I am leaving, I appreciate even more. I notice
how beautiful the place or person really is, and any issues they
may have pale in comparison. Yet we are called to move on. In the
same way a relationship can be over, with no critique, just knowing it is not our place anymore: we had our time together, ex-
changed what we had to learn, and split with gratitude and grace,
knowing that all things must change.
      Good bye Pacific. It had been my dream and, in search of par-
adise, I had found it. I now knew that the key to paradise is always
in our own pocket. I knew that the future of humanity lies too, in
our own hands.

FRIENDS TRIED TO HOLD US BACK, their own fears fuelling their
warnings, but I replied I would rather take my chances and risk
the bombs and bandits than to face a sure slow death by boredom.

I had that niggling feeling I had something more to do in life. I felt it was time for celebration and sacred gatherings.

I was no longer scared of the "big bad world." I knew that shit doesn't just happen, it is attracted. Nothing can affect us that we have not invited in. And it feels better to live life in celebration than in fear. *Even if* my own death was coming up ~ which then seemed sort of inevitable at some stage ~ I felt the best preparation is always to be as far as possible in one's personal evolution, to live and enjoy to the max. I wasn't anymore concerned about dying, I was concerned about living. When our preoccupation with survival falls way, a fundamental shift in attitude takes place. As my teenage daughter once pondered, "If I could die tomorrow, I don't want to lose today by worrying about it."

Hence the diagnosis of "terminal illness" sometimes cures people. Forced to face their fears, they quit their job and enjoy living their last days to the fullest. This free-flowing approach enables them to release all the pent up feelings, the blockages and the stuck-up energy that created the dis-ease in the first place. And as their life energy starts flowing again, they heal. "Miraculous," the doctors say…

Thus the fear of death can help us to jump over our own shadow. We drop all the procrastination, the hiding, the hoarding and the holding back which are linked to our expectation, or fear, of the future. Suddenly, living for *now,* our energy is released to flow and flower.

> *And the day came when the risk it took to stay tight*
> *in a bud became greater than the risk it took to open.*
> ~ *Anais Nin*

And this free-flowing energy is healing us, and our planet.

CHAPTER TWENTY-ONE

The Bright Side
of Struggle and Strife

*People have to really suffer before they can risk
doing what they really love.*

~ *Chuck Palaniuk*

AT TIMES when things weren't looking that hunky dory, I joked that we were surely lured onto this planet by a sleek tourist brochure: "Visit Planet Earth." There were glossy pictures of food and fun, smiling faces, and beautiful waterfalls. It's not surprising therefore that on grey days we may feel a bit ripped off. At times I have considered lodging a complaint for false advertising at the travel bureau when I get back home!

Whoever does their marketing up there must be doing a damn good job because heaps of people are coming here these days. Perhaps there's more to this place than meets the eye? Perhaps there's a special offer on, a package deal: "Visit Planet Earth: a rejuvenating health retreat for body, mind, and spirit."

REST ASSURED, struggle and strife is certainly not my favorite topic. Nor perhaps yours. Yet, looking at the bright side for a change, we become a lot friendlier with it when we know how much it has guided us. We then see it is not a random occurrence and even, dare I say, *not* a mandatory field in our earthly contract.

Even a seasoned traveler can become settled in and forget that there is more in life. We have all had experiences of holding on ~ to a person, a job, or where we were living ~ when it would have been easier, smoother, faster and more progressive, to let go. We cling to what we know because it feels secure and comfortable ~ even if it isn't. Our player part gets bored, knowing we are ready for the next move, and decides to scoot us along a bit on the playing board. So, whenever we get a bit too comfy or complacent, life, co-operative as always, catapults us into the next arena. We rarely feel ready for it. We rather tend to take it as a personal insult. "It's so unfair, how can they do that to me?" We may feel unappreciated, dumped, or kicked in the butt, rather than just realizing the great opportunity for growth it offers: a new experience, new territory, new qualities to develop within us. We cling, kick and scream, and refuse to budge. By resisting the change that is on offer, we suffer.

Acceptance usually comes when we have run out of arguments, steam, or tears. When we can't fight anymore we surrender, we are forced to give in to our higher good. Begrudgingly, we let go. Looking back we can see how the upheavals pushed us forwards, and those who instigated them were our helpers. We can even begin to see it as our own making. Eventually, and this is the beauty of experience, when such a situation arises we realize hey, hold on, this has happened before. It feels like losing everything but it is in fact just a transition, an opportunity for new growth. From previous times of opposing the flow of life and trying to force our own version, we realize the futility of that method and decide to spare ourselves the stress and distress. Once again, our heart's desire to remain in a happier space leads us to grow. We learn to look closer at what life plunks on our doorstep, sensing that it has always been in our favor.

It's very normal for us small beings to be slow to take on the unknown, feeling not up to it. But, like turtles, we only make progress when we stick our neck out. The reward for looking out of our shell is usually a better view and a better feeling. After some time we develop trust.

Life is very ingenious. If we don't flow and don't grow, if we resist and fight with what life delivers, we suffer. Through not wanting to suffer we finally stretch ourselves to accepting what is. It's only by accepting what really is: "Ok, I'm really stuck in a traffic jam," that we can start making better choices: "Fine, I'll meditate!"

We need to first accept the fact of a situation, including the most bothersome fact that we, somehow, created it! As long as we resist facing what is, or placate ourselves with false hopes and expectations, we are missing the gift the event holds for us. It may be the gift of tolerance, of compassion, of trust, or self discovery. It may birth other talents we never knew we had, such as unleashing our own power to do something about it.

We often experience hurt and, being the brave little souls that we are, then brush ourselves off and put on another smile. Life is all about being strong and having fun, so we won't let anything stop us. This has its merit, but it also has its place.

Mostly, as we toughened up not to feel the hurt, we were just covering it up, another plaster, another façade. This stifled our real feelings, and isolated us from our true self and also from others. Even braver, we may have found, is to acknowledge when something hurts us, to look at why and how we attracted it, and what it could be telling us. To avoid feeling and processing our pain, we often take refuge in the brighter parts of our personality, ignoring the small child within. We may distract ourselves with false hopes, entertainment, compulsive activity, drugs or recklessness. Now I am not saying we should make mountains out of molehills, or that we can't be optimistic, kid around and have fun! Playfulness is often the greatest healer and dissolves a lot of those little molehills. But if we hide in escapism, if we refuse to recognize the truth of the situation, it then manifests through physical or strong emotional pain that we are forced to look at. If we bury too many molehills we will end up with a mountain.

Sickness, for example, develops from continuously repressed emotions. It is the symptom of inner conflict, showing us that something inside us is not in agreement. It is our body's way of saying: "Look what you are feeling!" So you can consider the physical symptom which finally manifests not to be the sickness itself, but the red flag. It's friendly-wise telling you there is some dis-ease within you and prompting you through pain, the last resort, to look for the root cause. It is a wake-up call, hinting us to change course, and challenging us to become healers. So when something hurts us, rather than burying molehills, we want to listen to our smaller parts, see why it hurts them, and find new ways of dealing with it. Then it doesn't have to grow too big to overlook.

Often it is just our ego that gets hurt. We may have set ourselves up for disappointment through attachment and expectation. We slot people towards what we look for: this woman is beautiful, she will make me happy; this man is just what I need; this is the *perfect* place. We dig a trap, fall flat in it, and then blame life.

We could have had high hopes that an existing situation would change, or perhaps even higher hopes that things would never change. The pain is not to punish us, but to help us "get real." To get back on our own feet and back in touch with the essential.

THE AMERICAN SOCIETY, for one, may be experiencing such grounding. It was easy to predict from the outside. Living on credit is like living on hope: one becomes dependent and one's energy is vested in the future. The pioneers had founded the New World on principles of freedom and democracy, and it soon became an inspiring example to the world. At this point it was hijacked, the runaway child was recaptured. You might ask yourself, how come America rates as having among the worst education level in the world? Is there a lack of intelligent people, of good teachers, or of money? I will let you come to your own conclusions.

Through no fault of their own, but through their TV's silly and shallow shows, which promote an obsession with stars and over-consuming, parts of the society were molded to be rather superficial. Through the creature comforts, as well as through education and media encouraging competitiveness and insecurity, many became isolated.

Therefore, life steered numerous people to reconnect to more real values, such as simplicity, appreciation, and openness; to drop some façade and look deeper to the real things in life. Some strife caused people to pull together and recognize the good qualities in others. I have great faith that the American people ~ the melting pot of the planet ~ are still pioneers at heart, playing a large role to carry in, this time unstoppable, the spirit of the new world.

*Eventually we become less enamored with struggle and pain,
and choose to work smarter, not harder.*
~ Dannion and Kathryn Brinkley

SUFFERING IS NOT BECAUSE LIFE IS CRUEL to us, but because of
our own imbalance. It shows us we've gone too far to one side.
We may have become blocked, so energy is not flowing through
us. We are no longer in tune. Our distress brings us to realize there
is an easier way, we are off course, we are not following the script
of our lives.

It is still in the nature of humans that we learn from pain ~ because, often enough, only when something becomes unbearable
do we actually do something about it! Until it does, we tend to put
off dealing with it. "It'll sort itself out; I can handle it; It makes me
strong; I'll get to it later . . ." This procrastination, this hanging-on,
stems from our feeling powerless or lacking self love.

A woman was complaining to a friend about how badly her
partner was treating her. He suggested, "You could leave him."

"Oh no, I couldn't do that!"

The friend shrugged: "More pain is needed."

That is the function of pain. It says, "In this place there is a
problem!" It calls us to notice parts of ourselves we were not aware
of. The greater our tolerance to pain, the longer it takes us to get
the message. Eventually our suffering wakes us up. It brings us
back to reality, maybe back to earth. *It puts our attention onto ourselves.* It may bring us to a space of honesty where we can face
what really is. Through greater awareness of ourselves, our needs,
our insecurities and our patterns ~ we become more genuine,
more whole, and more loving.

Some events in life bring us down to the ground. They make
us more humble. We stop fighting, we surrender. We may become
aware of the greater plan, that of our evolution. So the sicknesses,
the accidents, the breakdowns and the deaths stop us in our tracks.
We cease the outward motion: aspiring, appeasing, achieving. We
slow down, we look within, we may begin to consider our own

death and ask what lies beyond. Society emphasizes and applauds the "male" qualities of outer strength, success and possession. Suffering puts us back in balance by turning us inwards, enabling us to feel our feminine side: care and sensitivity, humility and compassion, acceptance and let go.

> *When you lose, don't lose the lesson.*
> ~ *Dalai Lama*

When we have "everything under control" we can become a bit proud and insulated. But when things go wonky, or worse, pear shaped, our smaller part resurfaces, and we become more humble and open to others. To notice and express that part of ourselves keeps us in tune with ourselves and with our evolution. And if we do so out of freewill, we find life does not force us to. It may feel like a tough love planet, but if we want it easier... it's easy: all we have to do is to be softer ourselves, play the "tough cookie" a bit less, and be more open and more honest. What comes to us is never a punishment from life or from a judgmental god, only an *energetic* consequence of how we are.

OUR SUFFERING IS A TURNING POINT. It offers us the opportunity to re-evaluate the situation, ourselves, our life. It may push us to let go. Hanging on may feel like a choice but is rather the standard reaction, the default setting of our human insecurity. One day we come to the shocking realization that we never really chose anything, we were sleep walking, following our unconscious settings. We were living on autopilot, reacting rather than choosing, moved by our repetitive emotional patterns, rather than truly considering our options.

When we're winning a game, when we are successful, we really get into it. We get caught up in the excitement of it, it feels good, it feels real to us, and we don't want to stop playing. When we're losing however, it doesn't have such a hold on us. We tend to remind ourselves: "it's just a game." Hence it is often those who have experienced hardships, poverty, injustice, tragic deaths, and war who grow more detached from the social game. It is those with heavy pain bodies, and other sensitive ones, who are motivated to seek what lies beyond. They are the ones who ask *"Why?"* and find answers. It is when we have really had enough of struggle that we are ready to move on. Our hurt becomes one of the greatest boosts to our understanding and evolution.

> *If life didn't hurt we wouldn't look behind it.*
> ~ *Deepak Chopra*

To sum up, suffering shows us we are in resistance mode, off balance, or out of line. It helps us to be more realistic and more present. It makes us aware of what we don't want, and illuminates why we are getting it. It prompts us to turn within and pushes us to look deeper. Eventually we start to make changes, more conscious choices. It has guided us to reconnect and to expand. Our struggles have shown us the beauty of the human spirit ~ our humaneness and our strengths. As we overcame our sorrows to find back our faith in life, they stretched us further than we ever thought we could go.

Our suffering has, little by little, pulled our heartstrings, opening us to feel and to share. It brought us to compassion, for ourselves and our fellow humans; in times of deep sorrow, our heart pangs are its growing pains. Can we see how it has helped us, yes. Do we want more of it? No. Thanks anyway. We can choose other heart-opening situations ~ such as communion with nature, deep introspection, loving encounters, sharing groups and singing circles ~ where we may feel as though our little heart is bursting at the seams. It is indeed stretching: we are increasing its capacity to carry love.

CHAPTER TWENTY-TWO

New Horizons

*The real voyage of discovery consists not in seeking
new landscapes, but in having new eyes.*
~ *Source unknown*

LOOKING AT OURSELVES and at our lives, we can see, in retrospect, that what we thought was good at the time was not always that great, and what we thought was awful was often really not that bad. Thus we begin to take life as it comes and to feel at ease, at peace. The human pursuit of outer gratification stems partly from the fear of what might come up if we stop running. So once we have looked *within*, and found that we, and life as such, are actually okay, we can slow down and relax.

*People miss their share of happiness, not because they never
found it, but because they didn't stop to enjoy it.*
~ *William Feather*

Our inner pain had accumulated, perhaps through many lifetimes of burying those molehills, not realizing that every single one was of our own creation. It came from not understanding the mirror game, not knowing that *we too are creators*. Through feeling separate we grew in pain and thus the pain grew. As each misunderstanding piled on top of the previous ones they grew into mountains of mistrust, resentment, and hurt: suppressed shadows of stored pain.

This lifetime is our prime chance to recognize this and to drop the hurt complex. When we take our experiences, like losing a game or fellow tokens leaving the board, no longer just on face value, but peep behind the scenes at the machinery that runs the show, we get a new view on life. There is far more to this reality than we can possibly comprehend. We can stop dwelling on our hurts and get over the feeling that there is something wrong with the world and we can do it better. Earth is our healing place. This is our chance to realize it is the perfect set-up, to drop our resistance and separatist viewpoint, and to go with the flow; accepting with trust that which we cannot yet understand. Once we wholeheartedly agree to life, we become in tune with it. And once we are in tune with life, aligned with our own evolving, we become potent creators.

～

> And he said unto them, 'If a man told God that he wanted most of all to help the suffering world, no matter the price to himself, and God answered and told him what he must do, should the man do as he is told?'
>
> 'Of course, Master!' cried the many. 'It should be a pleasure for him to suffer the tortures of hell itself, should God ask it!'
>
> 'No matter what those tortures, nor how difficult the task?'
>
> 'Honor to be hanged, glory to be nailed to a tree and burned, if so be that God has asked,' said they.
>
> 'And what would you do,' the Master said unto the multitude, 'If God spoke directly to your face and said, 'I COMMAND THAT YOU BE HAPPY IN THE WORLD, AS LONG AS YOU LIVE.' What would you do then?'
>
> And the multitude was silent, not a voice, not a sound was heard upon the hillsides, across the valleys where they stood.
>
> ~ Richard Bach, ILLUSIONS

Life was never meant to be a struggle. It does not ask us to suffer. For long we felt it to be our destined way, yet our strife was only showing us how to join the flow: to seek inwardly for our true Self, for our own relationship with Life. We have always been on a journey of discovery, a journey of reconnection.

In the path of our happiness shall we find the learning
for which we have chosen this lifetime.

~ *Richard Bach,* ILLUSIONS

It is indeed our heart that steers us towards our dreams. We may not be able to eliminate all sorrow from our life in an instant, but we reduce it tremendously by understanding its purpose of showing us our track. Because of the mistrust inherent in our sense of separation the human race has carried hurt since Eons. We are now, each of us, dissolving this mindset.

Almost everyone carries in his or her energy field an accumula-
tion of old emotional pain, which I call "the pain body".... It also
partakes of the pain suffered by countless humans throughout the
history of humanity. This pain still lives in the collective psyche
of humanity and is being added to on a daily basis.

Any emotionally painful experience can be used as food for the
pain body. That's why it thrives on negative thinking as well
as drama in relationships. The pain body is the addiction to
unhappiness.

~ *Eckhart Tolle, A* NEW EARTH

I can just picture our little spirits cringing when they were in-structed they would have to don additional "pain bodies" when they entered Earth's paradigm. They surely shook their heads in utter disbelief when they were told that, once in human form, we can even become reluctant to shed this part of our personality!

Sharing bad news and complaining about life in general, has been a widely accepted form of social exchange for genera-tions. Now there are many progressive circles where that is no longer the case. Aware of how it affects their feeling, people no longer let themselves be drawn into it that dead-end street. This is not about being unrealistic or rosy-eyed, it's about where we give and direct our life-energy, and how we rewire ourselves *to create a lighter reality.* Remember that whether we are repeating old pat-terns or following new ways, we are reinforcing that particular wiring *in our bodies.*

Surrender the pleasure of pain. "What?" we may cry indignantly, "I don't enjoy pain at all!" Watch attentively your feelings when talking about the news, or a sickness you had, an accident or how someone died. Notice the attention it seeks, and how voicing horror and regret suits the pain body just fine. Sorrowful experiences may have become part of your identity. Appreciate them as part of your journey to maturity, and let them go. On the road one learns to travel light. We have to leave the old experiences behind in order to collect new ones. If we pick up a stone as a souvenir from every bit of rough road we traveled, we soon get bogged down by the weight of our backpack.

When we are caught in the lower frequencies, such as regret and resentment, frustration and anger, depression and blame, we are holding our own valve closed. We may self-indulge in feeling bad, stewing over petty issues. This is a "luxury" that many people on our planet don't have time for. When large landslides block the winding Himalayan roads, the locals get on with the job of clearing tons of rock, slowly but surely by shovel, with no drama and no fuss whatsoever. Through acceptance we remain calmly in our center. If we are attentive, in times of emotional crisis, despair or depression, we may notice that part within quietly waiting for us to get over it.

There is a famous story of an Indian king who has a ring engraved to uplift him in times of defeat, and humble him in times of triumph. The inscription reads: "This too shall pass." Remembering this keeps our emotions in perspective so we are not pushed off balance. It helps to reduce the pendulum swing: if we don't get too smug from our successes we won't need to be reminded that we have another side too.

We can see that our suffering has helped us to become more: to understand, accept, open, and love more. We may evaluate ourselves by our outer achievements, yet it is only this personal expansion that we take with us. We may choose to focus therefore on our inner relationship, so it isn't forced upon us. When we are loving enough to forgive and accept ourselves unconditionally ~

whatever we think we are, or are not ~ then we no longer feel bound to strive or to learn from hardships. We thus stop to create our own suffering by pushing, punishing ourselves, or resisting life's flow. As we move beyond personal struggle, into a position of respect, softness, and acceptance for ourselves and others, we see our lives change, reflecting that new awareness.

When I say we may be over suffering, that we may not need it anymore as a tool for growth, people look at me as though I was trying to change the laws of the universe. Well, life is in constant change, is it not? It evolves. Because of the density of matter, a certain amount of resistance is intrinsic to the physical world. So downloading the light of love into matter has indeed required a certain amount of overcoming, a certain amount of working against resistance. Yet soon enough, consciousness will become fully merged with matter, and the very source of our struggles will cease to be.

"No pain, no gain" has been so drummed into us that, for many, it is difficult to imagine that life's lessons could happen in a different way. One good example of this is the ingrained belief that childbirth *requires* pain. Yet natural ways of delivering life are proving not only painless but even ecstatic. This may seem unbelievable at first and even irk some, as it seems to devalue our own efforts and experience. Yet, our human mindset, *and with it our experience*, is changing.

The only way we can really leave a relationship, a country, or a lifetime is through love, not resentment ~ just knowing we are moving on. Otherwise we will be carrying stones on with us. In the same way, we can now understand the purpose of our suffering and be grateful for it, because without it we wouldn't have got here in time ~ and know that we are moving on. I am sure I'm not the only one who feels ready for that.

I sent an email to my "Wonderful World" group:

Beautiful people,

We all know that Life kicks us in the butt sometimes to help move us on. It does work! So we assume that being kicked in the butt is a necessary part of going further in life. I say, just because this is the way we've been doing it since eons doesn't mean it has to stay like that! I'm over it. The Stone Age didn't end just because we ran out of stones... We can choose a different way.

There is the universal law of Attraction, and the universal law of Allowance, but I have never heard of the Universal Law of Kick-in-the-Butt.

The universal law is that Life evolves. It keeps attuning us to the rising level of consciousness on Earth by coaxing us to evolve, to grow in integrity and love. So if we don't like to be kicked in the butt (and I, personally, don't) we do best to acknowledge our higher aspirations and visions for ourselves, being willing and eager to take on new spaces, to stretch and to expand. That's part of the new paradigm on offer: we have to co-create it. A new world, if we can be it. We have to be able change our minds in order to change our lives.

So yesterday I planted a seed: "I am increasingly able to expand and to evolve through only enjoyable experiences." Can we believe this is possible? All we need is to believe enough in ourselves and in this wonderful world. Through watering the seed it softens. By feeding it, it takes root, it becomes anchored. By tending it, it grows and blossoms. Perhaps you like to join in the gardening...?"

Suffering has matured us to this point, like a good camembert cheese. It doesn't need more maturing. Take a long last look at the role of struggle in your own life. It is time to lay down the inner and outer fight.

We may live in the illusion that we enjoy drama and confrontation; but once we've been through that all one hundred times before, once we realize there is nothing wrong and we created it all ourselves, we get over the buzz of blaming others and bringing justice to the world. After countless conflicts are we ready now to see that peace is not boring? It is a place of merging that fuels a brand new start.

It is the storms at sea, not the smooth sailing, that make a good story, and that we enjoy embellishing and telling to others. We look back at these as the fun adventures on Eartheyland, which is a cool change of viewpoint from how we felt at the time; but, to be honest, we wouldn't choose to go through them again! They may well have helped us to get here, to build our individuality and self worth; we may even have become fond of struggle because it increased our sense of inner accomplishment. But once we have crossed a bridge, we don't really need to pick up the bridge and carry it on with us.

> *There are a growing number of humans alive today*
> *whose consciousness is sufficiently evolved not to need*
> *any more suffering before the realization of enlightenment.*
> *You may be one of them.*
> ~ Eckhart Tolle, THE POWER OF NOW

However heroic and however compassioned, none of us are able to take on the pain of the world, nor do we need to. That, too, may have seemed part of our personal value. Yet, to go beyond this old paradigm requires a shift of focus. Where we put our energy is where we go. We all harbor a vision, one that is planted deep within our soul, both a memory and a prophecy of a more evolved world.

Celebration

I WAS RECENTLY AT A WONDERFUL CEREMONY in Bali for the reconnection of our energetic circuitry through sonic code and sacred geometry. I felt all the beautiful people around me, and the deeper purpose of our gathering. I thought to myself, "Yes, it's happening. Through the work we have all done on ourselves we are creating a new world." In response to my thought, one line came clearly through: "Our success depends on our ability to let go of suffering."

I recognized in a flash the full scope behind that simple message. It meant not only to drop our pain bodies, not only to realize there are no victims, but also to drop our journey. For to step into a new reality, where the vibration of struggle cannot exist, we will have to willingly leave behind everything that brought us to that door. To step over the threshold we can't take any of that baggage with us. So let it go, piece by piece, the earlier the better. We will not be able to tell our children, "Son, you don't know what we have been through to get here," as our grandparents used to say, "I lived through the war..." That past will no longer exist for us, and if it does, it may hold us there.

If we wish to enter *the reality* of peace and harmony we will have to leave all struggle at the door. You may be surprised how difficult that can be for many. It has become so ingrained, so much part of our self worth, that our suffering and our overcoming, our fights and our victories may have become our identity. Yet as great as our journeys have been, as awesome our missions, as powerful our triumphs, they belong to the realm of duality we are being asked to transcend. And in exchange for surrendering our stories, surrendering what may feel like a large part of ourselves, we find a clean slate: A new beginning.

This does not belittle our lives or our work in any way. In order to reach somewhere we do have to hold our vision and work towards it. Then, comes a time when we realize the work is done. This time is now. It's time to let go of the wanting, the yearning, and the pushing, and feel it is done. It is on its way. I think that's where many are now. It's time to celebrate. Through our gratitude and our celebration, we affirm our trust.

CHAPTER TWENTY-THREE

The Portal of Trust

Wisdom begins in wonder.
~ Socrates

WHILE I WAS IN THE SMALLER ISLES of the South Pacific, it seemed as if the rest of the world did not exist. And once I left there, the reality of those islands faded instantly away, like a dream, as though they were in a different dimension. It has to do with the predominant presence of the intuitive mindset in which they bathe, secluded isles of stillness, in the midst of the vast ocean, under the vast skies. The indigenous populations still hold, for the rest of us, that less conceptual, more unified mindstate. It links them to their intuition and to deep-seated trust.

Our intuition lives in misty realms; hunches against reason, spaces we can glimpse but not define, recall but not remember. Our intellect, limited by language and physical time-space perception, cannot grasp what lies beyond. And yet these spaces are as real as anything we can touch. More so even. The intangible energy that we begin to sense is the very essence of which our world is built. Quantum physics is only just starting to perceive the immensity and the complexity of what we *cannot* see.

Everything about this world is a mystery. Our own body is an incredible example. Science tells us that each tiny cell contains enough information to fill 1000 books of 600 pages each. Each microscopic cell contains six million pages of data. Ungraspable. We don't even know what "six million" looks like.

There are 200 billion stars in our galaxy, and an estimated 100 billion galaxies. That's only in this universe, there are more... If such inconceivable things are true, then what is not possible? And what is our place in this miracle of life? We are such a miniature part of the whole and yet, we are a part of It.

Does this mystery not stir in us some wonder... and in our awe perhaps awaken our dormant trust? Can we allow this mystery to lead us to surrender, through trust, as a child does? This innate trust may have become buried deep under layers of logic and skepticism, under years of disappointment and disillusion. We may be ready now to review our point of view. Our rational mind can always see more sides. Therefore it lives in split and in doubt, and so can we. Our intuition is undivided.

> *The human mind is not capable of grasping the Universe. We are like a little child entering a huge library. The walls are covered to the ceilings with books in many different tongues. The child knows that someone must have written these books. It does not know who or how. It does not understand the languages in which they are written. But the child notes a definite plan in the arrangement of the books - a mysterious order which it does not comprehend, but only dimly suspects.*
> ~ *Albert Einstein*

The billion piece puzzle

IN OUR EARNEST ATTEMPTS to see reality as it is, we have to finally admit that there is a huge scope of realities. And whatever we can see is still just a tiny part of a massive universal puzzle.

Let's say it's a billion piece puzzle. Let's say our physical reality is one million pieces, of which we, collectively, have found only one thousand so far. Out of those, we can barely find a hundred that we can individually put together. Now, does this 100 piece corner give us any idea of the whole billion piece puzzle? It's good to step back sometimes from the little bit we are working on to remind ourselves just how vast Life really is. We are only aware of the tip of the iceberg: a minute and simple part of this multi-faceted planetary life which works wonders without us knowing how.

People travel to wonder at the height of the mountains, at the huge waves of the seas, at the long course of the rivers, at the vast compass of the ocean, at the circular motion of the stars, and yet they pass by themselves without wondering.

~ Augustine

Studying anatomy, we become aware of the miracle that is the human body: how it all functions and interacts, and the tremendous degree of connectivity between all the parts. Consider your 50 trillion miniscule cells, each containing those six million pages of data, each perform trillions of interconnected actions every second. This is the same unfathomable design, and the same degree of interconnectivity, as in the outer world.

We are part and parcel of an interconnected whole. Be aware of the wondrous, mysterious nature of the world we live in. Obviously, we are not managing our life all alone. We have tremendous support. To find our faith back in Life, to dare to trust again, is not naïve. It is simply a very logical conclusion.

We can indeed feel that our world is a perfect set-up and everything is on course. Surely our destiny is not in the hands of a few would-be rulers, but in the flow of Being ~ of which everything and everyone, however wealthy or deluded, is just a miniature part. Can a small handful of people, out of their own fears, stop the universal evolution of Consciousness?

No amount of drugs, fluoride and fairy tale education could permanently suppress the longing of the human spirit for peace and love, for light, wonder, awe and yes, worship.

~ UNCENSORED magazine

That "the dark side is winning" may be loudly broadcast to demoralize the alternative population, in a desperate attempt to prevent the inevitable: the critical mass of humanity tipping the scales. Yet the truth of the situation is what we can feel within ourselves and looking around us. Is the dark side winning, or are we becoming more conscious, more genuine and more loving every day? We are each the source of our reality.

Some sensitive ones may feel that the dark is indeed winning because of the inner turbulence they are going through. Repressed shadow material rising, such as deep fears that result in strong re-activity, can cause us to lose balance. Our personalities being thus both dismantled and stretched may even appear like losing con-trol, losing sanity. Yet as we agree to loosen our own patterns of suppression, so the control around us also lessens.

And as we strengthen our inner connection, we are not so easily affected and disempowered by our own doubts, other's emotions, setbacks, news and scare tactics. Recognize that there is purpose and oneness behind all the apparent opposites and chaos. To be honest the world needs *big* changes and we should welcome them. Do we really want to be part of a soul-destroying system, and continue amassing material wealth, social status and fat cells? If we do not trust in the Whole, then where *are* we putting our trust? In the belief of the power of a few misguided egos who may try to control our lives against the increasing awareness on the planet? If we do not see the Light, then where are we looking?

Everything is happening at once. These are times of collapse and of great flowering, times of simplifying and times of great abundance. Times of transformation and times of celebration. Times to give all we have and to receive everything in return.

Trust in yourself. Trust in the greater force that flows through you. Trust in the process of life. And trust in the power of the human heart.

I LOOK AT ALL THE BEAUTIFUL CHILDREN, and people doing their best with the tools they have, and I know that they will not end up struggling just to survive. Life is fair and intrinsically loving. We did not join this game to fight against unbeatable odds or to be punished for a sin we never committed. We joined to learn to love within a fear-based paradigm. And, through the power of our hearts, to dissolve the current reality and create a new one. To stay open, not through ignorance and illusion, but through trust. Knowing in gratitude that, as we do our best, the universal laws respond accordingly.

~⌒

IT IS NOT SO MUCH that we need to regain trust so that we can relax, but rather that *when we relax we regain trust.* Any fear and pain we feel is always due to our sense of separation. Remember it is our "smaller" part, our left brain character, that feels separate. When it gets insecure, embrace it, reassure it, build the inner bridge that bridges the gap. The most strengthening thing we can do for that part within us or others, is not to talk away its feelings, but to hold an open heart space for them, until the waves of fear subside again into the ocean of peace. For it is there, deep within, that we all feel our sacred bond.

Separatism, the by-product of our labeling mind, avoids our *direct* experiencing. Our average 50,000 thoughts a day fragment us in myriad tiny pieces, scattering us all over the place and carrying us away from our center. In shifting to our right hemisphere we slow down enough to be able to disconnect from our momentary concerns. It feels like sinking within, to our inner knowing, and reconnects us to our sense of oneness. We can feel it sometimes with others when we lose our borders, we overlap, we merge. In sharing joy, or music. Or in a rare moment of silence between friends. We may feel it sitting alone on a cliff top. Or lying awake in the night with the stars. We were never really separate, we had just forgotten.

This is why the indigenous peoples and eastern races are generally more centered and more grounded: they have not pushed the development of the conceptual left brain only, they remain more balanced. They can easily switch off and thus regain the sense of connectedness to all that is. Hence, they have more trust.

Trust is the key that opens the door to love. Whenever we lack trust we close up and we disconnect. The mind raises doubts, our borders go up, we then feel separate: we become disquiet, insecure, or afraid. When feeling low, it is by putting our personal dramas aside that we open up again. Tap into trust. Come back to love. Recollect that sense of oneness, cast the light of trust upon your concerns and they dissolve. Because they have no real substance, they all result from our mistrust, the pain of separation. Light a candle and the darkness fades away. It has been said:

> *Darkness is not real, it is just the absence of light;*
> *fear is not real, it is just the absence of trust;*
> *hate is not real, it is just the absence of love.*
>
> ~ Osho

I found a "porthole" that works for me and when I am in doubt, lost in the small picture, I look out. I look out from my daily reality at the sky, and I reconnect to a larger sense of life. This always lifts my temporary feeling and one day was quite remarkable. I was walking down a noisy, crowded, polluted street in Kathmandu, disliking it intensely. I looked up at the sky. It reminded me that I am connected to something else: The current of Life. I am on a larger journey. This is just a small event on my way. I suddenly felt a few centimeters taller and as though I had a large, quiet, private space all around me. I felt as though I was alone in the street; others were there, but fainter. I reached a group of six street boys on the corner, little eight or twelve year olds, smoking cigarettes, who always hustled tourists. To my surprise they ignored me, as though I was not part of their world. Only once I was some way past them did they call out for money. It felt like having been shifted into a slightly different space, a different reality.

BE VERY AWARE OF WHAT KEEPS YOU in a state of anxiety, be it your own daily concerns, the mainstream media or the "alternative" media. Because whatever we think, do, or feel, we are sending out a certain frequency. It doesn't matter what is making us insecure, as long as we are scared of *something:* Be it bird flu or swine flu, anthrax or SARS, bees dying or chemtrails, global warming or planet X, Y2K or 2012, hell or doomsday, the dollar crashing or the euro crashing, the Russians or the Muslims, the "illuminati" or the aliens... *I can't keep up with all the things I'm supposed to be scared of!*

Whatever keeps us in an anxious, closed space disconnects us from our source of power. Whenever we indulge in thoughts and feelings that reinforce our worry and fear, we are giving our energy to that camp. We are either feeding Fear or Love. We are either painting the shadows darker, or holding the light that dissipates them. All that is required of us is a shift of feeling. The Shift that is happening on the planet today is that shift of feeling.

Let's face it. There is no one else to blame, not the wife, not god, not the government. The set-up is perfect, it always has been and it always will be. It is us who have been in the dark. We have been closed through fear and through trust we start to re-open. The turtle emerges from under its shell. The chick peeps out of its egg. The seed opens. The bud blooms.

And as we find our trust again, through seeing that life has always been our friend, we start to open the valve. The valve that *we* have been holding closed. And as we do so, love pours in.

> *To absolutely know, in your heart of hearts, that this is a joyful, positive and uplifting universe to be in, and it can be nothing else ~ since all is One, and the nature of that Oneness is to Be Love Now.*
>
> ~ David Wilcock

CHAPTER TWENTY-FOUR

The Change of an Age

Be realistic, prepare for a miracle.

~ Osho

THERE WERE TIMES it seemed we were getting lost in the maze, caught by the quicksand of hurt and reactivity, spiraling downwards. Now, all around the world, people of all walks of life are changing more rapidly and profoundly than ever. Even those who previously displayed great resistance to such "airy fairy" notions are now talking about finding balance, centeredness, and softness. It's marvelous to watch how our blinders are being removed, our tunnel vision is widening, the "mind-fog" is lifting, and sails are being set to reach for other shores.

These are the days of spiritual renaissance on Earth. The changing frequency of the planet is opening us up, so deeper issues are rising to the surface. Unethical situations are becoming unbearable and this obliges us to deal with them. Many, feeling off balance and unhappy, are slowing down to work things out, and are quitting abusive situations. Credits are collapsing and economies are slipping because the established systems no longer fit with the rising vibration. It is very powerful and hardly subtle. It is changing every one of our lives.

In the last decade we may well have experienced more or less difficult times in our relationships, our profession, and our living situation. The old ways didn't work anymore and life had to be reshuffled. What is at the base of these changes?

A presentation on the Mayan Calendar made things clearer for me. There is no doubt among researchers about the astounding complexity and accuracy of this ancient astronomical calendar.

Rather than just counting linear time it is a map of the Ages that indicates the interwoven, cyclic nature of our reality. Scientists and visionaries agree that we are, right now, at the end of one Age and at the beginning of the next one: an enlightened era, the "golden age" that multiple ancient traditions have foreseen. Every birth requires a renewal, a process of transformation.

Some researchers are cautious to overstep the boundaries of mainstream history, while acknowledging that the Mayan Long Count Calendar can theoretically stretch over millions of years. Dr. Calleman's in-depth research explains how this astronomically intricate and precise calendar describes eras of evolution. This calendar shows that, since the appearance of simple life forms on Earth about 16 Billion years ago, life evolves in cycles of ever quickening growth. These cycles, or ages, provide the background, the basic setting, for all development on Earth. They correlate accurately with the evolution of species, anthropological data, and historical events.

The Age of Power, from 1755 to 1999, was supportive to the modern development. During this time there was the founding of the USA and other superpowers; the industrial revolution, and the boom of technology. Rising out of that era, and standing on its shoulders, came the next phase: in 1999 we entered the Age of Ethics and Integrity. We are on a set schedule of ever escalating consciousness. These changing eras confirm and explain our feeling of life both speeding up and taking on a new focus. Despite efforts to discredit this empowering information, a growing number of people can confirm the transformation described in the calendar as they feel it happening within themselves.

The events "predicted" by the calendar, clearly matched what we were seeing on a global scale. Many people felt old set-ups starting to fall apart in 2000. Non-ethical relationships and corporations simply could not hold together on this setting. At this stage, power can only be sustained through integrity. That is why so many corruptions are being revealed in this decade and power structures are crumbling: the whole economic system, the monetary set-up, the over-productivity, the working chain and the abuse of natural resources are unethical. Many people were goaded to adjust their ways, and drop unfitting relationships, jobs and habits. The breakdown of old methods, superficial values, air-castle economies and excessive commerce helped us to evolve towards more sensitivity, real values, greater appreciation, self-reliance and maturity.

> *The Mayan Calendar is a calendar of the Ages that*
> *condition the human consciousness, and thus the frames*
> *for our thoughts and actions within a given age. That's why*
> *everything flowing at this time has to do with the global*
> *awakening taking place.*
> ~ Carl Calleman, The Mayan Calendar and the
> Transformation of Consciousness

The latter half of 2008 was the deepest cycle, the turnaround point of that age: "The dark night of the soul." Fuelled by my own experience of disharmonic relations I wrote the following tirade as part of a larger essay on the topic:

> *This is the age of integrity, of finding our personal truth; a time to redefine our values. A time for honesty and commitment, being true to our feelings and straight in our relationships.*
>
> *This is the age of Ethics, of relinquishing power games. Realize that we are all one. We can't afford anymore to steal energy from each other, either emotionally or financially. The age of power is over and the separatist ego is struggling with the shifting sands. Yet when we dare to move beyond our insecure left brain personality we are rewarded by the discovery of our blissful spirit: a peaceful loving character aware of its connection to all others.*
>
> *What we pursue out of separatism will lead to continued dysfunction, to more and more struggle. The paradox is that the separatist ego that urges us to compete to survive was actually pushing the human race to global suicide. It is time now to surrender towards the collective shift of humanity. It is time to move from 'me' to 'us.'*

Excuse me guys, I am just knocking at the door… but if we don't stop clubbing each other and start looking at the bigger picture we won't have a bigger picture to look at! Consider all of humanity to be one body, and each of us to be its cells. As Deepak Chopra points out, to keep that body healthy: Selfishness is not an option. Aggression is not an option. Competition is not an option. Nor is hoarding, superiority, exclusion, withdrawal, over-activity, or generation gap: Not an option.

In our relationships and our societies it is time to get over the petty differences that have been amplified to keep us divided. We all want peace, plenty and harmony. It is time to use the strength of our unified vision to receive it. We are all children of the Earth.

This is the era of humanity's healing. We are now reconciling our inner and outer relationships; regaining balance and harmony between the male and female energies both within and outside of us. As things speed up, as in an old clothes-dryer, if the load is not balanced it starts to clunk around, making itself loudly heard so we can adjust it. If we are in balance, like a spinning top, then we remain steadily centered as life speeds up. We have all had to make adjustments in our lives because the old ways of operating became gradually more unsuccessful. It is the same on a larger scale. Although the façade is still just holding up, we can expect disclosures of all kinds and massive changes in social structures and governance.

We have abundance on this planet. If the Chinese want to work more for less, why compete? Thank them and relax. There are brilliant advanced economists and engineers just waiting their cue, ready to step in with alternative systems and new energy technologies. Costs would drop hugely and no-one would have to work more than a few days a week. It is possible, but not imperative, that a certain degree of collapse is necessary first. Neither focus on this aspect nor resist it. Stay grounded in trust, and keep your focus on, put your energy into, the desired outcome. Remember, birthing doesn't have to be painful.

It helps to understand the spirit of the times so we can move with it. Then there is no struggle against the current but a tremendous chance for expansion. There is simply no point resisting the flow. It is a monumental cosmic current that takes everything with it. Earth is moving in small cycles around the sun. Our whole solar system is moving around a larger sun. And the whole thing is moving in an incomprehensibly fast yet vast slow motion... an infinite dance of stars and planets influencing each other gravitationally, creating geometric patterns in space. The changes of the Ages are written in the stars ~ surrender now!

Experiencing ourselves as part of this evolving of humankind, we can feel that everything happening is indeed okay. Our evolution is on course. When we reconnect to this flow, we feel the relative pettiness of all our concerns and a great sense of peace. We also feel how non-sensible it would be to try to forge our own way against it. Do you sense it sometimes when you look over a wide landscape, or out to the ocean, up at the open sky? I call it the river of life.

What all awaits us is beyond us. Don't limit yourself with disbelief, or any belief. If we are not too linear in our imaginations we can go to so far unimagined heights. Everything we can imagine as possible is possible. Everything we can't imagine is possible as well.

Life is developing so fast that we want to stay as free as earthly possible. Don't fix yourself, for we have little idea of our potential and destiny. It is the very energy of letting go of what one knows that enables the next stage to enter our lives.

> To take, you must first open your hand
>   Let go
> To breathe in, you must first breathe out
>   Let go
> To be warm, you must first be naked
>   Let go.
>   ~ Lao Tse

We are on a schedule. Time is not quickening but the amount of happening is. So it is normal these days to feel overwhelmed by events, like we can't keep up. Better get used to it. It may feel like you are losing your mind...don't worry, you are! Our mind can only handle 24 frames a second but consciousness is speeding up. Our mind is like a donkey being pulled behind a racecar. We are re-discovering our intuition because events will be happening too fast to think it out.

~ Ian Lungold, THE EVOLUTION CONTINUES

THE SENSATION OF LIFE SPEEDING UP is mounting, and day by day things are becoming more transparent, and hence fuller. We may well already feel that the inflow, our own inner expansion, is happening so rapidly that the part of us that is used to processing and controlling things can't quite keep up. This is not a cause for worry but a sign to release our mental hold on life and flow with it.

As we let go life becomes simpler. We are not really "losing our minds," we are naturally shifting from the overuse of our active left brain to our rather dormant right hemisphere, our intuitive side. Our left brain control structures are loosening, losing their grip on us; our sense of self dissolves as we expand and become more instinctive and spontaneous. It may feel like losing everything we are, yet it takes us to new dimensions.

Instead of the rational way of conceptualizing, dissecting and labeling our world, we are, due to less separation, regaining our ability to experience it directly. We are moving from the "male," left-brained way of identifying and analyzing, which separates us, to the "female," right-brained way of feeling and merging, which unifies us. From a separatist, detail consciousness to a holistic overview. Duality is the way of the mind. Wholeness, integrity, is the way of the heart.

This is an age of deepening spirituality. Science, in particular quantum physics has recently been able to discover and describe the subtle mechanics of the energy realm, the world that ancient traditions knew intuitively, experientially. Yet we have little time now to wait for the scientists to meticulously repeat thousands of experiments before we can dare to believe in anything new. Our in-tuition is our in-built teaching, our personal guidance, our inner knowing. This insight is within all of us and we become increasingly used to listen to it. When the mind is overdone it is a natural shift to turn within. The speeding up finally obliges us to slow down, and stay in touch with our small part to ground ourselves. It brings us to focus more on the now, the present moment, which centers us. It is the doorway to our own inner knowing.

Too much work, brain activity, TV shows, movies, media input, noise disguised as music, and legal drugs, distract and desensitize us. Our rational mind nags us with its doubts. Yet, if we listen, we can hear the call of our inner voice. The voice of our intuition is a quiet knowing, a soft whisper. It is the voice of our higher self that we often hush with our "logic." It is the voice of our heart, of our conscience, and of our soul.

The reason to follow our conscience is not a moral one. It is not good versus bad, saintliness versus sin. It is open valve versus closed valve. Openness is simply the only way for us to tune in, to connect.

> *Your conscience is the measure of the honesty of your*
> *selfishness. Listen to it carefully.*
> ~ *Richard Bach,* ILLUSIONS

Our integrity is not a matter of morality, it is a matter of wholeness. It is our guidance, our stability and our connection: the strength of our core.

Many fear their own strength as they have previously abused it. Yet once power is based on integrity, aligned with the flow, it becomes dependable and creative. Perhaps we are scared of our own light. Few dare to shine and to stand out. Yet we all have the skills inherent for whatever we came to do. All that we are being asked to do is to express, in whichever way suits us, the sacred energy that we are. To neither hide our light, nor get lost in the illusion of our ego's grandeur. To let this light shine through us, and to grow in beauty and love as we express the living spirit that is within us all.

Dr. Calleman's study of the Mayan Calendar shows the exponential expansion of our consciousness. Each new age is 20 times shorter than the previous one, yet the same amount of evolution takes place within it. Our awareness expands every era at a rate 20 times faster than in the previous one. He describes the current Age, from March to November 2011, as being the Age of Co-Creation.

Together with our opening and personal discoveries we start to see more potential, possibilities and synchronicities. As life continues to speed up exponentially, ever more information, understanding, and options present themselves to us at the same time.

Like a child, with less time, less mind, between us and the happening, we shall become less reflective and more responsive. With less fear-based resistance and less mental involvement, our connectivity and creativity boom. When led by our heart, our spontaneous responses carry us from one fulfilling moment to the next.

Whatever we are, feel, and attend to, will be increasingly reflected directly back at us. Living from a space of integrity, we are in agreement with ourselves, and thus with what life delivers. We become steady and focused, no longer distracted or tossed around by conflicting parts within. With acceptance and self approval we stay quietly centered inside. We steer our ship, through clear and calm waters, towards the new dawn.

It is hence through our integrity that we harness the power and the focus to create. Therefore, throughout 2011 our ability of conscious co-creation is greatly heightened. Indeed, in this time, we make the choice if we wish to be part of creating our destiny of a united human consciousness, and thus serve as evolutionary co-creators. The shift will happen through those who choose, knowingly or not, this path.

Wonder World

Our intuition lives in misty realms; hunches against reason, spaces we can glimpse but not define, recall but not remember. Our intellect, limited by language and physical time-space perception, cannot grasp what lies beyond. And yet these spaces are as real as anything we can touch. More so even. The intangible energy that we begin to sense is the very essence of which our world is built. Quantum physics is only just starting to perceive the immensity and the complexity of what we cannot see.

CHAPTER TWENTY-FIVE

Our Energetic Oneness

~~~~~⌒

Concerning matter, we have been all wrong.
What we have called matter is energy, whose vibration
has been so lowered as to be perceptible to the senses.
There is no matter.

~ *Albert Einstein*

IT IS VERY TIMELY that we regain, now, awareness of our inner, energetic existence. That we regain a sense of the energy, of the spirit, that is the essence of life.

Our view of the world is changing fast from the cut-and-dry explanations we were given in school. Scientists, at the end of their Latin, started to look further and agree that there is far more than we can see. Nowadays we can find confirmation in quantum physics of what the world mystics speak about since ancient times. Physicists tell us now that less than 10% of the physical world is solid matter. What is the rest, that which we don't see? Energy: Subtle matter. Matter, in fact, is dense energy.

FOR A START, nothing is as solid as it appears; because between and within the atoms that are our building blocks is a vast amount of space. The distance between the smallest existing particles of physical matter is greater in proportion than the distance from the Earth to the sun. So the space that is all around us is also within whatever looks solid around us, and also within our very bodies. They say our atomic matter fits on a pinhead, the rest of us is energetic space. It is joked that with all that space within us it is no wonder that we can feel so spaced out!

Simply seen, an atom is similar to a solar system: the planets are the electrons that circle the ecliptic around the center sun. The universe is formed by trillions of solar systems ~ planets circling around stars ~ in space. Our bodies are similar. They are formed by trillions of atoms ~ electrons circling around its center ~ in space. So matter is neither as solid nor as stagnant as it appears.

Picture the fast spinning blades of a fan forming a circle, yet when it slows down we see that it is not solid but has gaps in between separate blades. In a similar way the base of a tornado has the density of iron although it is only air rotating at high speeds. It is this density of vibration from the high speed at which the electrons buzz around the nucleus of the atoms that creates the *impression* of solid matter. With this constant motion, this field of magnetic energy within them, atoms are now found to be more like a vibrational frequency than particles of matter. It is this rapid vibration that makes us feel solid. Our body is just vibrating energy. What's more, quantum physics has observed that our subatomic particles are actually pulsing in and out of physical, three-dimensional existence.

This is partly why, without your body, you feel the same. Your energy body is very similar to your physical one, just less solid. You can likely feel this vibrating energy when you lie down, close your eyes and quietly observe how your hand feels. Although you can't see your hand you may well *feel* how it is *alive* and perhaps a tingling, a warmth, an almost tangible ball of energy vibrating in your palm.

There are simple ways to notice the energy in ourselves and others. When a person openly smiles there is partly a change of facial expression, muscles moving, but largely something energetic, *their aliveness,* that shines through. Babies' smiles show their inner bliss. People in love glow with the radiance of that high vibration. I have seen an elderly man's face become instantly twenty years younger when illuminated with a positive feeling and a most beautiful woman's face suddenly fall apart at the thought of a threat. The physical substance is the same, what changes the face so drastically is the resonance of the energy it contains.

Sometimes you can feel a partial separation of your energy

body from the physical. You may recognize this when you are drifting off and suddenly jolt awake, or when you pass out. I suspect this is also the reason we get dizzy at heights: it's an ever so slight separation from our body when we look down.

Every form has an energetic body, an energetic resonance. Kirlian photography, fine enough to pick up the vibration of subtle matter, showed this already in the 1940s: a photograph of a person with only one leg clearly shows the missing limb as a fainter image on the print. A photo of a plant also shows the shape of a leaf that had been picked off.

In earlier days it may have seemed logical to believe that there is nothing more to us than our physical bodies, no more to the world than meets the eye, but now, with the wide range of current discoveries, that rather becomes illogical. "I'll believe it when I see it" no longer makes sense. For what we see is only the very tip of the iceberg. The world we *see* is less than 10% of our reality. The remaining 90% is the underlying energy field within all matter, the living energy that binds every atom. Similarly there is some 90% of our brain capacity we don't use, and over 90% of unused DNA. Mainstream science labels this "junk" DNA. (No comment...) Much of who we are, most of our potential, lies dormant. The larger part of ourselves and of our world is yet to be discovered.

Hidden within the fabric of the physical world, enfolded within this dimension, are multiple others ~ each layer less dense, more subtle, more energetic. At the center is stillness. Motion increases through the layers, creating greater and greater density. The material world is a cover, a screen, an illusion of solidity.

When you realize that we are not solid, you may well realize that we are not separate either. That which is unseen, that energetic space within us and between us, is what connects us all to each other. Picture, simply, that the air that is outside of us is the same substance that fills the space between, and within, the atoms that form our bodies. It is the same space that is within everyone. So, at the base of our being, as all ancient traditions have said, we are all linked, we are one. And this air around and within us is not just inert space. It is known as "prana" in ancient Hinduism, as "chi" to the old Chinese culture: our life-force, the vital bio-energy, the Breath of Life. It is a field of conscious energy that permeates the whole of existence. Our spiritual oneness is not an idealistic notion, it is an energetic fact.

Quantum physics now confirms this. As the blockbuster and mind bender film "What the Bleep Do We Know?!" describes:

> Science has told us that we are separate, a random lonely mistake on a random lonely planet. This idea of separation has created many problems. But at sub-atomic level, you and I are literally one. We are all together, one, at the very base of our being. Empty space contains unbelievable energy. We are all alive, and connected, through this one energy which is a teeming, electric-magnetic field of possibility or potential. Science and spirituality merge. Consciousness is the ground of all being.

Consciousness is a big word and an even bigger concept. It is our life force, the life force, the conscious living energy within all existence. It is our energetic base. It is our true identity. It is the power within.

We are all connected. At the base of our being, we are all one being.

> A human being is a part of a whole called by us universe,
> a part limited in time and space. He experiences himself, his
> thoughts and feelings as something separated from the rest...
> a kind of optical delusion of his consciousness. This delusion
> is a kind of prison for us...
> ~ Albert Einstein

So we may see ourselves plainly and only as a physical body, therefore separate from everything else ~ and hence, all that happens to us is largely by chance. Or we may recognize ourselves to be an energetic being, within a body, and everything to be interconnected. We may see ourselves to some degree as a hapless victim of meaningless circumstance, or as a part of the energy of all that is and the co-creator, wittingly or not, of our own life. Through paying close attention to this aspect we start to notice, and to trust, that we are part of a mysterious conscious unity. We no longer see everything as separate and conflicting, but as parts of one living energy, united in cooperation.

Then nothing is random because everything is inter-related. There is nothing, not a single bacteria, that works out of line. Although our planetary life may look like pure survival, in fact all life forms are supporting each other. We can either feel that bacteria are threatening our health, or realize that they are at the base of our very existence, and that any sickness is *not* accidental but informative. Once again, over 90% of life on this planet is mi-crobial, invisible to the naked eye and existing since the dawn of time; without it other life forms could not even exist.

Our energetic existence ~ that we are each an inseparable part of the one energy field that permeates *everything* ~ explains how we are indeed able to influence the world around us: both organic and non-organic matter like cameras, vehicles and RNG (Random Number Generating) computers. It also explains, reversely, how our subtle, energetic bodies can be affected by electro-magnetic in-terference from our environment: such as TVs, computers, mi-crowaves and cell phones, and disharmonic, chaotic noise disguised as music.

Knowing that a huge part of us is purely energetic may also clarify how our *feelings* greatly affect our bodies and how contin-uous and unheeded negative emotion creates sickness. Accumu-lated residues of toxic waste, whether absorbed from food or environment, or created by our own emotions, are stored away as tumors, the body's rubbish bins. Yet there is nothing the body, the heart, and the spirit, cannot heal. Even for "terminal" cases, the success rate from natural detoxification methods, both physical and emotional, is phenomenal.

As we change our vibration, tumors go into regression and can disappear, dare I say, even overnight. It is scientifically shown that, exposed to a certain frequency, such as by ultrasound, they can vanish within minutes.[1]

---

[1] See Greg Braden on "You Can Heal Your Life"

There are many ways to release both superficial disturbances and deeply ingrained emotional patterns from our energetic, our *subtle* physical body. Countless books, sharing groups, techniques and workshops are now focused on clearing our old blocks, which in turn opens us to fresh feelings and new information. Since everything comes to us first on the energetic plane, attracted by our underlying resonance, deep healing is triggered by working directly on our etheric body. Thus energy work like cranio-sacral, sound healing and hypnotherapy effectively releases unresolved emotional experiences, tensions and blocks from the cellular memory of our bodies.

Indeed a massive healing and shifting of the human psyche is taking place daily on the planet as each of us does this work of freeing ourselves in one way or another. In doing so we lighten the collective mind field, eventually liberating the whole body of humanity of its burden of accumulated blame, hurt and fear.

WE HAVE SEEN THAT OUR BODY is formed by energy; it is a conglomerate of organs and other parts, vibrating at various frequencies. Sound too is a vibration, and a most powerful one. Through resonance it literally influences the energetic frequency, which is why sound healing is found to be so effective. You can clearly feel how sound influences you: how the noise of the neighbor's lawnmower and the drone of background traffic drain you; how music changes your mood and the atmosphere in a room. On an energetic level it affects our bodies, plants and other organic matter. Plantations of hardwood trees have been seduced by soothing music to grow at an accelerated rate, one third faster than usual.[2] Whereas potted plants next to drum kits usually die! Certain sounds resonate with particular feelings and stimulate their flow ~ and not only for humans... Faced with a mother camel totally ignoring her newborn baby, innovative zookeepers played romantic music to her thus arousing her maternal instincts to feed her baby.

---

[2] Peter Tomkins and Christopher Bird, *The Secret Life of Plants* and *The Secret Life of the Soil*

Back in 1787, physicist Ernst Chladni became famous through his discovery that sound waves affect matter by vibration. A certain note, played to metal or glass plates covered with a fine layer of sand caused the sand to adopt a particular pattern. Each note, or frequency, creates a different pattern. The sand shows, reflects, the geometry of the vibration: the higher the harmonic, the more complex the pattern produced.

In the same way, our emotions also emit a distinct vibration. Japanese professor Dr. Masaru Emoto showed this to the world in his well known experiment in which different feelings are projected onto water samples. When frozen, the water samples crystallize into distinctly different ice patterns. The feelings of hate and anger form scattered pictures while those of love and peace form beautiful harmonious shapes.

When we realize just how profoundly vibration affects matter, the implications are far reaching indeed. Because sound thus arranges matter, it is suggested that the universe was indeed "sung" into existence.

CHAPTER TWENTY-SIX

The River of Life

There are things known and there are things unknown,
and in between are the doors of perception.

~ *Aldous Huxley*

YEARS AGO, in Darwin, Australia, we met a young "wwoofer." A *what?* you may ask. WWOOf stands for "World Wide Opportunities on Organic Farms," and is an extensive program for travelers to be hosted at farms and other nature related projects, to help out and learn some skills. It's usually a great cultural and personal exchange for wwoof hosts and wwoofers alike.

I'll never forget the moment I met Claudio. He was 18, with big round eyes, and felt right away like part of the family. We invited him to come camping for the weekend. Our daughter was 14, and they lay quietly on the bed at the back of our bus, watching the sunset flare across the outback sky, while we drove to a clearing in the forest. It was not an official camping spot and early the next morning a police car drove through, oddly enough, out there in the middle of nowhere. We couldn't exactly pretend we hadn't spent the night there as Claudio's tent was an obvious tell tale. Rather than reprimand us, the officer asked if we'd seen a large, hairy guy with tattoos who was wanted for some acts of violence and was on the run in this area. Well, we hadn't, but, true or not, it sure stopped us camping in the woods!

There are moments in life that feel meaningful. On that camping trip I bonded with Claudio, sharing stories on the edge of a lake, while our daughter was swimming lengths. He was the sensitive type. He told me that his elder sister was very successful and there was pressure on him to achieve. He was returning home to Austria in a few days, after a year on the road, and I told him he wouldn't be able to re-adapt to that type of society. I only wish I hadn't been right.

A COUPLE YEARS LATER, we were in Fiji checking our email. The last mail we'd had from Claudio was signed "love and light," and I felt that was so beautiful coming from a 20 year old boy. This new email was in German and it was only two lines. I reread it, a couple times, hoping I'd got something wrong in the translation. Claudio had killed himself. I fell apart, there in the internet shop, weeping. Not again! I felt I could have read the signs: an 18 year old listening to Leonard Cohen... I felt I could have invited him over, paid his ticket, anything!

I bawled my despair openly, totally, unabashed, heedless of anyone else around me. And then, while crossing the crowded city street with my daughter, an odd shift happened. Something separated within me, detached me from my feelings, and I was watching myself as though from a distance: there she goes, enjoying the movie drama. It occurred to me afterwards why we have the expressions: to be "out of your mind," or "beside yourself" with grief. I was distraught, in anguish, in pieces, and yet knowing at the same time that everything was okay.

We met in a dream some time later. I asked him why he'd done it and he told me he was depressed, had no money, no girlfriend, and wanted to go to Berlin. I can recall the atmosphere as an aimless space, with a feeling of helplessness which I didn't feel comfortable in.

One year later, still in Fiji, we were invited over to a small, private isle, quite some way out from the main island. It was, in the chief's small open boat, one hell of a ride. We left the comfort of the shore, headed towards the edge of a reef where the breaking waves loomed ever higher. I remember thinking, "we are not going through that!" The next moment a towering wave crashed over our little boat's bow, soaking us all. I reminded myself to be less adventurous in the future, if indeed I had one, and remained wet and seasick for the rest of the journey. An hour later we landed on a gem of an island: a palm-clad haven, ringed with pristine, brilliant white sand in a turquoise lagoon.

I HADN'T TAKEN ANY PSYCHEDELIC substances since that potent mushroom soup 20 years earlier. Over that period I had "lost" a number of brothers and sisters of the road and I was curious to find out more about life and death. The previous week I had met a traveler I connected well with and, as we talked about the nature of the spiritual world, he reminded me that: *He who looks outside dreams, He who looks inside awakens.* He then gave me a small bag of Ayahuasca, a sacred plant used by South American shamans to access our mirror world, the spirit space. I planned to take it on the anniversary of Claudio's departure.

The day came, out there on this tiny pacific isle. My partner prepared a space amidst the trees while I sat on the timeless beach, far removed from the ways of the world. I drank the bitter brew, and watched the colors become vibrant and the waves roll in slow motion. The contours took on a sharp, outlined quality. The movement of the waves and the birds became disjointed, like an old movie slowed down so you begin to see the still frames. The scenery became very surreal, crisscrossed with bright energy lines like an Alex Grey painting. Sacred geometry patterns were hidden in the trees and hung in the sky. Admittedly, as realities begin to seriously shift, the first reaction is "*Why* did I do this?" Our familiar world falls apart and the easier we let it go, trusting in the trip, the more we enjoy the ride.

I guessed it was time to retreat, while I could still walk, and moved gingerly into the jungle. The shrubs and the roots seemed sculptured, laid out like a work of art. I felt I was entering a sacred temple space, the sandy path beckoning me into the depths of the sanctuary. I curled up in the center of this virgin clearing, the air pregnant with expectancy. A bird skull lay there in the sand. I closed my eyes, and fell.

I remember being surprised about the distinct feeling of falling. I thought one would rise in consciousness, but I fell. It was as though I was retreating into the center of myself. I dropped down through the layer of my thoughts, my sense of me left behind, swimming on the surface, all my worries floating away. I fell through many layers of my being, coming to rest somewhere deep within.

What is happening on such a journey is we are accessing our own inner wisdom, the field of all knowing. We are, if you like, opening a door to our higher floor. The intention I had set was to know more about life and death and our physical world. And so, without the barrier of my conscious mind which limits us to this reality, the answers were revealed.

Thus it became clear to me how we are all just actors, each of us playing what we believe in, and what we want to be. That we are all collaborating with each other: intertwined, interacting, and interconnected. And that we are free at any time to stop playing our predestined role and write a new script, to take the steering wheel of our life and change track.

I was shown that thought generates life forms: that is the creative process. We have been like runaway thoughts, blowing in the wind. We are now learning to focus and direct our intent so as to become conscious creators. It is our imagination that creates our reality. This is where magic begins.

I was told: "To enter into relationship, to work with others, you have to take on a personality. Realize though that it is just a front, fitting to what you want to be and to do. Don't become too attached to it and don't hang onto it. Allow it to change, to expand and to flow. Become more familiar with the *inner* You." Our personality, I realized, is just like our dressing, essentially useful to relate to others. It is a protective shell we wear to cover the fragile nakedness of Being. And in the same way we choose clothes that suit both our inner feeling and our outer circumstances, it mirrors who we are and who we think we should be.

I laughed out loud when I recognized that what we feel is us, our body, is just part of that personality ~ just a physical side effect really, a reflection of ourselves in the world of matter, the expression of our own creative impulse. It is our costume, our outfit for this earthly life. Our bodies are the way through which our one energy, the divine life force, plays with matter. We are both creator and creation.

I had expanded once more to that far larger sense of identity, a vast field spanning all time and space. One could say we have a hierarchy of bodies, all overlaying, ranging from our solid body through increasingly subtle energy bodies back to our essence. Yet it is far less complex than it sounds. It is very simple. In that space there is no doubt, no worry, no separation; we are pure being. Once again I recognized that I was both a part of, and one with, All. I was reunited with my infinite nature, seeing that we are all truly infinite. Each of us is a part of the Whole, and in a sense is the Whole. Humanity is one consciousness, one Being, fragmented in a multitude of seemingly separate life forms.

I felt, yet again, my eternal existence, and the blatant fallacy of death. Dying ~ changing form, transformation ~ is part of the constant flow of Life. Consciousness *is* Life. The life force within each of us. As units of consciousness, as sparks of life, how could we die or end? Nothing can disappear from within the Whole. Where, indeed, could it go?

We are consciousness living in matter. Without a body we are the same consciousness, just without the limits of time and space. Wouldn't the world be a different place to live if we were all granted this experience of our connectedness, our oneness and our eternal being?

Between the revelations that surfaced from the depths of time, I reveled in the ever-morphing exotic energy patterns playing, like a kaleidoscope of colors, within me. It is impossible to describe these dimensions, even in full Technicolor, yet, ever the optimist, I try! The closest portrayal of our energetic reality I could find is this one: Imagine each of us is a color, and all together we are many colors of liquid oil paint swirled on the surface of water. They are all touching each other, so every move any one makes alters the shape of those around it. It is thus, as all the colors slowly swirl, that every act and every thought influences others and forms a different picture. We are, conscious or not, co-creators of our reality.

I explored some spaces I am unable to describe. I was aware of other beings and glimpsed areas I knew I'd been to before, but I was not able to access them because my focus was not clear enough. Truth is I was often laughing, finding the trip quite funny, like surfing a gargantuan multidimensional network. So this impressed on me the tremendous value of our focus, our will and our intent. It is what enables us, in that realm as in this one, to move in the direction, and attain the spaces, we wish to reach.

Downloads of innate knowledge occur during such a journey and our conscious mind is certainly not able to grasp, comprehend or integrate it all. One most powerful revelation is unforgettable. As I lay there on the sandy soil my body became the Earth going through Creation. I watched in awe as massive Amazonian forests formed in my hand, felt mountain chains rising within me, and rivers rushing through my veins.

I queried the possibility of Earth changes in the current times and felt the logic of the reply: "Earth is undergoing inner struggles because everyone is blocking the flow of energy. Energy is fluid and needs to circulate freely. Because everyone is hanging onto energy instead of letting it flow we may need some shaking to release it."

I realized that, in multiple ways, we all obstruct energy from flowing freely. Emotions, instincts, love, knowledge, power, and money are all forms of energy. We hold onto it, hide it and hoard it. The energy becomes blocked, causing pressure to build up.

"So what can I do?" I asked. "The best you can do, all anyone can do, is to be as open as you can, so energy flows through you. Be open to receive energy and to release it. Don't hold back, share it, pass it on. Keep it flowing. Be as water, going with the flow, or be a boulder standing in the way. Whatever we do not let flow will be finally shaken loose."

I asked about healing and the answer was plain: "We have chosen this life as an opportunity to clear our own feelings. We heal when we slow down and expose, open everything. All hurts and grievances accumulate because they are held inside; closed wounds fester." Since that day, I resolved to notice whenever I am holding anything back in any way, and to be as open and honest as I can. This has made a huge difference to how I feel and to what I receive.

It is hardly possible to describe the sense of rebirth, and the openness, fragility and reverence one feels after such a trip. I felt my nakedness, temporarily bared as I was of the mind patterns and structures that normally formed my personality. As the effects of the shamanic plant slowly ebbed, I moved back out to the beach, alone with the vastness of the open sea and sky.

Lying in the sun-kissed sand, I recognized a massive slow motion current, like a vast river, which flows inexorably on, behind all of life. It is behind the movement of the stars, and heedless of our business or retirement plans. It has far greater prospects for us. It has its way, it has its timing, and everything is right on course.

CHAPTER TWENTY-SEVEN

Magical World

~~~

I have no special talent.
I am only passionately curious.
                    ~ Albert Einstein

The Answer lies Within

WE DO NOT have to take shamanic medicine plants to access some degree of inner knowing. Contemplation and meditation also slow down our brain waves, enabling us to drop within, and our inner wisdom to surface. We can find all the answers we seek through intent, sustained focus and quietness.

Once when I was 13, I was up late at night doing my philosophy homework for the next morning. It was dark and quiet and as I was focused on it, pulling ideas "out of my head," the essay took on new proportions. I was surprised at what all came out, it felt a bit beyond me, and I was quite chuffed with the result. A week later, the teacher handed back the papers and as I was eagerly awaiting an excellent grade, she announced to the class, to add insult to injury, that I got a zero because I had asked someone elder to do my homework! My heartfelt objections were to no avail as the teacher could not find another explanation. I was less upset about the zero than the injustice of it. With my Aquarian sense of fairness I thought I would have made a good lawyer, until I found out that is not among the required criteria!

It is interesting, that in the right circumstances, we are able to tap into further knowledge. Indeed scientists, visionaries, the greatest artists, all pull from this source of spontaneous inspiration.

So it does not matter whether one is anyhow educated or good in school. Anyone can access the answers they wish for, through enquiry, reflection and contemplation. If you have enough interest and focus on a certain matter, the answers will come. They come when we are open enough to receive them and quiet enough to hear them. When we are not so distracted by the "fussade" of the world. And sometimes, if need be, we find them through our surrender. Listen to your true feelings, and to the soft voice of your intuition. It is our link to our expanded being.

The answers come in unsuspected ways, sometimes so loud and clear you have to laugh. It is as though we put the question out there and the reply comes in with the next delivery of "Daily memos for planet Earth." We are tapping into a collective mind-field of greater knowledge, just as our computers tap into the World Wide Web. Not that we can instantly google the *Encyclopedia Galactica* to check up on the meaning of life, or access the "2012" file in God's library. Have you noticed how we always get the next bit of information just when we need it? Our filters protect us from the overload we are not yet ready for, as it could blow our minds!

There is a mass of researched evidence for a collective mind field. It shows that we are indeed all joined on the subtle plane. In an experiment together with the chief of police, a group of professional meditators were able to lower the crime rate in Washington DC over a few days by 25%. They numbered only 1% of the city's population. It has been shown too that any number of ordinary people holding the same intent has tremendous weight. That's where the power of our individual and group intention comes in.

The "100th monkey phenomenon" has been repeatedly observed and validated since the late '50s. Its original discovery was made when monkeys on one Japanese island were learning to wash their sandy food. Once a certain number of them had got the idea it was instantly picked up by many monkeys on other islands and the mainland. Despite some attempts to discredit it, is by now very widely accepted in both wildlife research and studies of social development.

The BBC have run a number of experiments on this theory, concluding that when the answer to something is known by enough people then the human race can now tap into the answer. When enough mice from a group have learned the maze, they all suddenly know the maze, even if they haven't run it before. Rupert Sheldrake, well accepted by the scientific community, says we program the collective, "morphogenetic" field with our discoveries, enabling others to then access the information. The 100th monkey "theory" demonstrates that when a critical number of people reach a certain awareness, then this understanding spreads directly through the population. The percentage needed to anchor the knowledge, to alter the mind field of the planet, is found to be very small indeed.

> *Never doubt that a small group of thoughtful, committed people*
> *can change the world; indeed it is the only thing that ever has.*
> ~ *Margaret Mead, anthropologist*

Nothing is separate from the energy field of consciousness of which everything is made. Information spreads to "disconnected" populations through the fabric of this one field. A cat can feel when its kittens are in strife hundreds of miles away. Our interconnectedness explains too the likes of telepathy, ESP and remote healing.

The more right-brained, the less separate, more open, we are, the easier we tap into the collective knowledge. It indeed makes you wonder that some autistic people are able to memorize and recreate maps of a whole city after only a few minutes of viewing, give the results of multi digit multiplications within seconds, and play instruments masterly, all with no training.

This "super-intelligence" is not limited to humans. Some fish will lay more or fewer eggs depending on how many of their species are already living on that particular reef. A certain tree will produce toxins instantly as a zebra starts to eat from its leaves, and, as it does, so will all the nearby trees of that type.

We don't need to have all the answers, but we do have to wonder... Allow yourself a "beginner's mind," the childlike feeling of curiosity, awe and mystery. This alone opens us up. We start to grasp now that the wisdom of the ancient indigenous traditions was aware of this connectivity between all living forms, the plants and the animals, the peoples and the land, the elements, the Earth and the stars.

There are volumes of scientifically demonstrated data, such as in the thoroughly researched book *The Field* by Lynne McTaggart. Every link gives us now so much information that we really want to allow our intuition to grasp the essence rather than use our minds to evaluate all the content. You may have noticed that our instinctive first hunch, when uninfluenced by the doubts of our minds, is always right. Where does that insight come from? From our inner knowing.

This gut feeling is what senses, for example, the wonder behind the massive and beautiful, artistic crop circles: sacred geometry expressed on the canvas of the Earth. Something tells us that this is the work of supreme intelligence and not made by an army of hedgehogs running around at night, by teams of obsessed humans with planks and string, or by a covert government project. That, indeed, they cannot all be explained away. Many thousands of these designs have appeared in fields and in ice worldwide over the last 30 years, some simple, some extremely elaborate. There is written evidence of crop circles as early as the 12th century. Eyewitness accounts describe these geometric masterpieces appearing within seconds.

We joke it is an art project of some alien college kids.

Nature Nurtures

Trust like a child trusts its mother,
for the Earth is our mother and we are its children.
~ Chandra

I WAS AT A SMALL FIRE CIRCLE in Bali one evening and a beautiful cross-cultural couple was singing simple African songs, songs of the Earth and the spirit, which really opened my heart. I saw these two as children of the Earth, those whose love of this planet, the plants and the little creatures, not only beautifies the garden but also enlightens this physical plane.

I have great respect for the sensitive, the intuitive and the indigenous children of the Earth. They are so in tune with the changing seasons through their hearts and their connection to Gaia. Gaia is our planet's name from antiquity; she is a living example of cooperation, harmony, and balance; a sophisticated, self-regulating organism, displaying inherent intelligence. Embodying the yin principle, she leads the way into this feminine cycle of deepening spirituality. She knows her children, and who is who, by their resonance ~ not from reading the "Who's Who" guide.

We have become so distanced from our natural feeling of appreciation and reverence for our planet. Earth is not dirt. Earth is our mother, our playground for fun, and our classroom for love, expansion and all things sacred. Gaia is our doorway to the galaxy.

Searching, searching, searching
But you are already home
Lost in your thoughts
In the Earth you are found
                    ~ Susu Ibu, Lyrics

Deep within each of us is a feeling of peacefulness, of belonging, of silent being; it is part of our intrinsic nature. It is the inner feeling too of our Earth, imbued as she is with spirit. By tuning into her we reconnect with our essence. Through her we are reminded of the harmony, the abundance, and the spirit within. Gazing out from her hillsides gives us perspective on our daily lives. Strolling in nature or lying in the sand, we soak up the deep feeling of peace that emanates from the land, the trees, and the breeze. The wind and the sun and the waves subdue our restless minds. The river carries our thoughts away and we drift into a space of calm, reminded of the beauty of simply being. When you go home or back to work, carry that core feeling with you, remember it is always there, beneath the clutter, at the base of our being. Once you have identified that feeling, you can find it always within you. Whenever you feel things are lifting off too much, or going too fast for you, the Earth is your anchor.

Through appreciating the beauty of the natural world, the

flora and fauna, we open ourselves to feel the life energy within it all. And as we become aware of this living energy, which is every-where, we start to feel the harmony, the tranquility and, gradually, a sense of trust. We are part of it all. The spiral in your fingerprint is repeated throughout nature in plants and in shells, in your cin-namon roll, in cloud systems and in the galaxies, all spiraling to-gether through the universe.

Earthsong

She lay beneath the starry sky untouched by human hands
The tides the rhythm of her pulse upon the shifting sands
The mountains rose the rivers flowed into a fertile sea
And she breathed the living spirit in balanced harmony

And man struck by her beauty quickly took her by the hand
He grew strong from her bounty and overtook the land...

Then man felt he was separate, as he went in search for power
He took what he could get from her and the love affair went sour
By lust pushed forth to conquer, till no sacredness remains
But in the end he loses believing that he gains...

Now she lies abused and bruised under a bloodshot sky
Stripped naked of her forests and the riverbeds run dry
Her seas are being gutted and the air is full of smoke
Amidst the barren fields the crowded cities choke

When will man understand that he builds on sacred ground?
And realize why he is missing the love he could have found
As she lay beneath the starry sky untouched by human hands
The tides the rhythm of her pulse upon the shifting sands.

Magic Moments

Magic is a natural part of life.
> ~ Stuart Wilde

NEPAL ENCOMPASSES THE HIGHEST mountains in the world and a special spirit, both soft and powerful. Eight years after we left, we took our daughter back there to see the place where she brought us all together. We rowed across the lake from Pokhara's tourist strip and showed her the one lone little house that was built on stilts above the water. We had lived a whole year there at the time. We reminisced on the verandah. Wondrous things had happened here. It was here that I was sitting quietly minding my own business one day when what can only be described as a bolt of light shot up my spine. I am not the only one to have had such spontaneous kundalini experiences. It was here, on the same balcony that I had written my first poem, "Little sister come and see…" Interestingly, it turned out that our daughter is a natural poet. Long before we had heard about the upcoming transition, she wrote:

> *I shall pray under great silent trees of light*
> *and dance like the spirit of fire, spirit of water*
> *And I shall sing, like flowers out of pure freedom*
> *A full blossoming flower, with all colors in my center.*
> *These golden raindrops, falling on my heart*
> *sing me a song I remember long ago*
> *Generations, generations and generations,*
> *Find, after all,*
> *The truth of All.*
> > ~ Chandra, age 8

We couldn't spend the night at the house so we opted to stay just a bit higher up the hill. In the middle of the night there was a powerful spring storm. Thunder roared and lightning lit up the mountain lake. We felt the impact as it hit the lightning rod on our lodge. The Nepali family downstairs spent the night hiding under their blankets. The next morning was quiet and clear, as it often is, and we walked back down to the lake. The storm had set off a landslide, and the little house on stilts, together with a large portion of the hillside it was built upon, had disappeared into the deep water. It was as though it had waited those eight years for our return, just to vanish that very night.

When our daughter was 21, she returned to Nepal with friends for hiking. We rented some lousy kayaks and paddled around the large lake. It was very wild, green vegetation all around, except in one particular spot. Exactly where our house had once stood and slipped into its watery grave, blossomed a bush of large bright yellow flowers.

There are some magic moments in life. During that last visit, one clear and crisp autumn morning, I was sitting on top of Sarankot ridge, which looks over the lake on one side and the snow clad Annapurna mountain range on the other. In that beautiful setting, I was reading about the Renewal, the magical realms and the creation of new worlds. In a flash I was reminded of the second poem I had written in that little house, just across the lake from where I then sat on the ridge, over 21 years before. It was one of those moments when the light shines through and one is simply awestruck by the vastness, the mystery and the interconnectedness of it all.

ON MY RETURN TO BALI, I found the original page among my poems and read the faded words:

As I watch the new sun rising, spreading love over the land
I know that it will never more be cold
For I feel the gentle wind bringing laughter on its wings
It whispers all is good and life is golden

At dawn I swim the crystal lake which mirrors all I see
And feel all the love my heart can hold
For I can see new flowers growing out of heaven's earth
And I know that we stand now at the threshold

When there is an eagle circling ever in my dreams
I feel that this world is growing old
As I fly the silver moon to clear my cluttered mind
I know that all life's secrets have been told

When the thunder rocks the night and lightning splits the dark
And love calls out its beauty loud and bold
When all the stars join hands and dance
to greet the newborn galaxy
I know the magic world will now unfold.

CHAPTER TWENTY-EIGHT

Window into Eternity

Life exists only at this very moment, and in this moment it is infinite and eternal. The present moment is infinitely small; before we can measure it, it has gone, and yet it exists forever....

~ *Alan Watts*

ONE OF THE WEIRDEST incidents in my life provided me with yet another insight into the realm where time warps. It demonstrates that every situation can be your friend! As I was stepping out of a minibus, near a beach in South India, the dodgy driver decided he wanted more than just my money and made a grab at my breast. I was stunned. My mind stopped and, with it, time stopped ticking. Everything went into *extreme* slow motion. I was caught totally by the moment and, my mind gone, my instincts took over. I watched my arm reach out, *ever so slowly* and deliberately, and yank a cable out, *ever so slowly*, from under the dashboard. Trying then to grasp what was going on, I found myself switching in and out of that surreal reality a few times as my mind switched on and off.

As our brain scientist describes after her stroke:

Without the time keeper of my left brain, my life s-l-o-w-e-d to snail pace. As my perception of time shifted, I fell out of sync with the beehive that bustled around me.

~ *Jill Bolte Taylor, MY STROKE OF INSIGHT*

Our minds, always focusing on and jumping between the past and the future, actually miss the present moment. I once watched an Indian man in an ashram who was in that state of being totally "in the now." He was tying a knot in a rope around a cow's neck, with such a sense of presence and purpose, you could really feel how he was completely absorbed in that action, fully in the present. From my own brief experience I knew how it felt. There is nothing else in the world happening, you are just there, fully captivated by the moment, tying that knot.

You can observe the same in very young children. For them each moment is fully alive and actual, and each expression is total. Each action has, in that moment, a sense of meaning and fullness. The next moment it is gone.

> *My right brain is all about right here, right now.*
> ~ *Jill Bolte Taylor*

THIS IS WHAT SITTING or slow movement meditation is aiming at: to "be here now." The thoughts, the mental noise, may run on, but you are not lost in them. It feels like sitting silently in a big, empty hall while a distant radio is playing in the background...

> *Suddenly, a great stillness arises within you,*
> *an unfathomable sense of peace.*
> *And within that peace there is great joy, there is love.*
> *And at the innermost core, there is the sacred,*
> *The immeasurable, That which cannot be named.*
> ~ *Eckhart Tolle*

"Bringing your mind home" is a meditation term. You bring your mind back into the present. You can watch your breathing, or focus on your heartbeat. You can gently remind yourself: I am here, right now, and I will never be here, in this moment, again. Look softly at the light playing in the trees, notice the silence behind the bustle, in the gap. The noise ~ the activity, the traffic, the busyness ~ comes and goes while, like the sky behind the clouds, the stillness is always there. When the constant chatter and concerns of the mind, or left brain, pause, we return to now. It feels like sinking within oneself, to one's base and inner knowing; our right brain character lives, blissfully, in the now.

The time is now, for it is the only time that actually exists. There is great peace found in the now, for we are no longer striving. There is a sense of wholeness and of homecoming. It feels like we are reunited with simply Being.

Through intense focus on being in the present, this state of presence also occurs in sports where it is commonly known as being "in the zone." Immersed in surfing, skiing, running or dancing, we disconnect from all the bustle around us and we click into the present moment. The vividness and intensity of this momentary awareness is well portrayed in the movie "Peaceful Warrior." Such glimpses also happen to musicians when they become one with their instruments. That sacred feeling of union is there all the time. It is only our ceaseless mind activity that blocks it out.

You start noticing that the ethereal is present everywhere. In the slow swaying of the trees, and in the evening light, in the sound of a river, and in patterns of light dancing on the water. In the feeling of poetry and music, in butterflies and flowers. In the presence of an ancient tree, or in a sunlit clearing in the forest. In the writings of the mystics that speak directly to your soul, stirring the memory of beauty within.

Slowing down takes us out of the dense world into the subtle. You may have felt something of this spaciousness in a close silence between friends, before you kissed someone, falling into a deep hug or eye contact, or spacing out to quiet music. You can approach it by tuning in closely to the world around you, through your senses, such as noticing the feeling of the sun and the water on your skin. Or notice the gaps between your thoughts, like small spaces between an incessant stream of cars, like the stillness of the everlasting sky behind the passing clouds. No force is required, and no expectation on yourself, or on such a happening. It is not important to reach the goal but to enjoy and embody the way. Just through quiet observation and allowance you may slip spontaneously into it. It is a gift.

ON A DESERTED ISLAND in Fiji I wrote:

The Land from whence we came…

I am the moonlight, I am the mountain, I am the sound of the waves on the beach
I am the wind blow, I am the silence, I am a question just out of reach
Follow my footsteps, search in the shadows, where will I find me buried in time?
Flickering feeling, a moment fleeting, if I am nothing then what is mine?

I am the calling, I am the falling, I am a child tossing in sleep
Lost in a daydream, seeking the surface, beckoning faintly far from the deep
Am I my tears, am I my laughter? Am I my lifetime covered in snow?
A cloud drifting, a flame burning? If I don't know me then what can I know?

Summoned by magic, call of the twilight, I hear the ocean whisper my name
Borne by the wind, under the starlight, Call of the land from whence we came
I am some petals caught by the sunrise, I am pure wonder held in trance
Flight of a bird, soft fall of a snowflake, I am the moment, born unto silence.

***

IT IS ONLY WITHOUT OUR MIND, spinning out its own little story line, that we can be in the now. That's why when the car crashes, the bad news breaks, or the silence overcomes us, it creates a gap in our life's continuity, in our plans and in our thoughts. Stopping is a window to a different dimension. At the London underground stations, where loudspeakers constantly repeat, *mind the gap, mind the gap* to warn the train passengers of the space between the train doors and the platform, the daily commuters must be getting the hint. Mind…the…g…a…p…!

My own experiences were varied, due to circumstances, but in essence they were all the same: brief openings to the bigger picture. The silence when I was a teenager sailing with my father, and again by the river bank with my brother and sister; the shock of the car crash and the early morning meeting with the cobra; the uplifting moment in the streets of Kathmandu, and the gap in Tonga where I felt unconditional love.

Only through the portal of now do we access our larger picture. Usually our mind keeps pulling us forwards or back into the past, and we thus spend most of our lives lost in thought. Indeed humanity has been lost in thought since a very long time. It will be very freeing to be over the obsessive activity of our left brain fixated mind and to thus return to the state of blissful union which we are all seeking, in one odd way or another. That state is always present ~ it is us who are not!

And it is certainly rather curious that what should be the most natural things in the world have been so far the most elusive to us humans: just to Be, to be Here, and to be Now. Yet, with the pausing of our left brain, any one of us can, at anytime enter instantly, with no preparation or diploma needed, this state of Presence. Indeed, we are already there. We are like the funny drunk who spends all night walking around the outside of the park, holding onto the bars, calling, "Let me out, let me out!" It can be helpful to know, while we are on our journey to fulfillment that we have already arrived. We are already, on some level, not only everything we have ever aspired to be, but also far greater than we can possibly imagine.

As important and worthwhile as our momentary life story is, it's just a drop in the cosmic ocean. And we are that cosmic ocean. Keeping this perspective in view, it is all small stuff. Use your mind, enjoy your personality, however don't get too identified and be intrigued to go beyond them. For you are infinitely more. Think big. Universal scale. One day we will be faced with a much greater identity, that of our soul. We may become instantly aware of many lifetimes. In the enormity of our soul journey, all our concerns are but details. In the face of that immense cosmic being that we are, our cultural and personal history here is just a minute aspect.

And yet, do not worry, you will still feel "this is me," for your sense of being you remains exactly the same. Do you still feel like you are the same person inside as when you were young? Your body and all outer conditions have changed but your life force, your sense of "I am," remains the same. It always will.

WHAT IS HAPPENING TO TIME? During my first, unexpected, discovery of being not limited by a fixed time-space perception, a five minute song seemed to last an hour. I could hear every single note arise, climax, and linger; all the notes intermingling and harmonizing with each other. I was in a state of consciousness where I was *experiencing* far more within the five minute time interval than usual.

These days we can feel a powerful increase in the intensity of experience, of happening, of realizations. This expansion is due to our shifting more towards our right brain hemisphere, away from separation, more into the present. We are becoming more connected.

Our left brain personality, trying to keep up with all the details on its "things to do" list, feels it has less and less time. This obliges us to release our own pressure, to simplify our lives and move towards trust. As we do so, we start to feel how much more we are actually experiencing, expanding, and becoming than ever before. Indeed, each year we seem to be living far more than we ever have.

So what is the "end of time?" Time, as we know it, is linear and moves from the past to the future. To do so it depends, solely, on our mind. Without our minds there is no recollection of the past and no projection of the future. When we stop to heed these, when we fully enter the present moment of now, linear time stands still and expands. What is for the left brain the end of time is for the right brain the discovery of endlessness. The tiny moment of "now" is a portal into eternity. The ocean falls into the dewdrop.

For the mind this is rather difficult to grasp. It is not that time stretches eternally into the future and the past. Eternity is a zone of timelessness. Time "ends" when we enter the zone of non-time. It is not scary to step out of our mind, into the mindless, timeless state. It is the end of separation. It is re-union. It is blissful.

Our mind limits our perception to a very small picture of reality. In linear time our life is laid out like a book, each chapter being a different phase, one after the other. Yet, in reality, like in a book, all the chapters exist at the same time. We can indeed open the book anywhere and choose to read any chapter, paragraph, or line, in any order. We may also picture the chapters as different lifetimes, seemingly one after another; yet they are all bound together in the same book, all existing simultaneously. Like the different time phases, the characters in the book appear to be multiple too; and yet, in the same instance, we are all one.

CHAPTER TWENTY-NINE

Eartheyland:
A Day at the Movies

What I'm talkin' about is a game.
A game that can't be won, only played.
~ *THE LEGEND OF BAGGER VANCE*

SEEN FROM this side, expanding our reality seems like hardly a trivial matter. To keep things in perspective, it helps to bear in mind that life on Earth is much like a day at Disneyland. Some come here because they love the rides. Some come to accompany friends or family. Some most enjoy sitting on the benches, people-watching and writing reports on life in the park.

On entry we get our ticket and accept the terms and conditions: donning a left brain personality that makes us forget our origins and life beyond the park. Thus we become engrossed in the rides, pursuing excitement and experience. Sometimes we are on the teacup, sometimes on the roller coaster. The bench is where we recoup between rides. If we hold back out of fear we may feel in the end that we missed out on the fun; but if the rides really don't turn us on, or make us queasy, we may be the contemplative type who is happy to sit on the park bench.

Imagine a waterslide park to be a giant, three-dimensional game of "Snakes and Ladders;" we climb up the many ladders to the top and then hurtle down the long snaky slides. After lifetimes of twisting and turning, being spun around and shot down shocking chutes we may just enjoy chilling out by the pool, merging with the sun and the quietness. Well deserved, I say, it is not a waste of a ticket! After so many rides they start to lose their grip on us and we no longer feel the need to prove ourselves or get our money's worth of thrills. We begin to question and to figure out the machinery: the set-up behind the scenes.

"Dying" is as simple as walking out of Disneyland. When we leave we return to the parking lot, back to our usual life which we had temporarily forgotten in the distractions of the park. We are still the same person; we just broaden once again our perception and our activities. Our unfulfilled desires, ambitions and grievances are what attract us back to Disneyland, or another park.

Eartheyland 2000

A GALACTIC GAME is now being played to lighten up Eartheyland, offering wonderful opportunities of fulfillment to the participants. Eager souls are rushing in, taking body-tokens to play on this colorful board, planet Earth.

The park keepers are also working on the upgrade of this beautiful park. Improvements are scheduled to be completed in 2012. Amazing new features will be introduced. The new park standards are based on higher integrity to ensure the safety and enjoyment of *all* life forms within the park, as well as for visitors from abroad.

A lot of thought, energy, and creativity is being put into this project and we can all feel it in the increased intensity in the air. Old, dysfunctional structures are being taken down. Many of us were so engrossed in the thrills, they didn't notice the air castles were on the brink of collapse. Others, who had become bored of the rides, started to look behind the scenes and revealed many illusions in the machinery that once seemed so real. Non-ethical hoaxes and hierarchy which were detrimental to the health and happiness of the majority of participants are now being disclosed and disempowered as they are not up to the new standards. Hidden truths and ancient teachings are now being revealed as they contain the blueprint and designs for the new structures to be built.

As usual, the work is a bit behind schedule. Many aware players are pushing their tokens to work overtime, putting all their focus on the remodel to make now manifest, according to the grand plan, these long anticipated changes.

We are all being prepared for the greater knowledge and new energy that is yet to be downloaded into the game. As always, kids are the quickest to catch on to new ideas and technologies so they are of utmost assistance in this transition. We all came to play, to support and to benefit from this upgrading.

The human tokens we chose came with a body-mind we felt we could deal with, work with, and help raise to greater understanding. Through loving and maturing our human character, whether it tends to be weak, insecure, stubborn or aggressive, we help to raise both its ability to participate and the whole level of the game. Helping our "human-becoming" to drop its resistance and its outmoded behavior patterns is a most useful contribution and may well be the winning move.

Only those who do not approve of the upgrade, or downright refuse to go with the flow, may find their tickets are not valid for the improved version. For a time it was considered by the committee that some areas of the park may have to be re-landscaped but that should no longer be necessary due to our combined human efforts to partake in the changes.

This is the time for "all hands on deck." There are some fields where our unique talents are most suited now and you may feel an urge to fulfill whatever you intended to do here. We are each a note in a cosmic symphony. If you are not sure what your role is, practice the inner game of tennis: focus on the point where you want the ball to go, rather than worry about how you have to hit the ball to get it there. Look ahead to where your own focus is taking you. "We always steer in the direction we look at" ~ as my driving teacher would frequently remind me! We hold the steering wheel. Universal laws are logical and simple: we go in the direction we look, we slot into the reality we believe in. Uphold your vision as if your life depended on it because, in one way, it does.

If Eartheyland life feels like too big a mission, remember that we chose to play. Your spirit-player knew the stakes and that his token was up to it. It respectfully leaves the token free range yet offers help and guidance. It knows that if the token can be encouraged to drop victimhood and resistance, and to co-operate in this partnership, then the gap between them can be bridged. To build this relationship within us is the most recommended preparation to play the upgraded version of "Eartheyland 2000." This connection within us builds a bridge between humankind and the stars.

~~~

You are the ongoing energy of life
scampering around in this particular playground.
~ Lynn Grabhorn, EXCUSE ME YOUR LIFE IS WAITING

YOU ARE AN INFINITE, ETERNAL SPIRIT, playing the role of a mortal being. How on earth, you may wonder, did you get this job? Personally, I reckon my soul buddy Rob asked me: "Do you want to go to the drive in?"

And I replied, "What's showing?"

He said, "Whatever you like. There's a lot to choose from. I am most attracted by this great epic drama, Eartheyland 2000. It's a perfect plot which plays on many levels, an intricate intrigue seemingly between the power of light and dark forces. It's also an interactive game: the outcome of the blue planet depends on the viewers, and the outcome for the viewers depends on their hearts, which are portals to another reality. Imagine that! And you can choose from all these different roles. They don't give you many tips on how to play at the start though, so you do have to really figure it out by yourself, looking for clues as you go along. Once you get the idea it becomes a lot easier."

I hesitated, "Hmm, sounds a bit challenging...I'm not sure I'm up to that."

He encouraged me, "Oh come on, it's really just for fun!"

Never one to be left behind I sighed, "Okay, just remind me of *that* when the time comes. I guess you might appreciate some reminders down there yourself! Anyway, there's nothing to lose. Count me in!"

And so we all came, for the greatest movie in human history. We wouldn't have done it for less.

In the beginning, perhaps, after a couple billion years of hanging out together in Blissland we all got bored and created this theme park Eartheyland. To make it interesting we decided we would play blindfolded, or rather "mindfolded." We wouldn't remember who we are, that we've known each other since forever, that in fact we are one being, or even, most unbelievably, what bliss feels like! We set ourselves goals, intentions, and clues along the way, making sure not to discover them too early, lest we say, *"What did I volunteer for?"* We chose roles we could identify with, which suited our beliefs and our desires and would enrich our soul.

I'm sure many of us spirits thought they'd be fine off because they would never forget that it's just a movie. "How hard can it be to remember the obvious? This Eartheyland business is going to be a piece of cake!" I can picture my own eager, earnest self, anxiously rehearsing some keys lines, as one does before an exam, prior to taking the final plunge into the earthly plane. I knew damn well the amnesia that occurs on arrival through the tunnel of birth, which takes us from one dimension to another. It is similar to moving from the dreamworld to the waking state: that which was so obvious a second ago, just disappears. We will leave through the same trans-dimensional tunnel. Dying is waking up.

So in my childhood some simple lines resurfaced from within. For most of my life I thought *I knew* these elemental things. I finally realized they were rather the particular topics I needed to bear in mind! These shreds of basic wisdom arose from my subconscious, like the remnants of a dream we cling to in the morning, in the hope of remembering more: No one else can make you happy; Whatever companions we have on the way, the journey of birth and death we do alone; Above the clouds, the sun is always shining.

WE ENTER THIS WORLD LIKE we go to a movie hall. There are many movies playing at the Eartheyland cinema hall and we are attracted to whichever one fits with our feelings and our beliefs.

Soap operas are not exactly my style, but some people love that kind of drama, also in their daily lives. A deep personality would likely choose a thought-provoking epic. Some like adventure movies, others prefer comedies or romances. I used to find tragedies meaningful; it fitted to my outlook on life, until I had enough of them to get over it!

A sensitive, light-minded person is unlikely to choose a horror movie. But some people enjoy them; it excites them and feeds their pain body. Some with unpleasant lives may have judged themselves as bad enough to deserve to be punished in that way, or just got pulled into their reality by being in a victimized or abusive vibe. It is the same as in our daily lives: much happens to us unawares through the law of attraction, until we start to make more conscious choices. Nothing is random. We "live," "die," keep on living, are "recycled," all perfectly in accordance with our awareness, our own judgment, our vibration, our energetic resonance.

Perhaps, from the multiple healing projects on offer on Earth, such as alleviating heavy pain bodies, self doubt, self hatred, addiction, etc, we picked characters that we felt we could handle and would benefit both us and our co-actors. Some very bright spirits may have indeed chosen dark issues to uplift and enlighten those areas of the human psyche. It seems that at least one heartache and one death were compulsory subjects to experience! Our spirit player takes on life with a light attitude of "Let's see how this goes!" After all, it has nothing to lose.

> *Souls often choose familiar places or sceneries to live in. They volunteer for bodies which are to be killed, have fatal illnesses or accidents. Souls involved in large-scale tragedies are not caught in the wrong place at the wrong time with a capricious God looking the other way. Those who die in infancy do so as a lesson for the parents. One subject chose a short and difficult life as a crash course in humility. Commonly I see some choosing challenging lives to catch up with learning after easy ones.*
> *~ Michael Newton, Journey Of Souls*

I met a brave woman once who was mourning her mother and her son. One day she saw her little son, as though behind a veil, jumping up and down, exclaiming, "I'm okay mummy, I'm okay!" Another time her mother appeared above her, and looking down on her grieving curtly said, "Lighten up girl!"

Among other authorities, "The Tibetan Book of the Dead" describes that after leaving our body we pass through layers of our energetic being towards the bright light that is, in fact, our own essence. We pass through increasingly subtle layers of our personality and corresponding "realities." As in daily life, we are attracted to whatever we resonate with. As in daily life, our strongest beliefs, feelings, and opinions are what overwhelm us and pull us back into the drama ~ the play, the movie. Our leftover regrets and desires catch us and *whoosh,* we are sucked back into that "reality": be it money, fame, pretty girls, starving people or wildlife becoming extinct. The fewer attitudes and attachments, habits and hurts, doubts and unfulfilled desires remain with us, the further we can move towards our inner light, towards our core.

Perhaps our spirit player is sighing sometimes like a resigned parent: "He really insisted on chasing that girl, on making a million, on saving the turtles, on becoming famous… And now I have to again wait for him to get over it!"

Aiming for the bright light, our highest possibility, is like attempting to fall asleep, or to meditate, or remain conscious in a lucid dream. As we sink inwards towards our core, we can easily get caught up in our thoughts again. The practice of meditation is to maintain our presence: to neutrally observe our thoughts without becoming lost in them. Eventually we disengage and experience our thoughts and emotions as separate from us. In the same way, we are all becoming more aware now of our thought patterns and how they affect us. We are learning to detach from the pain body, not to follow disempowering thoughts. As we identify less with our viewpoints, we become freer from judgment that entangles us in the situation we are judging. We are managing not to be so easily tricked by emotions that draw us into unwanted discussions or situations. We are all learning in this way to have more control over our destiny, to recognize our subtle choices and where they take us. That is the great opportunity that life here today offers us. It is what we are most discovering and establishing in this era of human history: to recognize and to use our creative power, our power of choice.

So when we die, same as in our daily lives, it is our predominant feelings that determine our continued destiny. We move on in the same way we live here: either pulled unconsciously into the next movie, or following the script we have written for ourselves. It is the same when we are given the extremely rare opportunity to collectively create and participate in the birth of our new planetary reality.

CHAPTER THIRTY

Wilde and Wilder

It's easier to ridicule than it is to investigate.
But less profitable.
                                        ~ Steven Greer

PERHAPS TAKE THIS as an exercise in widening.

Life is not always that straightforward for us Earthlings ~ multidimensional beings that we are, squeezed into disposable containers and tossed mindfolded into a limited version of reality, without as much as a *Lonely Planet Travel Guide to Earth.* At least the food is good down here and we get hot showers and internet while we work out the acceptance thing!

Lonely planet, however, it is actually not. We may be on the outer edge of our spiral galaxy, still the most intrepid travelers are flocking to see what's going on here. It seems that an intergalactic aide mission has been set up for planet Earth and beautiful beings are crossing dimensions to visit.

It's inevitable that we locals would feel inferior if we saw these tall white travelers with high-tech gadgets whizzing around our globe. It would blow our fragile self esteem. Many a native culture has lost its own identity by the apparition of the white man and his sophisticated technology, and of course, an advanced, ethical race would be very careful not to do the same to us. Wouldn't they?

Some describe the ethereal beings they have seen, moving trans-dimensionally into our world, radiating warmth, nobility, honor, and a silent power and dedication that is sacred.

There's something stunningly beautiful and majestic
about these beings, and they seem to be waiting and
watching over humans at the same time.
                                    ~ Stuart Wilde

Others have a vested interest to keep us ignorant of our ances-
try and our interaction with other beings. One can better give this
amazing topic the deserved curiosity, without fear, if one hasn't
watched the inevitably scary Hollywood movies. Our DNA is an energy pattern that is found throughout the galaxy and thus creates
similar life wherever it can. Hence our cosmic cousins are humanoid.
Like us, they come in different colors, shapes and sizes. Those who
are able to cross space and time are of course rather evolved.

Way back in 2001, which feels now like a lifetime ago, I was
handed some pages of witness testimonies to the extraterrestrial
phenomenon. There were some big names in there such as astro-
nauts Edgar Mitchell and Gordon Cooper, and Werner von Braun,
the father of US rocketry. There were members of the British Ministry of Defense, including Lord Hill-Norton former head of the
Ministry, two Commanders of US underground nuclear bases and
John Callahan who was high up in the FAA (The US Federal Aviation Authority). There were other high-ranking military, aviation
and NASA personnel. I was always curious about this topic, as we
all are, yet still I suspected the conference advertised wouldn't be
conclusive. I was wrong. It was our 12 year old daughter who insisted we drive the 100 kilometers to watch it. We had no idea of
the revelation in store.

· That memorable night, we were shown a video of a Press
Conference held in May 2001 at the Washington Press Club, spon-
sored by the White House correspondent at the time of the Clinton
administration.

"Disclosure Project" was formed by Dr. Steven Greer in a
joint effort to bring out the hidden truth behind our interaction
with off-planetary races, and the sophisticated free-energy technologies since long developed, that would transform our social
power structure. All in all, we saw six hours of testimonies from
dozens of military, corporate and scientific witnesses. The evidence was dry, non-sensational, and undeniable. When we walked

out of that room, a new dimension of life had opened. The sky never looked the same again.

It's not that I ever had a problem with believing in the possibility of extraterrestrial life. In such a vast universe, it is plainly logical that we are not the only planet with intelligent life forms. However, it was the closeness and the extent of the interaction that surprised me. Fear of ridicule, for one, keeps the topic well smothered. Even I felt shy at first of broadcasting my new discovery in case people thought I was wacky. I wrote to my friends, "If you want to think I am gullible and stupid that's understandable, but do your homework first."

Steven Greer has briefed members of Congress, CIA Directors, senior Pentagon officials, international heads of state, senior scientific leaders and other officials worldwide, to inform them of this secrecy. He has notified numerous insiders, working within the military-industrial complex, of the covert agendas of the backstage world rulers. There is much dissention now within these covert operations. In tune with the changing times, many working in these highly classified areas and members of the secret "elite" are now undergoing a change of mind and heart. Having understood the exact agendas and the level of deception they are collaborating with, many are not, or no longer, in agreement with such plans. Aware that they can assist to bring out the new energy technologies, they are now coming forwards. "Well, I thought we were keeping this secret so the enemies wouldn't get it," or "I thought we had to keep it quiet not to collapse the economy," or, "…to protect the oil industry."

Disclosure of the existence of off-planetary cultures has been on the menu since a long time, and is now imminent. The question is: which version will we get? The false picture of hostile aliens can further justify the push for tight control by a global government. This agenda was already known of by Werner Von Braun back in the '70s, potentially including the threat of a hoax alien attack using UFOs, which have been built on Earth since decades. Perhaps this move can no longer be pulled off at this stage of insider awareness, yet it is still recommendable to be informed. Genuine UFOs are notably identifiable by their low profile.

THERE ARE ALSO many stories that we have been genetically either upgraded or downgraded by an alien race. It is like political parties: whichever one you choose you get the same thing. It is wise to avoid duality, drama, and swallowing *any* picture that puts us in a position of powerlessness. As with any information about hidden powers behind the scene, what matters is not what power anyone may or may not yield over us, but what power *we* have. In truth everyone on this planet, whatever rank or social position, has *the same creative power.* We all have one heart, one vote each.

Whether "bad aliens" are designed to scare us ~ programmed, bio-robotic life forms ~ or whether they are only the energetic manifestation of our own dark, not yet reconciled, shadow; whether we have been upgraded or downgraded… the trick is not to feed any dualistic picture, *not to give your energy to any camp, but your own.* Your heart is your strength. Love is always our protection.

There is so much we can focus on that is rock solid, practical, and beneficial. And as we start to discover more about our wondrous world, we recognize that things are really not as they seem. Our logical, linear minds find answers the best they can, but these are, truly, only concepts. The day will come when we see our reality from an expanded viewpoint, and we shall be more than amazed about our world, our lives, and ourselves.

~

THE EVIDENCE OF FREE-ENERGY technologies is now widespread in the scientific community and reaches back more than one hundred years to the inventions of Nicolas Tesla. However, almost none of the available information has been made public. It can make you very mad or sad that our world has been denied these advanced technologies that would have given us *all* a very different life on this planet. Yet these feelings empower us to take our governance into our own hands. By now we have all had *so enough* of pollution and abuse on all levels that we are really ready to move on to a new world. A sustainable and abundant flow of free energy is available to us. When the energy dynamics in our own lives are largely cleaned up, these clean, free-flowing energy technologies will be the expression, the reflection, of the increased awareness on our planet. We will inherit these technologies when our actions display the same level of integrity.

This is the time to take the reins of our own life and lift ourselves beyond victimhood and thus beyond abuse. Then we can openly relate with our galactic neighbors in the spirit of cooperation. We cannot just be "saved" for it goes against the law of freewill.

The integrity of these advanced ethical races requires them to leave us alone to develop our own maturity. They cannot interfere or infringe on our development as they would become karmically entangled with us, putting us again in a position of dependency. However, same as with the technology, some information has been passed down to us, through various channels, in order to assist our progress.

Our history and our evolution are interwoven with other races. The archeological evidence of ancient higher cultures is undeniable. There have always been different levels of civilization on this planet at any one time. Planet Earth is a galactic melting pot of races from different places; a nature reserve, an island in a cosmic sea. These visitors are both from our future and our own higher consciousness. ("Extraterrestrial" in that they are a part of ourselves that exists outside of Earth's matrix.) The mind boggles.

To glimpse the holographic nature of life, consider that each solar system is just an atom of a much larger being. And to conceive that this all lies *within* us, imagine that each atom of your body is in fact a solar system. The universe lies within... Modern physics confirms that time is not linear and to traverse distances in the universe is not so much a physical matter as it is transdimensional. The way out there lies within. The mind gives up...

AMIDST THIS MIND-BLOWING INFORMATION, our heart is the one thing that connects all of us. Our cosmic cousins have, like us, similar human feelings and expressions, somewhat more refined and delicate. They have crashed, been shot at, and been arrested on our planet, and if faced with hostility they can, like us, feel lost, alone, and scared... and a long way from home.

A New Dawn

When the seed is ready, the outer casing breaks open and a shoot, a sapling, a tree, bursts forth. We take this transformation for granted.
Yet it is one of the wonders of nature that the information for a gigantic oak is contained in a tiny acorn.
A seed is programmed to be mature at a certain season. For the seed to open, the time and the conditions must be right; it has a certain window of opportunity.

CHAPTER THIRTY-ONE

Generation of Transformation

I saw them across the twilight of an age
The sun-eyed children of a marvelous dawn
The great creators with wide brows of calm
The massive barrier breakers of the world.

~ *Aurobindo, visionary*

THERE IS A TIME to grow enclosed, and then there comes a time to open. Having developed our own individuality, having built our relationship within ourselves, we are ready to truly embrace others. We can dare to drop our sense of separation, which has so far protected our growth, and open ourselves to merge with others without losing our integrity.

We use our personality and wisdom, the individuality we have created through our own life's experience, to the benefit of all. Understanding our interconnectedness, the mirror effect, our shadows, our soul connection and the roles we play, we no longer see others as separate or against us, but as mirroring aspects of ourselves.

As we each develop more self approval, more openness, and more compassion, we take things less personally, and communication starts to flow more smoothly between us human cells. With our channels open, very rapidly things are getting better. As we all become more in agreement with ourselves, humankind, as one body, is also becoming more in agreement with itself. We come to see that despite different paths, different walkabouts, we all are on the same journey. As we grow in trust, as we open, share and acknowledge others experience, we begin to expand exponentially.

It is a natural process of evolution. First we strengthen our individual personality until we are ready to drop resistance, and then we join together. *The Global Brain* by Peter Russell describes how single units that hitherto had developed separately start to naturally exchange and unite once they reach a large number. They then form a greater and far more advanced organism. Thus it takes about ten billion atoms to create a cell, and ten billion brain cells to form a brain. They grow first in separation, and once they are fully developed, the dots start connecting rapidly.

The reflection of humanity's increasing exchange, sharing and smoother communication is the advent of the modern technologies, which allow for a broader and faster flow of information. We can observe a conscious uniting happening now on the planet through the interaction of billions of people. Never before has there been so much new, freely available information, as well as feelings, being shared. Never before has there been such a network of connected energy and people around the globe. It shows that the human mind and heart is expanding.

Modern day mystics confirm that there is indeed a huge shift of identity taking place on the planet as we now move from a single sense of self to a wider feeling of collectiveness. We are in the process of forming a unified humanity. The key to these times is to identify with the one collective being that we truly are.

～

In the late 1950s God hears the sound of the blues coming from a remote corner of her universe. She puts her other duties aside, listens closely and feels some faint discord is going on down there. It seems that in a cell of her small left toe there is a strain of sorrow being expressed. She sends a warm healing thought to that area, and planet Earth is hit by a wave of love, peace and understanding. Flower children begin to blossom.

Barely a moment later God becomes alerted by a stronger vibration in the same toe. She sighs, tunes in again and hears Sid Vicious

*and Johnny Rotten, followed by Ronald Reagan declaring war on
her favorite weed. There are faint calls for help and the tiny cell
Gaia appears to be choking. Decided to fix it for once and for all
she visualizes a powerful beam of light embracing and healing the
area. The information and love carried therein sparks a new wave
of spiritual awareness and re-generation on Earth.*

When threatened with extinction, a species needs to evolve in
order to survive. Increased awareness from the '60s spread across
the world, largely underground, and birthed an irrepressible generation that began to emerge in the '80s. Whether you call them
"indigo" or "crystal" children, or simply new agers, these "new
children" are spiritually advanced. Surfing the wave of the new
dawn they reach across all countries and through all parts of the
population, from the most alternative to the most mainstream.
Their appearance on the scene is of course partly due to the efforts
of the previous generations who have paved the way and contributed to the changing mindset. No lives have been in vain, no
work has been wasted. Our youngsters are good news and good
energy. Some see them as the rescue team or the reserve squad, or
the return of the wise souls. They are also here due to our dreams,
our prayers, and the planetary transition. They play a leading role
in this unique era of human evolution where consciousness is becoming *fully embedded* in our world. They are the beautiful expressions of humanity's flowering.

Many of the younger generation have a less competitive character and a more holistic understanding of the world. They have
greater openness, innate intelligence and awareness, increased
sensitivity and indeed, ethics. They have lighter pain bodies and
greater presence. We do not have to worry about our kids for they
are naturally more in tune, more equipped than we are to flow
with the changing times. However, we may not recognize their
talents because we cling to old values. We may need to revise our
own views! These days "lacking ambition" can simply mean trusting, "lazy" can mean relaxed, and "irresponsible" can mean not
responding to the old social structure but rather in tune with the
new. In Australia once I overheard a high school teacher say,

"Don't push him to toughen up, he's a snag."

"A what?" I asked.

"Oh, a SNAG: a Sensitive New Age Guy."

And that, in Australia, shows the times have really changed!

The times have changed, we can relax, we no longer need to strive for our living, or plan for our pension. Our souls have greater plans. Some of these astute and powerful children may be keeping a low profile, biding their time as indeed are many others. I have noticed that behind a façade of social conformity and normality, large parts of the population are far more open minded, aware and alternative than they outwardly appear. The changes are happening largely below the surface.

A few last words from our brain scientist friend:

> Western civilization is a pretty challenging environment for my loving and peaceful right brain hemisphere character to live in … It is my intuition and higher consciousness…. It is filled with gratitude for life, content and compassionate, nurturing and optimistic, friendly and smiley. It knows we are laced together, life is good and we are all beautiful just the way we are…. It is agile and creative, not bogged down by the past or fearful of what the future may not bring. Freed from all perception of boundaries it proclaims 'I am part of it all. We are brothers and sisters on this planet. We are here to make this world a more peaceful and kinder place.'
>
> ~Jill Bolte Taylor

Some of this new generation are very bright indeed: "Mummy, why are we enclosed in this limited time-space reality?" Some have "extraordinary" skills that are in fact a natural expression of a developing consciousness. They display amazing psychic abilities, like telepathy and clairvoyance. Some have even, in controlled experiments, opened flower buds with the power of thought. You may doubt it, but they are taking these advanced youngsters very seriously in China, Russia, Central and South America, among others. These capacities for ESP are dormant in *all* people and will, as the veil lifts between the worlds, be awakened.

Born in the early '80s, an Argentinean boy says:

*Now that this world is starting to be less physical, other
children like me are going to come. Human beings are different
now. They are going to be more open. I am here to calm the
people who are frightened by the changing energy of Earth.
New children are being born. I am just one of them, one of the
first ones. Humanity is changing. The connection with the
spiritual world becomes more open.*

> ~ *Flavio, Vengo del Sol, age 7*

We may well have to bow to wisdom from the mouths of babes.

—

THERE ARE MANY "FRINGE DWELLERS" on the planet: those who
have never fitted in. They could never quite make sense of the game,
or believe in the rules. They were the most affected by the seemingly
dysfunctional face of the world but, in these times, they lead the
way. It is the most sensitive who, like receptors that pick up what is
going on and inform the others cells, first sense the winds of change.
Human evolution has always been led by the most sensitive, the
most flexible and the most adaptive among us. They may be our
parents, our friends, or our children. Support and encourage them
as our guides. They hold within them the memory of distant realities, refined values and ideals, and a sense of innocence, brotherhood, and peace. They are those that hold the dream for us all, and
in doing so they anchor that frequency on the planet and thereby assist it to materialize. There is nothing that can kill this dream, for
within it lies the memory of our larger being to which we are eternally linked. They are those that never forgot.

You may say I'm a dreamer, but I'm not the only one...

> ~ *John Lennon,* IMAGINE

These sensitive folk are not just idle daydreamers, giving
their power away to illusionary hopes, but indeed a worldwide
web holding, through their presence, a unified and clear vision of
a new Earth.

In past ages they would probably have been called contempla-
tives. There is no place for them, it seems, in our contemporary
civilization. On the arising new earth, however, their role is just
as vital as that of the creators, the doers, the reformers. Their
function is to anchor the frequency of the new consciousness on
this planet. I call them the frequency-holders. They are here to
generate consciousness through the activities of daily life,
through their interaction with others as well as through
'just being.'

　Their task is to bring spacious stillness into this world by
being absolutely present in whatever they do. There is conscious-
ness and therefore quality in what they do, even the simplest
task. Their purpose is to do everything in a sacred manner. As
each person is an integral part of the collective human conscious-
ness, they affect the world much more deeply than is visible on
the surface of their lives.

~Eckhart Tolle

All over the world, as they quietly tend their fields, cook their chapattis or bathe in the rivers, the indigenous populations, the people of the land, are a large part of fulfilling this role on Earth.

Other sources speak of some souls that originate from afar, which could explain why they never felt at home here. Although already evolved beyond victimhood, they chose to incarnate on Earth at this time to inspire, assist, and guide the birthing of a new paradigm. To do so they had to take on the same patterns that held all humanity in their grip, despite the considerable risk of getting stuck in the mindset of victim consciousness.

Whatever the possible different origins of mankind on this planet, whatever your age or race, nation or star, we are all sailing the same boat now. Each of us is of equal value. Each has their role to play on board. We are all working together as one. We *are* One. One love. One people. One Soul.

Silent (R)evolution...
On the surface of the world right now there is
war and violence and things seem dark.
But calmly and quietly, at the same time,
something else is happening underground
An inner revolution is taking place
and every individual is being called to a higher light.
It is a silent revolution.
From the inside out. From the ground up.
This is a Global operation.
A Spiritual Conspiracy.

We are quietly working behind the scenes
in every country and culture of the world
Cities big and small, mountains and valleys,
in farms and villages, tribes and remote islands
It is of no concern to us who takes the final credit
But simply that the work gets done
Occasionally we spot each other in the street
We give a quiet nod and continue on our way

We are slowly creating a new world
with the power of our minds and hearts
Our orders come from the Central Spiritual Intelligence
We follow, with passion and joy
We are dropping soft, secret love bombs when no one is looking
Poems ~ Hugs ~ Music ~ Photography ~ Movies ~ Kind words ~
Smiles ~ Meditation and prayer ~ Dance ~ Social activism ~
Websites ~ Blogs ~ Random acts of kindness...
We each express ourselves in our own unique ways
with our own unique gifts and talents

We know that quietly and humbly we have
the power of all the oceans combined
Love is the new religion of the 21st century
You don't have to be educated to understand it
It comes from the intelligence of the heart
Embedded in the timeless evolutionary pulse of all human beings

Be the change you choose to see in the world
That is the motto that fills our hearts
We know it is the only way real transformation takes place
Nobody else can do it for you

Perhaps you will join us
Or already have.
All are welcome
The door is open

                              ~ Anon

CHAPTER THIRTY-TWO

Why Not You?

We all have the power to make a difference.
A new Earth begins with a new you.

~ *Eckhart Tolle, A New Earth*

MY FATHER was an adventurer and a natural sailor. As a lad he built an extension on his motorbike so he could still ride it with a broken leg. He traveled Far East Asia in the '50s, and sailed a Chinese junk solo across the northern Pacific in the days of the sextant. He wondered how it would feel to be alone in a rip-roaring gale in the midst of the ocean, and he found out. It seemed then that nothing could stop him. Such ventures enlivened him, as running a business killed him. He was the type who would go out to buy a practical family car and come back with a sporty convertible. I remember driving down the highway at night with the roof open, us kids curled up behind the front seats to keep warm until we fell asleep. In later life he rode around the countryside on an old classic motorcycle...the wind in his hair. My mother loathed his bike, yet after he died it was the one item that left her weeping when the buyer took it away. For it was the symbol of his dream.

This book is for you, and for all those who have put away their spirit for a "normal" life. Follow your dream, for it is nothing less than the call of your soul. Perhaps a distant land lures you, or a childhood fantasy beckons from long ago. Perhaps a friend whispers your dream to you when you have forgotten, an inner urge awakens or a romance laid aside...

You may still remember, after this long and winding journey together, that I first went to India in search of the meaning of life. What did I finally find? All roads lead back to our own front door.

The meaning of Life is not discovered by one person
and then displayed so others may find it without searching.
Your life is the ultimate opportunity to create meaning.
                                                    ~ Osho

To get the most out of our lives is really a matter of choice. These days an inspiring number of people are looking at what more they can be, do, and experience. You are, we all are, special beings. Not because we are brainier, richer, or better looking than others, but because our true nature is so amazing we can't even conceive of it. We have come here to get closer to our larger being, not to be a cog in the system's wheel. Maybe take some days off to think about that.

Don't forget your dreams for they are
your directions on the map of life.
                                    ~ Chandra

My father would say, "You can be anything you want to be," to which my petite mother would rightly reply, "I couldn't be a heavyweight boxer."
"And would you want to be?" he would ask.
Anything. You. Want. To. Be.

You are never given a dream without being given
the possibility to make it true. You may have to
work for it however.
                            ~ Richard Bach, ILLUSIONS

There are heart-opening success stories of those who have overcome debilitating feelings and "terminal" conditions, that show the awesome power of our spirit and our human heart.

*There is nothing we can imagine to be, do or have that we have
not got the power to be, do or have. All the theories in the world
are useless unless there is action, positive change, and healing.*
                                        ~ Louise Hay

No one else can live your dream for you. Don't worry: "How
will I accomplish it?" We can only, need only, and are only asked
to do one step, one page, at a time. Drop disempowering doubt
and looking too far ahead. We ground ourselves by keeping our
focus on what we can do now. Rest assured, whatever is good for
our own evolution is good for the whole and will be supported.

Years ago in Fiji, visiting someone in the evening, a rare thing
happened: I watched a movie. Out of the usual shallow plot I retained a few profound lines: "You don't wait for things to happen.
You make them happen. YOU make them happen." It was among
the first stirrings of change.

When repeatedly asked, "But where are you originally
from?" I would joke, "Honestly, if I knew where I was from, I
would go back there!" Yet I finally realized: if we are not happy
here, the point is not to return to where we came from but to do
what we came for. For now we know:

We are the ones we have been waiting for.
                                        ~ Hopi wisdom

THERE IS NO SAVIOR GOING TO POP OUT of the bushes and do our
job for us. The big challenge here for us little humans is to simply
allow the creative force to flow through us.

It's about our own evolution. The future of the world doesn't
hang on your shoulders, but yours does. We just want to fulfill our
own potential, and that is our contribution, to ourselves and to the
whole. I do consider it a bit above my talents to save the world! But
I will do whatever leads me to greater openness, expression, expansion and joy. Honesty is our best friend. Insisting that we are
happy where we are can make us blind to what we truly feel. Have
the courage and self reliance to make constant adjustments on

your way. If something doesn't happen in our life it is simply because we didn't do it.

> *The fact is whatever you think the world is withholding*
> *from you, you are withholding from the world. You are*
> *withholding it because deep down you think you are small*
> *and you have nothing to give.*
> ~ *Eckhart Tolle, A New Earth*

.   We cannot see, from our limited perspective, the ripples of all our thoughts, feelings and actions. Yet we are beginning to recognize our influence, and therefore our responsibility. Not because of egoic aggrandizement, but because of the interconnected and interactive nature of our world. Each of us has their specific personality ~ the sum of their experiences ~ to offer. Each of us has the same life force within them. And none of us got here by mistake. Each of us is a unique combination of life experience, personality, expression and talents. You are unique, original, and no one else can take your place. The fulfillment of your destiny is in your own hands. You are not doing anyone a favor by not letting your light shine. When the crunch comes you won't get any medals for playing small. Some reluctance is natural for us humans and yet this is not a time to hide in modesty. In our shyness not to be special, superior or elitist we tend to undervalue ourselves. We may not believe that any single contribution is worth much, and yet we each have our role to play as part of the one body and soul of humanity. Our actions are the seed of our future.

Drop what you don't like, encourage what you do, do what you can't leave, forge ahead ~ without leaving your little child behind ~ and let your beauty shine. Through inner reflection on who we are and what life is all about, we remember the sketch we outlined for this life. Don't panic if you don't feel up to it. When the time comes, if we just clear the blocks, our latent abilities will surface.

This is illustrated by a funny cartoon. I don't remember the original animals so I'll make them up. In the self help section of the library, a number of different characters are sitting around studying books. A giraffe is reading, *Dare to stand tall.* A tiger is engrossed in, *Be wild! A beginner's guide.* A bat is reading, *Enjoy your nightlife!* An eagle is studying, *How to fly high and improve your vision.* An elephant has, *Think big ~ why weight?* And the dodo is puzzling through *To be or not to be? ~ A survival handbook....*

We only have to unlock and rediscover our intrinsic talents. We brought all the tools we needed for whatever we intended to do. We are not expected to be or express any more than what we are. It is more than enough. Many great people who have had far-reaching experiences concur: however simplistic it sounds, just to be kind and cheerful is a huge contribution to our world. It influences not only our own day, but all those around us. Ever philosophical, this sign graced an Indian school entrance: "It is nice to be important, but it is more important to be nice."

We do not need to do great things.
Do small things with great love.
    ~ Mother Teresa

It is so rewarding to see rapid results in our happiness and our relationships as we put our focus on loving our self, and others, more. *Work on your inner beauty and all else will follow.* It is not so much what we do but rather how we do it, which type of energy we express, that counts. Fulfillment is not only found in the goal, but at every step along the way. Hence, when a sage is asked what he would do if the world were to end tomorrow, he replies, "I would plant a tree." Whatever you are doing, whatever vibe you are sending out, you are joining a network of people all around the globe who are doing the same.

Shared laughter is almost as powerful as love. With love and
good cheer flooding our spirits and infusing our hearts, the likes
of confusion, doubt, worry and fear do not and cannot exist.
    ~ Dannion and Kathryn Brinkley

You may be an infinitesimal part of the universe but you are, undeniably, a part of the collective consciousness on planet Earth.

Through our daily choices and our work of uplifting and expanding ourselves, we are assisting human consciousness to rise. So don't hide from your ability to serve, not save, the world. We are each, through our own evolving, a gift to Earth's evolution and we are fully supported when we willingly align with the bigger picture.

> *There is an arising presence, an evolutionary impulse of the universe. Consciousness is flowering: through your form it wants to flower. And you thought you were a little person, needing things and having to protect yourself. You are here to enable the divine purpose of the universe to unfold. That is how important you are!*
> ~ Eckhart Tolle, *A NEW EARTH*

Your answer is maybe? Maybe you are the answer! You are a spirit being, a star child. Even your cells are made of stardust. We have been given the keys and god is in the back seat praying!

> *The Beings of Light believe in us. Perhaps it is time we more fully believe in us as well. We are heroes and heroines to have come here at this time.*
> ~ Dannion and Kathryn Brinkley

It is not by chance that we are here at this turning point in history. We wanted the job, we got it. Our position is, "creator in training" and for a start, just to try out our skills, we have been given the minor task of changing the Earth paradigm. We are displaying now our creative powers. We are consciously choosing to paint a new picture, creating a new world. The world we have dreamt of and prayed for. It is our birthright.

Follow your dream, your heart and your integrity. If you feel you have work to do, do it, in the spirit of celebration. Hold the vision, lightly and confidently. We are not crusaders; indeed, force displays doubt. Keep your vibration warm and at ease. This *is* our time.

Our deepest fear is not that we are inadequate. Our deepest fear is that we are powerful beyond measure. It is our light not our darkness that most frightens us. We ask ourselves, who am I to be brilliant, gorgeous, talented, fabulous? Actually, who are you not to be? You are a child of god. Your playing small does not serve the world. There is nothing enlightened about shrinking so that other people won't feel insecure around you. We are born to make manifest the glory which is within us. It is not just in some of us. It is in every one of us. And as we let our light shine, we unconsciously give other people the permission to do the same. As we are liberated from our own fear, our presence automatically liberates others.

~ Nelson Mandela

It is easy for us humans to feel insignificant. Yet those who have glimpsed the bigger picture are those who can act upon it. We may know fellow tokens who are more unsure than us about navigating in new waters. It may then be our contribution to inform, inspire and reassure others, with a lot of love and care, through the most interesting epoch of human existence on this planet. Whether we have evolved here or chosen to come for the purpose of changing the world paradigm, it is through our intent, our focus and our hearts that we assist and support this transition.

Share what you believe in, empower yourself through whatever stirs you. Always remember, we are not alone. Picture yourself like the ground crew, receiving assistance from your creation partner up in the tower. Because of the laws of love and freewill we are left to find our own way home. Yet when we ask for answers we open ourselves to receive guidance.

When we start to serve the purpose we came to fulfill, in alignment with our greater journey together, we are rewarded by a sense of peace and contentedness, and become tremendously supported. Do your best to tune into whatever it was you planned to do here. It is what you do best. You have a cosmic contract with yourself. Your destiny is your own freewill.

Er...Me?

NOT SO VERY LONG ago, I wrote to a friend:

> *Seeing the transition ahead, I had been earnestly asking the powers that be what more I could do to serve the world in tune with my own evolution. I could have asked what I could do to have more fun!*
>
> *Well, no good deed ever goes unpunished! Lo and behold, out of the blue, I met this elderly international astrologer. From glancing at my daughter's birth chart, who wasn't with us, he gave an uncannily accurate description of her. He then looked at mine. He is a lovely, perceptive and gentle guy and he didn't beat around the bush:*
>
> *"Your chart is very clear as your planets are in their houses, so life is rather smooth and timely for you. All your five personal planets are in Sagittarius, which gives you strong vision and energy. It puts all your focus on exploration, openness, insight, interconnectedness, spreading light and wisdom. Those five planets are all in the 8th house so the themes of spirituality, transformation, death, resurrection and the beyond are predominant interests in your life."*
>
> *Yes, I had noticed, I am one of those who do not have the luxury to forget that we are on a journey here!*
>
> *"In the past you have allowed yourself to be held down."*
>
> *I nodded. So far, so good.*
>
> *He then said, siriusly,"This set-up makes you the archetypal prophetess. Your job here is to serve as a loving guide, to assist people through the coming transition."*
>
> *Er...me?*
>
> *"It is time to share what you know. You will be very supported in getting your message out there. You should be giving talks."*
>
> *Er....talks? Suddenly, writing the book everyone had been*

telling me to do looked like a good proposition! "Er...could I, maybe... write a book?"

"Excellent, it doesn't have to be a big book."

Good, I thought of something tiny...

"Then you can talk to people..."

At this point I was thinking to myself: Er... could I, maybe...skip that bit? And yet, I knew I couldn't.

"You will also convey your message through art and music."

That, I thought, even sounds like fun!

By then I had so often said, "Life always knows when we are ready, even if we don't" that I had succeeded in convincing even myself. So although I expected I would be kicking and screaming, I didn't. When the time is right we recognize the street sign. Instead of feeling alarmed, I quietly took it on board, simply accepting the inevitable: the time is now.

CHAPTER THIRTY-THREE

The Time is Now

~~~

Yesterday is history, tomorrow a mystery.
Today is a gift… that is why we call it 'the present.'

~ *Eleanor Roosevelt*

THE WORLD doesn't need saving. Yet there may be things we wish to accomplish for our own sake, for our own transformation and peace of mind. Perhaps it is just to make some space in our daily life, to read a good book, to pick up an old guitar again, or to do some quiet contemplation. If you are the more sporty type and such spaces really don't turn you on, then let's just say that these times require us to be on the ball! It is time to do what really matters: what *you* really want to do. From there the answers will come. Tuning into our own inner guidance we will always know the right next step, at the right time.

Taking on life and expansion is our contribution to our own happiness as well as to the whole. It is what we came here for. These are hardly times to consider, maybe, perhaps next year, I'll start to look into it, I'll go on holiday, I'll make the move, I'll follow my dream. We may have put a large part of our lives on hold for a bit, while attending to business, or family or other duties. When we find ourselves sitting in a part of the river that is not flowing, it's time to join the current again. Now is the time to reprioritize, to redefine what is essential to us, so that we make the most of our lives.

Aim for your highest vision for yourself. "Better late than never" has never meant so much. Our dreams await. And yet there is no pressure to reach a goal. The most, in fact all we can do, is to focus on the quality of our present moment. To live with gratitude and love, and to nurture our body, our mind and our spirit.

This is the perfect occasion to expand our borders, and explore areas that are new to us. You don't have to pack all your bags and buy a one way ticket to Timbuktu. Perhaps do some research, connect to people around you, go hiking or dancing, or put on some music and warble along... Or do buy a one way ticket to Timbuktu! Our priority is whatever helps us to reconnect, to release blockages and tensions, and to unburden our minds, our bodies and our hearts. Lighten the load, lighten up and loosen up. When there is really too much to cope with, drop it and go to the pool, the beach or the park. You don't have to save the world singlehanded before breakfast!

To retire sometimes from busyness adds a new perspective to our lives. Contemplation and meditation allow one to experience some of the stillness that is always there, behind all the hustle and bustle of daily activity. It is the stillness from where we draw our real strength. In quietness we remember, and the more we remember, the less we are bound.

IT IS BECAUSE WE HAVE BEEN HALF ASLEEP, caught up in unconscious patterns and dramas and working for a living, that the progress of humanity may appear to be slow. Still, the turtle is getting there! We really had to get to the base of things first: to delve deep into our subconscious cellars, bring in the light and warm them with our hearts. We now re-emerge triumphantly: more conscious, more genuine and more loving than ever before.

Picture the whole body of humanity sleeping. Some cells start to stir out of their slumber. They whisper, shout or sing to their neighboring cells: "Hey, wake up, remember, the dawn awaits..."

"What, me, now? Ok..."

We are all cells of the body of humanity, contributing to our worldwide awakening: "Yes, you, now."

We don't need more time, more preparation, more information or more healing. As soon as we can say to ourselves, "I'm okay now," and feel it, then we are okay now! To open up, to be ourselves as fully as we dare, is all that life is asking from us. We are a bud about to bloom.

Life is a stretch, between our survival instincts, which tell us to hang on to what we know, and our dream, our potential, which beckons us to let go and move on. It is not so difficult to find a path to our highest vision as it is to just take the first step and head for new frontiers, beyond the limits and constraints of our daily life.

"I'll stop working so hard when I've..." Why not now?

"I'll be happy when...I'll love myself when...I'll love my partner when..." Why not now?

We are not used to spontaneously acting on our deep feelings and our impulses. We tend to rationalize, to consider and to ponder, allowing doubts and hesitations to creep in and to discourage and debilitate us. It is time to move from our heads to our hearts ~ to benefit from the guidance of our right mind, our inner self.

Our priority this lifetime is to identify and release those repetitive thought patterns that inhibit the flow by causing the likes of mistrust, apathy or anguish to arise. It is these thoughts that take us out of "the now:" the present moment, our direct doorway to all that is. This is our true work: to each free ourselves so we reconnect to all that we are, and thus shine our light bright to raise the consciousness and the frequency of our planet Earth.

Hint: the cage is not locked.
   ~ Nova Knutson

GREATLY INSTRUMENTAL TO GETTING OURSELVES out of doubt, a sense of powerlessness or hopelessness, is the understanding that all is well with us and the world. Life is a play and everything is on course. We shall soon see that we are being given a tremendous chance to start anew. All we are being asked to contribute is to open our own doors and clear out the old so we are able to receive the gift of love. It is time to put into practice all that we know. It is time to open ourselves to the flow.

I simply cannot emphasize enough the value, the importance, and the rewards of becoming increasingly open to allow the flow through. As we open, in trust, we connect and abundance flows in.

In the same way that each cell in our body lets information and nutrients stream in, and toxins flush out, we open ourselves to recognize our interconnectivity, to receive evolutionary input, and to release stored pain. It is only logical that therefore the membrane of the cell must be soft, for a hardened shell blocks the flow.

Some yogis, believing literally that we each have a limited number of breaths for our life, practice holding their breath as long as possible. We may laugh at this great example of holding back, not daring to live fully. Yet we also hold onto our life energy, our feelings, our dreams and our money, for "later," out of feeling lack or inadequacy, or just waiting for the perfect time.

Songs speak so beautifully:

> *It's the heart afraid of breaking that never takes a chance*
> *It's the dream afraid of waking that never learns to dance*
> *It's the one who won't be taken who never seems to give*
> *And the soul afraid of dying… that never dares to live.*
> ~ Bette Midler, "The Rose"

What if we can't count on "later" being the same? What if later goes beyond our wildest imagination and the only way to reach there is to live and love fully now? What if the *very moment of now* is the only moment that is real, and hence our connection to all that lies within? Remember your dreams, reach for the stars, and invite them into your life through increasing presence. And next time someone asks you for the time, you can simply say, "The time is now."

CHAPTER THIRTY-FOUR

The Renewal

*All you have to do is gently and lovingly take back
your power and wait for the day when the intuitive people,
those with love and caring in their hearts, those with
a true spirituality, will inherit the earth.*

~ *Stuart Wilde*

AS I JOIN gatherings of people from all nations and of all ages, I look around and I feel that we are all brave souls doing, largely unknowingly, a labor of love. This is a unique time of transition, and we are all headed for great transformations. Remember we volunteered for this. Life is a balance of fun and homework, and when we understand what we are doing, that each of us is helping to free the collective human psyche from its burden of self doubt, pain and fear, then even the homework becomes more enjoyable.

This is a time of renewal. It is as though we are being turned inside out, and everything that is not in the vibration of love, every part that is not loved within us, and therefore around us, is making itself known. In increasingly subtle variations, our misgivings are surfacing from deeper levels to be healed. The density of our previous personalities is falling away as we all go through layer after layer of mental and emotional clearing to release the hurts of the human race.

So everywhere people are opening up and exploring new areas, shedding blockages and dropping borders. We are becoming more relaxed and genuine, spontaneous and open, trusting and contemplative. We are blossoming with the help of the cosmos, books, friends, support groups and perhaps, still, the odd kick in the butt.

Our human heart is growing in this way, for we can feel that we are all going through the same process and the same issues. In doing so we are taking down the walls that have stood between us. We come to appreciate and respect each other for our efforts and we birth greater compassion for our fellow humans. See the beauty and the courage in every human life. See the sweetness and the openness of the children all over the world. Many races, many lives, one smile. And as we notice the strength and the warmth of the human heart, we nourish that part within ourselves.

We ran from our pain, but life repeatedly faced us with it until we understood that we carried it within us and we learnt to look at it and to love it. So value the life you have led and all you have gone through, for it has brought you to this threshold in time. You don't need, you wouldn't want, to hang onto your past. Yet it was the way we got here, it was part of the flowering, the bridge that spans from our smallest part to our greatest dream. That journey was beautiful (at least in retrospect!) and its gift has shaped our soul and carries us to new dimensions. For as we dissolve our pain we change our daily reality. And the essence of who we have become will be the seed for a new paradigm.

> *Listen to the tide slowly turning,*
> *washing all our heartaches away,*
> *we are part of the fire that is burning,*
> *from the ashes we can build another day…*
> ~ Moody Blues, lyrics

THESE TIMES ARE ALL ABOUT OUR FLOWERING and our expressing, in a myriad of colorful ways, the fullness of the human spirit. It is up to us to feel out the new ways, for this road is being paved as we walk it. We are on the way to find out how openness, love, and joy, really feel. Feel blessed and honored to be here now, for this life is a packed present that we are unwrapping, layer after layer, to find the gift that lies within.

The tide has turned, the Shift has begun. This is an age of extraordinary potential for us to rise to a brighter dimension of human life. This is the time we have been waiting for: The birth of a new world, more sensitive and more refined, where we can freely express, without fear, the beauty of who we are.

A new world, if we can be it.

Imagine to be, back in a child's world
So free, a clean, beautiful mind
Unscarred, living for the new
With no worries for tomorrow and no regrets for yesterday
No care in the world and a smile always given for free

A brand new dream, untouched, undreamt and unbroken
A lifetime to explore potential
Reach the horizon and touch the sky
Dive the depths of the ocean and smile into the sun

The road is paved by you as you travel it
Your imagination, your map of reality as you perceive to create it
Your life, your vision you dreamt as a spirit soul
Only your heart knows the answers to your deepest questions

Visions mingle to guide each other
Through the sweeping rivers of life
To pool at the oceans of love
Eternally… thoughtlessly… drifting to an unnamed destination
~ a home of souls.

~ Chandra

It Is Time

A bird does not sing because it has an answer.
It sings because it has a song.
~ Chinese proverb

THERE ARE MANY PEOPLE on the planet who are aware, on some level, of the change that is taking place on Earth. The sensitive, the intuitive and the indigenous people can feel it in the air. People of all races and all age groups are gathering together, sharing and spreading the light through ceremony and sacred space, through song and dance, through art and all types of creative expression. We celebrate our wholeness, our diversity and our oneness. We express our humility and our power, our love for ourselves, for each other and for the divine.

Each of us is a unique individual, and each has the light within. You always have something to give: just being you is enough. This is not a time for holding back, but a time to get on the dance floor. Be true to yourself, and express who you are, as quietly or flamboyantly as you feel. Live more through your body and your heart: allow yourself to feel more, let love flow through you, play with water, light and crystals, absorb the sounds of nature and lose yourself in music.

Sing as if no one is listening
Dance as if no one is watching
Love as if you've never been hurt
Live as if heaven is here on Earth.

We are discovering a less mental, more intuitive, experiential existence, like that of a child. Our physical world is moving closer towards the fluidity of the spirit world. Tune in, open up and flow.

Our expression, our creativity, is the offering of what we have become. Humanity shall flower in an explosion of diversity, color, inspiration and love. We shall give ourselves, our journeys and our fullness, our passion and our devotion, up in offering...like the phoenix. And like the phoenix, from the everlasting essence of who we are, we shall be reborn.

MILLIONS OF PEOPLE ON THE PLANET today are working towards this vision, the prophecy of a new dawn. A vision that has been strengthened, formed even, by what we have all gone through. It is the powerful awakening of a dream that is planted deep within our hearts, engraved into our soul. It is the dream of freedom that so many have carried since so long, and now it is time that the fruits of our labor are born. Borne by the wind of change, the changing seasons of the Ages. Be thankful to our forefathers and to all those, from the elders to the youngest of us, who are giving their energy to this transformation. Aligned with the spirit of the Earth, our hearts beating to her pulse, we ride the cosmic wave to a new shore.

The Other Shore

Just like the wind can change direction
Just like the moon changes shape
I was a traveler heading to nowhere
Just like a ship without a sail

Eagles fly across the ocean
Magic islands, you're going home
Meet the woman you've been waiting for
She takes your breath as you walk in through her door

There's complete transformation
As you journey through the night
Feel the love, feel the wind
Feel the fire under your wings

And I will dream eternally
For you to find your way to me
Just like the stars are home to me
Inside your heart I will be

And I will lead you through the door
In time to reach the other shore...

The other shore, a warm embrace
Speaks of affection, and living grace
The other shore, the human heart
Awaits in silence...a brand new start!

CHAPTER THIRTY-FIVE

The Awakening
of the Human Race

*We are in the midst of a momentous event in the evolution of
human consciousness but they won't be talking about it on the
news tonight. On our planet...consciousness is awakening
from the dream of form.*

~ *Eckhart Tolle, A NEW EARTH*

WE ARE LIVING, without any doubt, at the most interesting,
powerful and rewarding era of our human history. We can all feel
a rising intensity, an exponential increase of happening, of knowledge and of awareness.

Our consciousness is rapidly expanding. Our days are filled
with new feelings and insights. There is a growing understanding
of ourselves, each other, and the world; a natural global uniting, a
flowering of cooperation, community and creativity; and a decen-
tralization of power as individuals and groups affirm their own
power of choice. We are waking out of victimhood, shedding limitations, growing in love... remembering. We had all wished and
sought for more in life. We are now discovering, through many
different approaches, that there *is* far more to our life than meets
the eye. That there is, indeed, some energetic interconnectivity behind the scenes of our physical world.

The British Encyclopedia confirms that human evolution is
speeding up. Humanity now learns in one month what just a few
decades ago took us ten years, what a century ago took us 50
years, and previously took us 6000. In 2011 the evolutionary inflow

will increase 20 fold from the previous decade. Consciousness is flooding in. If we follow the curve, we see this cannot just build exponentially forever. What are we gearing up towards? *Where is this mounting awareness leading us to?*

I have been dropping hints all along. If you have started on this chapter looking for information on 2012, I recommend you read a few previous key chapters first. *Beyond the Veil* reveals our own energetic existence, *Change of an Age* introduces "the Quickening" and the Mayan Calendar, *Window into Eternity* describes the "end of time."

We have seen, throughout the pages of this book, and our own lives, how life always supports and guides our awakening. How our struggles keep attuning us to the rising level of consciousness: showing us what is not in balance, redirecting our focus, and steering us to greater harmony, compassion, and self love, where true strength lies. We have recognized that this interactive world reflects our beliefs and stored pain, revealing our own unloved shadow parts so we may recognize them, embrace them, and return to wholeness.

Our entire lives have in fact, through building this relationship to ourselves, been preparing us for this next step. We are now expanding from our personal identity to our collective identity; we are working and uniting together, co-creating the next leap in humanity's evolution: the global Awakening of our human race.

Researchers, visionaries, and ancient prophecies confirm that the end of this current cycle will offer humanity an unparalleled expansion. The flowering of a new age. We can all feel that change is in the air. It's our choice how far we want to take it.

THE DAWNING IS WELL UNDERWAY. We are rapidly awakening to *all* that we are.

We are all becoming ~ every day more aware. Is it not just logical that in some years, due to the exponential curve, when enough people have woken up to our essential spiritual existence, that this enlightening realization then ripples through the Global Mind and awakens the whole body of humanity out of its collective dream: the illusion of existing only in physical reality, in a purely linear time-space dimension?

We have seen that our being always spans a wide range of dimensions, but our mind, our left brain actually, limits us to only being aware of the life we have within our physical body. This has been supportive to our individual development, but we are coming to the end of that gestation phase. We are soon to embrace our own greater existence, our expanded being.

There is nothing scary about reuniting with this inner self. On the contrary! I have described mine and others experiences. It is a homecoming, a merging with our spiritual identity, with our all-knowing higher floors. Accurately speaking, it is not even a reunion because we have never really been separate. We have just been largely unawares of the greater part of our own existence. When the veil lifts we discover that we are truly an eternal, infinite being playing our role here on Earth.

We are not human beings having an occasional
spiritual experience; we are spiritual beings having
an occasional human experience…
~ Deepak Chopra

Who would not want such an inner revelation? It is an eye-opener, a heart-opener, and a new beginning. We get to see the backstage reality ~ the energy realm that is the backdrop of our physical world ~ and how everything works hand in hand. Having long been isolated as separate individuals, this opening will reveal our connectedness, our oneness and our eternal, energetic existence.

The process of this birthing has already begun. We are now in a powerful preparation phase, as we release our restrictive patterns and beliefs, as we open our hearts to ourselves and to each other, and as we open our minds to our world and to our possibilities.

Our current strugglesome, fear-based paradigm is caused by our sense of separation, from our true selves, from each other and from the whole. Yet as we discover the interactive nature of the world, and the underlying connectivity that always coaxes our growth, we heal even our deepest hurts. Our core feelings are shifting. To see, as many have done, beyond our sense of separatism, beyond our limited 3D perception to the space where all unites, will lead to a world beyond fear, force, and struggle. A world that is the reflection of a unified humanity, united beyond abuse and victimhood, beyond duality and suffering. Where we all live aligned with, in harmony with, the one universal life force that is within us all.

A TIME OF GREAT EXPLORATIONS, discovery and fulfillment lies ahead. We are the carriers of change. We are the caterpillar undergoing metamorphosis. We are giving birth to a new world. Recognize that the more we open, *the more we allow to be possible, the more we allow for ourselves.* To make space for the new to come into our lives we do have to clear out the old. By willingly discarding the limiting beliefs and insecurities that keep us small we prepare ourselves to embrace the totality of who we are. If you tell a baby it will soon have to give up its bottle, it may well feel that to be a great sacrifice. Yet, when it reaches that stage, it will be most happy to throw it away to get a cup.

> *I must be willing to give up what I am,*
> *in order to become what I will be.*
> ~ *Albert Einstein*

All growth is a gradual process: a natural release of whatever cramps our expansion. A snake sheds its skin, a seed sheds its shell, a chick cracks its egg. How much choice do we really have in the matter? None. Our choice is not *whether* to follow the river's flow ~ it's *how willingly* we do so!

We have all come a long way in shaking off layers of superimposed conditionings, rigid structures and assumptions. Aligned with the spirit of the times, Eckhart Tolle points to the preparatory work of recognizing our separatist ego identity, its emotional reactivity, and the pain body. This awareness facilitates our freeing, as we shift from our separatist and hence insecure left brain character towards our connected, all-inclusive right brain personality. The old mindset is losing its grip as we are opening daily: releasing old patterns, opinions, judgments, concepts, and social roles ~ all that which is, in fact, not really us.

Truly, we must be willing to give up what we *think* we are, in order to become what we *already* are. It is simply a case of getting out of our own way. In deep meditation too, as on a shamanic journey, the limiting attitudes and structures of our outer character are left on the surface as we access the deeper realms of our being. Like falling asleep or going on holiday, we leave our concerns and our struggles behind. Simply by removing our attention from these outer layers we are put back in touch with our inner essence: carefree and at ease. We lose nothing except that which limits us; we gain what is always within: peace, love and understanding.

As our shells are loosening we feel ourselves becoming less bound. Like buds, we are naturally opening up to the new dawn. We are shifting from our heads to our hearts. All we have to do to blossom, to allow our vibration to be thus heightened, is to shed what is no longer fitting. This is happening spontaneously for we gravitate instinctively towards love and light. If we are sensitive, just following our feelings, it becomes finally impossible these days to do otherwise than to lighten up.

> *Those who tune into the new frequencies will find*
> *life growing more wondrous every day. Those who hang*
> *onto the old, in fear, will find things falling apart.*
> ~ THE STARSEED TRANSMISSIONS

The process of letting go is not necessarily comfy for our "pet human." Some may say, "Well, I prefer the devil I know to the heaven I don't." Yet as always in life, it is far smoother to go with the flow, willingly agreeing to our evolution, than to hold on tightly closed till the end, and therefore have to go through the intensity of the whole dissolution in one go. There is no point clinging to the rocks, while the powerful river of life is flowing towards a beautiful dawn. We may not know where it is going but wherever it is going we are going with it! Return to trust.

> *We cannot reach new horizons*
> *if we do not lose sight of the shore.*

The unknown, however promising, tends to insecure us little humans. Yet this is not the time in our human history to look the other way; it is the prime time to recognize that life has always worked in our favor. From a holistic viewpoint we see that everything is interrelated and, whatever the apparent intention and appearance, works in the same direction: towards our awakening. This realization prompts a vital shift in our core feeling, giving us a fresh outlook of trust and gratitude. It enables us to truly embrace life and the extraordinary events ahead.

If someone had told us years ago we would have to go through the change of an age, the dark night of the soul, face our subconscious shadows, undergo personality meltdown and withstand the obstacle course of threats that are being thrown at us, we would have crept under the carpet! Not only we made it through, we emerged stronger, warmer, and more genuine. Our human evolution is indeed well underway, unfolding in tune with the rising energetic vibration of Earth.

The walls that are coming down are the ones
that have imprisoned us.
~ *Don Alejandro, Head of the Mayan Council of Elders*

While we may still feel the remnants of our old patterns, we are, undoubtedly, all waking up. We can feel rapid changes and inner expansion. We can all feel *something* is in the air, and maybe an increased charge within us. Apart from our own considerable efforts, what is causing this exponential evolution of our species?

Scientifically, our whole solar system is receiving more light energy. In 1961, astronomers detected an unusual nebula of miniature light particles, photons, on a "collision course" with our solar system. It became named the Golden Nebula. It is a highly charged electro-magnetic cloud of photon bands, commonly known as the "photon belt," that covers an immense area of space. In 1997, Russian scientist Dr. Aleskey Dimitriev published a report on the effects of our encounter with this energy belt: heightened warming and an increase of energetic emissions on all planets in our solar system. NASA has now published more than 200 documents on the increase of photons throughout the entire solar system. These are indeed special times we chose to participate in.

It is the Galactic Core, our greater central sun, that pulses these cosmic photon waves spiraling through the galaxy. Carrying high frequencies of light energy, they charge all suns they embrace, directly influencing all surrounding planets. Scientific experiments have shown that light can carry a frequency ~ a resonance, a blueprint ~ that triggers spontaneous evolution by reprogramming DNA. The increase in energetic charge, the accelerated dataflow of light-information within these energy waves, stimulates an evolutionary boost on Earth, thus facilitating our shift in consciousness.

The Galactic Core, our galactic center, can be seen to be, physically and spiritually, our origin, the source of our being. Spiritually seen, the light, the intelligence it radiates, is the light of consciousness itself.

We feel internally the impulse of evolution
as our own desire to evolve.
> ~ Barbara Marx Hubbard,
> *Visions Of A Universal Humanity*

While entering this photon belt, we are also currently moving through a 36 year period that aligns Earth and our sun with our galactic center, and with the "dark rift" in the Milky Way that the Maya called the "birth canal." This occurs every 13,000 years, due to the precession cycle of the equinoxes. Spiritually, on the inner picture, we are aligning with our source. Among other ancient advanced cultures, the Maya foresaw this alignment as a great time of renewal for human beings on Earth.

When I first heard of the Mayan Calendar allegedly ending on the solstice of December 21st 2012, thinking of it as a linear time calendar carved in stone, I came up with the classical, "Well, I guess it had to end somewhere!" In fact, it does not end; it marks the finish of the current world age, and the beginning of the next. Mayan scholars concur that there are no doomsday predictions in the classic Mayan accounts.

*According to the Mayan creation mythology, such cyclic end-
points do not spell a catastrophic end to the world. That is a popular distortion of the true doctrine, mainly intended to pander to
sensationalized marketing plans for books that almost always
distort authentic Mayan traditions. One of these traditions is the
belief that time is cyclic, and the end of a cycle means transformation, renewal and rebirth into the new cycle.*
                                    ~ John Major Jenkins, MAYA COSMOGENESIS

I then proposed that the calendar was carved on a stone disc
~ to symbolize the stone age ending, at long last, in 2012 !~ and the
continuation of Earth's history was carved on a gold disc ~ which
is now either in a sunken galleon or in the vaults of the Vatican.
And indeed, the prophecies of multiple ancient traditions and indigenous cultures, including the Hindu, Hopi, Maya, Zulu, Abo-
riginal, and Waitore, predict not only a new age, but a golden era.
When will *this* be on the evening news? Don't hold your breath.
We can't expect the mainstream media to confirm such things for
us, it is just not their job.

*If one morning I walked on top of the water across
the Potomac River, the headline that afternoon would read:
'President Can't Swim.'*
                                    ~ U.S. President Lyndon Johnson

FOR SOME, 2012 IS STILL A CONSPIRACY THEORY: "Remember
Y2K, nothing happened." Personally, I wouldn't be too surprised
if that particular hype was broadcast partly to trigger precisely
this dismissive response. However, since we are ever more rapidly
becoming the conscious co-creators of our own reality, it is surely
wiser to stay open than to shut off our own possibilities in advance. This is hardly a time to lengthily debate, discuss details, or
wait for scientific proof. When we follow our curiosity, our feelings
and our intuition ~ our own inner source of discernment and wisdom ~ we take our life into our own hands.

We may have recognized throughout our life how the planets
and stars imprint and map our personal frame of mind and evo-

lution. Whether we relate most to astronomy that maps our solar system's journey among the stars, or to ancient spiritual teachings, to the Mayan Calendar's evolving Ages of consciousness, or the studies of our fossil records that show cyclic evolutionary leaps on Earth ~ all these different approaches come to the same conclusion: various massive cycles[1] can be seen to "end" around the same time. This time is now.

Note though that *it is in the nature of a cycle that it does not end.* It just reaches its completion point from whence the new cycle begins. The night turns to day, the winter turns to spring. The acorn becomes an oak.

BECAUSE THE MAYAN CALENDAR records colossal cycles in astronomy and human evolution ~ and these also have to be transposed onto the Gregorian calendar ~ it is difficult to pinpoint the completion of these cycles onto a certain date. Dr. Carl Calleman counts the cumulative eras of the Mayan Calendar to converge at the end of October 2011. Some sources speak of the December solstice, 2011. Most commonly cited is the December solstice of 2012. Drunvalo Melchizedek, the genuine spokesperson for the Mayan Council of Elders, relays that the window of opportunity within which the Shift will occur is open until 2015. His feeling suggests sooner rather than later. However, concerning with a certain "end date" can put the focus outside of ourselves and distract our attention from our own awakening where *we are currently co-creating* the happening through our daily feelings and actions.

Speaking of co-creation, some ancient traditions tell of great transformation being preceded by a period of purification. We know well from our own lives, especially in these times, that every renewal requires a cleanse: a clearing of old beliefs, old patterns, old structures. Visionary researchers propose that the huge upheavals some predicted to birth the golden age are precisely what

---

[1] The 26,000 years precession cycle of the equinoxes; the 225-250 million years cycle of our solar system's galactic orbit; Dr. David Raup's and Dr. James Sepkoski's 26 million years, and Dr. Robert Rohde's 62 million years evolutionary cycles discovered in Earth's fossil records.

314 THE POWER OF THE HUMAN HEART

we are now going through: a considerable shift in the human psyche. My own inner guidance tells me that earth-shaking changes are instrumental to move us and release blocked energy ~ hence they are only necessary if we obstruct energy from flowing freely.

If "2012" brings up images of doomsday from the Bible's Revelations, from YouTube or from "alternative" or "leaked" information, or if you've been watching the wrong movies, that's okay. Fear can prompt us to further enquiry and discoveries. Looking logically, the probability factor that an obscure planet X comes hurtling through space at this precise time of cyclic convergence to wipe out planet Earth is, still understated, rather less than infinitesimal. It is possible that fearful distractions of various kinds will continue to be used in an attempt to maintain the survivalist mindset.

Yet fear is often the fuel for our opening and for our transformation. It is a catalyst that pushes us beyond ourselves. At first we close and cling tighter, but eventually it helps us to open and gives us the get-up-and-(let)go. Finally everything serves our growth, all roads lead to our evolution. The beauty of the design is that our flowering is inevitable.

SO, NO DOOM AND GLOOM AT ALL? Perhaps, before the turn of the century, we were headed on a path to destruction. It is a path we would never reach the end of. Same as in a nightmare: when things get too bad we either become lucid or wake up ~ and recognize it was of our own making. In the same way that we each carve our lives and destiny by the choices we make, we averted potentially glum and gloomy possibilities for the planet by transcending the need for that reflection. Enough people all over the globe woke up and took their own lives and our world situation into their own hands. By doing so we steered humanity onto a new timeline where a new paradigm, a new way of being, awaits. It still remains our individual choice whether we follow our hearts and step onto that timeline.

It is a clear fact that "apocalypse" does not indicate catastrophes. The Greek root of the word "apokalypto" means *to reveal*, to uncover. The long foreseen "apocalypse" is the revealing, the unveiling.

Anyone awaiting for catastrophes will be disappointed as the
main event will take place inside of all of the ones ready for it.
~ *Mads Larsen, quoted by JM Jenkins*

Logically enough, as with any new discovery, any revelation,
we shall each take on board just what we are open to receive. This
is why we want to unburden and expand our minds and our
hearts.

The end of time will be very much like a strong wind that
passes over a calm sea and only those boats who have their sails
unfurled and are prepared will notice the effects of the wind.
~ *Wingmakers*

An unfurled sail indicates our openness, our readiness, our
willingness to go with the wind. Sometimes I do wonder if we
shall all get this Insight, or whether we may end up in parallel
worlds. Other times I see us all laughing, in retrospect, at the
thought that *anyone* could have missed THAT!

Pulsing from our Galactic Core, the cosmic energy wave, the
luminous photon belt, is at an ever-increasing rate en-light-ening
our solar system. Our inner awakening is stimulated, our awareness is heightened. We may well already feel that the mounting
intensity of changes and realizations these days is leading us up to
a threshold. Indeed, the rapid transformation taking place in humanity's psyche will culminate in a vast opening ~ the birth of a
new state of consciousness.

"APOCALYPSE" MEANING REVELATION, what is there about our
life that is yet to be revealed? Our own energetic existence.

Few yet suspect the magnitude of the Insight in store. If you
say I am taking this seriously, I stand guilty of the charge! We are
only talking about the most extraordinary, amazing, breathtaking,
awesome, and magnificent happening in the history of Earth. And
yet, it is simple.

The stream of conscious energy that is flooding Earth is already opening our inner eye and carrying us into a lighter vibra-

tion. As we release our burdens and our borders we shall all have, through an inner revelation, *the direct experience* of who we are at our essence: eternal spirit beings, united in our oneness.

> *Cycle endings such as the galactic alignment in 2012*
> *can be understood spiritually as an opportunity for human*
> *beings to reunite with their higher divine source.*
> ~ *John Major Jenkins*

In this interval within the zone of no-time, we access the state of all-knowing Consciousness. It is the discovery of our own life force, our own greater identity; a vast sense of self in the quiet, peace-filled, feeling of infinity. This is the "opening of the worlds," an inner opening beyond 3D. This is the end of our illusion of being purely physical, separate, mortal beings, the end of duality.

Our blinkers, our beliefs, our interpretations and our concepts will be shed. We will recognize through this most enlightening insight that we have been living in the womb of 3D: "dreaming," entranced in the play, believing the restrictions of the virtual-reality game Eartheyland to be our only reality. From that cosmic perspective we will see our life reviews and the interconnectivity of all life, and will come to recognize the oneness of our spirit: the unified being of humanity.

Do not expect the sky to roll open. This is an inner initiation. It is the touch of Grace, the kiss of life, a gift of love.

A LOVING RELATIONSHIP TO ourselves and an open mind are all we need to receive, integrate and maintain the higher vibration of cosmic awareness, peace and love that shall flood us. We will discover our internal, immortal reality without leaving our body or the physical plane.

Downloads of innate knowledge occur during such a journey and our conscious mind is certainly not able to grasp, comprehend or integrate it all. Nor does it have to. As the three experiences described in *Beyond the Veil* illustrate, there's no need to prepare anything really because we receive all understanding in that moment. It is likely that full awareness will come in waves to those who need time for integration.

> *At the moment a cycle reaches its end or culmination point, the*
> *still point manifests, time ceases and incarnated beings who are*
> *usually fated to always live within the field of duality and*
> *causality can catch a glimpse of eternity.*
> ~ John Major Jenkins

When the universe reaches maximum expansion it starts the cycle of contraction. These cycles are described in Hinduism as the out-breath and in-breath of god. The out-breath is the cycle of separation: manifesting into form, into matter. The in-breath is the cycle of transcendence, the return to unity, to oneness. In the mid-point between the two, there is a gap: time stands still. In other words, we will all enter "the now," we will all become totally present.

We have seen that "the now" is a crack between the worlds, a portal into another dimension. In its seemingly brief flicker, the lid lifts and we find ourselves in the spaciousness of the timeless zone, with all the time in the world. This is the state of full consciousness, without the limitations of our left brain, beyond linear time-space perception; the state of no-mind in which we experience eternity: the end of time.

WORDS BETRAY THE SIMPLICITY of this state. The sense of peace and "ah-ha ~ of course, how could I possibly have forgotten?" It is the state of direct experience. It is the consciousness of a small child, immersed in oneness. *Become like little children to enter the kingdom of heaven.*

We are making this step into timelessness collectively. Once outside of time-space, we are one with all that is. Everything blends together as we reunite with other planes and those on "the other side." We reconnect to the playful, expanded self that is our spirit, and the collective consciousness of humanity ~ both a part of, and one with, the Whole.

It can be described as the merging of the subtle planes with physical reality, a hyper-dimensional convergence, the interlacing of the celestial dimensions with 3D, the "opening of the worlds," or a multidimensional portal. You may be thinking: did I really sign up for this? Rest assured. We did. Willingly. Now that could either testify to our qualifications or to the excellent advertising talents of the celestial marketing board for Eartheyland!

OUR LANGUAGE CANNOT PORTRAY these expanded, ethereal spaces. It sounds like something outside of and beyond us. Yet the larger part of us, our own "higher floors" that we can tap into through meditation, already exists in these brighter frequency realms: It is all within us. The vibration is higher, lighter, not because it is ethically better but because there is less separation, and hence less fear. All language and all our conceptual pictures and understandings fall short. They only point the way to that which is beyond words. When all else that stands between us and our divine essence is shed, love is all that remains.

> *Love never faileth: but whether there be prophecies they shall fail, whether there be tongues they shall cease; whether there be knowledge it shall vanish away. For we know in part and we prophesy in part. But when that which is perfect is come, that which is in part shall be done away.*
> ~ *1 Corinthians 13, quoted in 2012: THE RETURN OF QUETZACOATYL by Daniel Pinchbeck*

This inner revelation of our infinite, eternal and unified energetic existence will forever change the way we feel, think and interact. All those who have had Near Death Experiences report how it changed their lives. Now imagine when everyone has had such a glimpse... That alone would change the world.

CHAPTER THIRTY-SIX

A Gift of Love

What the caterpillar calls the end of the world,
the master calls a butterfly.

~ *Richard Bach,* ILLUSIONS

THIS IS AN AMAZING time in humanity's long journey. Be proud to be part of this transition, this extraordinary portal of opportunity for which souls are flocking to Earth. We came to transform ourselves and, while we're at it, the planet ~ let's do so with style and enthusiasm.

If it feels like, once again, Life is what happens while we are busy making other plans... recognize that we wrote the script. We all wanted to change the world. We didn't realize just how powerful our group intention is! *The power of the human heart is nothing less than astronomical.*

It seems that they really took us seriously up there and are offering us sizeable changes. Not quite what we were thinking of perhaps...like some small changes in our figure, in our bank account, or in social structure...but the real thing. The surprising simplicity, the clarity and profundity of this cosmic revelation will forever alter our view on life. Our minds and hearts will be stretched, never to return to their current shape, never again to fit into the box.

Of course we may feel we are not quite ready and we are finding out a bit late. We may have had other plans for Christmas 2012! Our situation reminds me of discovering I was pregnant at six months, and then spending the first two weeks of my remaining time in denial. Yet life always delivers the next stage when we are ready, and whether we feel that we are or not, a significant part of us *is*. Learning to trust life more, we take what it hands us as a cosmic exercise in acceptance ~ once we do take the offer on board it is very empowering.

The word surrender has to us a negative connotation. But in fact it is most beautiful, because it is a doorway to the beyond. Surrender is full acceptance, allowance and approval of the way things are. It is the recognition that there is absolute intelligence behind the workings of the universe. It is our devotion, our total trust and our complete let go.

This direct initiation goes beyond anything we could aspire for ourselves. If you feel you haven't yet fulfilled all your other dreams, or have missed out in life, don't worry, this is just the beginning! Life so far has been the school, now we really start living. Allow yourself to feel excited. The most extraordinary and fulfilling period of our lives is just ahead.

On one level, *we are creating this happening through our readiness*. This Insight, this Awakening, is our graduation day. Our own journey of self discovery and growing in love culminates in the recognition of our spiritual identity. Already we are birthing our new state of being, where we all can live in the awareness of our connected, collective, and energetic existence.

Our entire lives have been a preparation, an embryonic period of gestation, in the enclosed darkness of the womb. Looking at it from the perspective of a chick, we soon get to peep out of the egg. Wow…is that what is all out there? Then we hop out and have a bit of a run around, stretching our legs and enjoying our newly found freedom. It's a brand new life and a lot to discover. We have all chosen to take part in this transformation and to receive its gift, a gift of love that we have all worked for ~ the keys to a new world.

Keys to a New World

SPEAKING OF PREPARATION, where is the place to be for this global awakening? The Med? The mountains? Over the moon? The best place to be is grounded in our heart. Our comfort is in our integrity, our anticipation, our gratitude, and our vision. To align with *our own evolution* is the safest spot on the globe.

There are groups and pockets in every country in the world where like-minded people are spontaneously gathering, knowingly or not, to facilitate their preparation and transformational work. We are naturally, from our beliefs, our focus and our vibration, attracted to people and places of the same resonance.

I was never sure if the tiny New Delhi office "Panicker's Travels" was really a good marketing name for a travel agency or not, but my experience in life shows me there is seldom a reason to panic. If it feels like a desperate move, it probably is. We don't have to all retreat hastily to the hills with a beginner's guide to meditation and a survival handbook. The appropriate action, the best choice, always feels right, feels easy.

You may think you have little or no control over an event of such magnificent proportions. Think again. As always, multiple realities are open to us. What we get depends, as in everyday life, on us. We will naturally gravitate, as we always do, towards where we fit: whatever we truly resonate with and believe to be possible. You are a co-creator: what you believe becomes your reality.

Argue for your limitations, and sure enough they're yours.
~ *Richard Bach,* ILLUSIONS

Within the frame of any paradigm is a wide range of possibilities: multiple realities to choose from. I spent long periods of my life living simply, for next to nothing, in lovely beach locations. Tourists on holiday there, preparing to return to work and the city life, would often say, "Well, one has to go back to reality." Realities are not in short supply. It is truly a case of, as in the witty book title by Wayne Dyer: *You'll See It When You Believe It.*

Move from a sense of foreboding to excited anticipation. By tuning into a positive reality, it becomes your reality. This is not doom and gloom. It is the most grandiose moment in human history.
~ *David Wilcock*

We have spent our whole lives to get to this point. Now is the time to give it our best shot. Our vote, our readiness, counts. If life feels like it has been a bit of a push, perhaps our player part knew we had a deadline. As we well know, deadlines help us to achieve our goals! Our dreams and aspirations are calling for fulfillment: they remind us of our path, the task we chose. The opportunity offered is up to us to fulfill: A new world if we can take it, create it, *be* it. This is our chance to become the change we so much desire. This is our contribution.

The current world picture still reflects some of our stored pain. We raise this vibration by acknowledging and healing *our own* hurts. By embracing our own shadows, and *choosing* a more encompassing and holistic outlook, we introduce lighter feelings into our life. As inseparable parts of the one human consciousness, we do this for ourselves and for all humanity.

As our own shift of feelings greatly affects our daily life and those around us, so too our collective shift of feeling, our planetary change of heart and mind, leads us to an entirely new reality. The opening of this doorway is already being felt in our lives. The veil is lifting.

WITHIN "THE OPENING OF THE WORLDS," the multidimensional window calculated to peak on a global scale in end 2011-2012, we will have a unique opportunity to shift to a new paradigm. The Hopi describe this shift as being created by the "unfulfilled longing of humanity" ~ a longing born from all that we have lived. The exact nature of this new world is not as important as our desire for it. Our highest vision will lead us through the days ahead. It is time to find it back, dust it off, and place it close to our heart.

> We always attract into our lives whatever we
> think about most, believe in most strongly,
> expect on the deepest level, and imagine most vividly.
> ~ Shakti Gawain

This is our chance to launch a new way of life, a totally new form of existence that is beyond abuse and suffering. Hence it is vital for us to shed, for once and for all, the hurts and the victimhood that caused our strugglesome and abusive world paradigm. By now we indeed know that we are not hapless victims of fate but co-creators of our reality: past, present and future. We are no longer held in the belief that life is all, and for always, about separation, struggle, and survival. We are shaking off the shackles that have bound us in doubt and mistrust, busting the seams of this fear-based paradigm, breaking out of the box. We all have different walkabouts yet *we are all on the same journey.* We are *all* shifting the human psyche from fight to peace, from hurt to appreciation, from slumber to awakening ~ from resistance to accepting the guiding nature of life, our mirror.

> *The more you trust that it is all for your higher good,*
> *the more life will reflect that belief. That is the essence*
> *of spiritual truth right there.*
> ~ David Wilcock

When we express this trust through our daily decisions, in our relationships and through our gratitude, our life becomes most clearly supported and aligned. We come to see that each of us has been given, indeed is, a piece of the puzzle. Each has their place and their contribution in Life's Play, each is of value. This is the ultimate healing of our hearts. As we appreciate every person for their part in our own journey, our own awakening, we start to glimpse the bigger picture. Humanity's journey has been a colossal team effort.

> *A main goal in our lives is to increase our ability and capacity to*
> *love. We have designed our lives with challenges… It is impera-*
> *tive we do not fear the challenges we have attracted to ourselves*
> *in order to promote growth. Armed with gratitude and good*

cheer there is no mountain we cannot climb in order to reach the
pinnacle of our spiritual power, as a Force of One.
                              ~ Dannion and Kathryn Brinkley

We are soon to recognize ourselves as part of the one Being
that is Humanity. At the end of this World Age, the end of this
round, the reset button is being pushed. As we return to pure potential, to the source of our being, we create a brand new game.
A new paradigm that is programmed by our hearts.

This is the dawn ~ of a brand new world
With my body and mind, with my heart and soul
I embrace a new way of living, a new way of giving,
and I release the old
With my body and mind, with my heart and soul
I embrace a new way of being, a new way of seeing,
and I release the old
We're stepping into Eternity,
with our minds and hearts set free
We're stepping into Eternity
We are embracing Reality.
                              ~ Kevin James lyrics, ONE

In this revelation I name the Awakening, we find ourselves in
the state of sentient awareness, of pure consciousness. Some may
feel this to be a visitation, the presence of a "super-being," while
others will recognize it as their own expanded, infinite consciousness. How much we can merge with that, how much we can take
on board, depends on our individual mindset and heartspace.
Wherever there is matching resonance, wherever there is an open
heart and mind that agrees with the vibration of the living spirit
within, a vibration of love and totality... the creator slips inside
creation. The ocean falls into the dewdrop.

DUE TO OUR INTERCONNECTEDNESS, a small critical mass of the
world population is enough to receive and stabilize this new, energetically higher frequency on Earth. As one spirit, one conscious-

ness, the whole of humanity will gradually shift to a totally new level of awareness.

~~~~~

As we start to glimpse the scope and the awe of this Initiation, this enlivening touch, we feel the blessing of this lifetime. Any transformation takes us beyond who we are. We surpass ourselves when we surrender: *this is the power that creates new life.* Birthing does not have to be uncomfortable, it can well be ecstatic. It just asks for our full agreement, our willingness to open and to give ourselves to go beyond. Our evolution is a natural process. The caterpillar doesn't need an instruction manual, or any help, to become a butterfly.

Yet do not shun or block your fears, for only by going through them, through the tunnel, do we come out the other side. Fear can bring us to the doorway where it transmutes. When we accept it, we surrender, we let down our walls, our resistance. In doing so we open ourselves to feel the love that is always there. We step across the threshold.

Any insecurity over this transformation we call "2012" gives us the drive to face our deepest fears and to get through them. It stimulates us to live, love and learn to let go. It may well be the very push that launches humanity into a new dimension.

Because of the non linear, fractal nature of time, the fact that 2012 marks the "end of time" shows that we reached, we achieved, we did it. Phase One of the human experiment, our individual awakening, is already completed: the calendar marks the end of that long epoch. So while we are working ourselves there, bear in mind that the result is, on another level, already accomplished.

It is great to know that "time is not linear," "reality is beyond duality," and "all is One"… still, we do want to stay close to our small parts, lest we leave them behind in the flood of exciting influx that is reaching us. There is a risk of flying too high, "Yeay, I'm off to the fifth dimension!" when our small part may not want to be going anywhere at all. Remember fear is in the gap, so familiarize yourself with the idea. It's a matter of heart to inform our-selves and to relate to the kid within and make sure it is comfort-able. Our littlest part may first seize up or attempt to hang onto something familiar. A rush on the emergency chocolate stash is al-lowed! Emotionally, we bridge the gap as we build our inner rela-tionship.

Our spirit is rearing to go, our mind may be collecting data, our inner child wants its hand held. Return to softness, return to now. Although we are of course one, this dualistic picture still serves our inner reunion and integration. Integrity is to acknowl-edge all our parts and to become in agreement with ourselves. Recognize the part within you and others that may well be scared. If part of us is kept in the dark, is in denial or on strike, we are de-prived of its support.

Maybe tack some tips on the fridge door:

Relax.

There is no point resisting life. It won't go away.

We never feel ready for what life gives us, yet we always are.

It's the best thing that could possibly happen to us.

We have already reached, we just have to get there.

Our heart is our anchor, our compass and our sail.

Our heart will always connect us to those we love.

We cannot do or be any more than we are in the present moment.

Keep your feet on the ground, your eyes on the horizon, and your spirits high.

Whatever happens, don't lose your sense of humor!

Although we may sometimes feel small and confused, as though we just got stuck on the board, remember Eartheyland is the game we chose to play. We are not alone here. We are always connected to our inner spirit player and hence up to *whatever* is going on. We are the means through which spirit is playing in mat-ter. Tune in for advice, and trust where it moves you to. Tune in also to its detached and playful feeling of "let's see how life un-folds." Be open, flexible and available ~ we are always guided.

Part of our inner relationship is learning to hear and to trust our in-tuition. It is always there for us, a direct message from our higher self. To focus our attention on the present moment is the way to tune out the mindfog and tune into our inner knowing. "The now" is our link to the totality of our being. Through our presence, through *gentle* focus on the moment, we connect to the sacred energy of who we are. When we switch our attention off our concerns and onto what we are doing this very moment, we may slip into the spacious state of direct experience.

If feeling overwhelmed, center on your heart, on here and now. We can always cope with the present moment. At one stage in life, when feeling seriously overloaded and under pressure, I realized that everything on my to-do-list was there because I had put it there. I cleared all that wasn't beneficial to my fulfillment and fun, and I am rather careful now what I all take on.

By putting "2012" on your priority list you are surely backing the winning horse. In fact, it quite alleviates matters by putting life in perspective. Lesser concerns fall by the wayside, our "problems" and petty differences become real small. It encourages us to make life-affirming choices and to align our daily activities with our vision. If we want to get somewhere, we do have to walk in that direction! Our future always depends on our decisions, our will, our focus, and our intent.

HOW CAN WE PREPARE though for what we do not yet know? Our situation reminds me of a most cryptic sign that was painted on the wall of an Indian restaurant: "Customers are expected to know the prices of items not on the menu." *Er...okay...* Not knowing where we are going actually incites us to live more fully *now*. Instead of surviving, just carrying on by default, we *choose* to live, we choose to thrive. We can no longer afford not to notice the feelings we hold and emit. The sensation we call joy is the frequency of the energy that is our spiritual being.

Do what you love. Be with those you love. We express our love in how we care for ourselves, others and our planet. As we open, we feel the intensity of the rising energy coming through us. Ground yourself in your heart and in the present. Feel your connectedness

~ through nature, friends, music, laughter, and sacred space. Tap into trust, be attentive, and be gentle on yourself and others. Listen to the elders, for they hold the gift of experience. Listen to the younger generation, they are the bringers of this new dawn.

As we move through the twilight days of our current world paradigm, bear in mind that we are all creating this transition with the power of our hearts and our dreams. Our vision is the fuel for our work here, our love is the spark. *See that all we do is in preparation, feel that all we do is in celebration.* Be grateful for this life and the tremendous, awesome, unparalleled opportunity to be serving and creating this transition from the old age to the new. We will see that being on Earth at this time is truly a gift. Honor it. Gratitude, appreciation, and self love are our keys.

From Separation to Oneness

> *A spiritual person isn't one who knows a lot,*
> *it is one whose heart is awakened.*

ALTHOUGH NO PREPARATION IS NECESSARY ~ for we can achieve through grace, or surrender, maximum openness in an instant ~ we do well to clear the way for ourselves, as it makes the road easier. We expand our hearts and minds not with conceptual information but just with our willingness to go with the stream. By softening our shells we adjust our own vibration to invite more flow through us. We do not need a degree in theoretical physics, or a diploma in Vedic philosophy, or even a million bucks. All we really need here is an open heart: the sensitivity to feel any leftover pain, the love to embrace it and the trust to move on.

Since that is our work here ~ to expand, to enlighten, to dissolve mistrust, fear, and pain ~ we are being continuously faced with any remaining shadow feelings within us. We want to become familiar with all these traits so we do not condemn them. This heals our hearts and hence facilitates our opening. It gives us a steady core of inner connectedness and calm through which we can best receive, assimilate and integrate the increasing influx of conscious energy. This is our essential groundwork.

    We can not just expect to be redeemed by Grace. It is up to *us* to redeem ourselves ~ with our own compassion. We don't have to be saints ~ just naturally kind is enough. See that the way we feel about others is the measure, the reflection of our own self judgment. Don't hold your breath for the sky to open and an irate God to strike down "the faithless" ~ such as all the good people who have been brought up in different cultures, or never even heard of JC! Everything lies within us. Although we may well experience other higher beings depending on our beliefs, this Awakening, this "download," is first and foremost an inner initiation. Through it we will experience unconditional love ~ and we want our own feelings to agree, to identify and to resonate with that higher frequency. How we instinctively merge with that vibration is the only Judgment.

    Logically enough, if we condemn ourselves we recreate our own suffering. When we finally bear, out of compassion, our own self approval and hence a loving outlook, we rise above hurt and blame to a new frequency. We can then welcome, feel worthy of, and take on, far greater love.

    Recognize that you always did your best. Value yourself for your efforts. The unconditional heart accepts all our parts, without condemnation of our weaknesses and insecurities. All our traits are a necessary part of the Play. It is our hurts that have empowered us all to become healers; it is our own shadows that have enabled us to expand, and to stretch our capacity to love.

    It is the contrast of colors that creates a picture. It is the play of the sun and the shade that is beautiful. Pure light is formless, pure matter is lifeless. Together they create *life forms*.

~

WE ARE, INDEED, COMING TO THE END of this particular, dualistic theme park. In the same way we allow what lies within us, we allow the world changes taking place. We thus spare ourselves the struggle inherent in attachment and resistance. Already we can see the old and the new world living side by side. When we put our focus not on upholding the old but on assisting the new, we are of the most service to the transition and to our fellow humans. As our own breakdowns are followed by breakthroughs, the deepest point is always a narrow gateway to a new era. It is our birth canal. We do well to welcome this 11th hour, the perfect global situation where our leftover un-dealt-with issues and feelings surface to be healed.

> *These times can look dark and troubled, but remember: the brighter the light, the darker the shadows. It is because we have already done the first steps in self love, that embracing the collective shadow is simply the next thing on the list.*

It is the darkest before the dawn. Yet the sun has already risen. Daily, because of the time it takes the light to reach us, the sun rises a while before we see it emerge from beyond the horizon.

As WITHIN THE BODY of a caterpillar when it begins to metamorphose, the first "human cells" that started to mutate, decades ago, were also bumped off by the "immune" system in a vain attempt to maintain the status quo of the existing paradigm. Yet as too many cells transformed too fast, it finally had to surrender to the inevitable transformation.

Cells multiply by doubling. One cell divides to make two, the two become four, the four become eight, and so forth. Because of the resulting exponential curve it can look like the end result is very far away when it is, in fact, very close. *A few moments before a test tube of cell cultures is full it will still appear almost empty.* Just one moment before it is full, the tube will still be half empty. Yet, with the last doubling, within an instant, it becomes filled.

As the caterpillar, before it cocoons, rushes frantically around in apparent confusion, so the activity on Earth may look now: senseless and scattered. In the same way, water molecules go into chaotic unpredictable movement just before they boil, and then crystallize at boiling point, out of the chaos, into a perfect geometric shape.

Yes, there will be a new world order. It will come through natural evolution. It will simply be a new world, in order, in harmony with our intrinsic Intelligence.

The caterpillar becomes a butterfly.

~

WE HAVE ALL HAD TIMES WHEN WE LOST FAITH ~ in ourselves, others, and our world. Through misunderstanding and mounting mistrust we fell ever deeper into the feeling of separation. This feeling is at the root of all pain. Once we recognized the degree of our connectedness, and that we are the source of our reality, we started to understand the game and hence to enjoy it more. Now we are on a journey of discovery of our interactive world, a journey of reunion and reconciliation with ourselves and with each other ~ the many facets of the one Being that we are.

Every child comes from the state of oneness. We grew in increasing separation, steered to focus on our inner relationship. Now we are ready to meet and merge with our own higher self. Each of us is returning towards the state of unity with all that is. For we have lived and we have grown, and we have come to embrace the understanding that, despite appearances, all is one and all is love. And in truth, we have never really been separate, for the whole is an extension of ourselves.

Our heart is our stargate to other realms. Our soul calls us to remember the land from whence we came. It was humankind's increasing belief in separation, and the accumulated hurt and fear thus generated, that caused us to "fall" to a denser level of existence, creating the current world reflection: a survival paradigm that includes the need for physical sustenance, pain, sickness and death.

It was not always so, nor shall it remain to be. For our spiritual immortality is a given. Once we realize that this is the case, and that there is indeed never failure but just our own judgment, never punishment but just reflection, never separation but just illusion, then the physical plane will reflect that understanding. The material world is always our mirror.

The physical realm is absorbing, exponentially, the higher frequency of consciousness. We have all been integrating, embedding, our spirit deeper into the material plane. It is through our work, our lives, that we are transforming in our very cells, knowingly or not, the laws of matter. This is where we are headed.

WE ARE BEING OFFERED MORE THAN than just a gradual, progressive change, *we are being offered a leap in evolution.* How far are we willing to go?

We have seen that because matter is intrinsically energetic, factually "dense energy," it can be rearranged by vibration: the higher the frequency wave, the more complex the pattern formed. In the same way, as the vibrational level rises we evolve to more complex beings.

We do not need to leave our bodies. Rather, our spiritual identity is merging more fully with our physical body. As it does, our bodies reflect this increase of energetic charge. We have all seen enhanced radiance, on a small scale, when someone is in love or bliss. So far we are like light bulbs that have been on very dim. As our spirit enters more deeply, or rather, emerges more visibly, the power is being amped up to full brightness. As we become less resistant, less dense, we are filled with more and more spirit-light. Esoteric scriptures speak of bodies of light. We are on the brink of, we are already undergoing, an energetic in-lightenment.

This is not magic, it's just that our current minds cannot quite conceive of radical changes. It is time now for an evolutionary leap in our linear thinking because this is what is on offer!

We have long been divided, separated from seeing our own divine essence. Through the Awakening we shall become aware of the totality of our being. We will then be able to maintain the awareness of our multidimensional existence, our cosmic identity, while remaining in physical form. We will function in two realities at once, part of our attention focused on our spirit nature and part on our form identity.

It seems likely that some will easily integrate this new state of cognition while others will stretch to this capacity over time. If I had not had some, albeit minimal, experience of this, I would think this is science fiction, out of reach. It is really not. It is our own current state of *full* being of which we are now simply unaware. It is our state of maturity. A baby eagle does not know how it feels to be a bird before it takes off, for the first time, to the limitless sky.

PERHAPS WE HAVE BEEN CLOSER to this state of awareness before. If there was a fall... nothing makes one appreciate one's freedom more than having lost it! There is certainly monumental and legendary evidence of previous high civilizations that were further advanced than we are now.

There is also living proof on our planet today of people who have what we see as "superhuman" abilities, mentally, physically and psychically. Yet once we recognize the underlying and interconnected energetic base of our being, these skills are no longer unbelievable or unexplainable. Psychic and "paranormal" experiences are considered normal in many indigenous, right-brained, cultures. As we open up, they are now becoming increasingly common. ESP capacities, such as telepathy, clairvoyance, or psychic healing are not only achievable but the inherent potential within each of us. It awaits in the 90% of brain capacity we do not yet use, in the 97% of dormant DNA.

Our DNA is our inherent set of instructions, our "software." Science shows that light carries information that can regenerate and rejuvenate cells, "rewrite" DNA and evolve biological life. (See data in Appendix II.) Thus life forms throughout our solar system are being affected by the current evolutionary boost. Vital organs, like the pinecone-shaped pineal gland, our "third eye" that receives light information and uploads it to the brain, are expected to become fully activated. Rather intriguingly, there is a huge statue of a pinecone, of all things, in the courtyard of the Vatican. The pinecone design is commonly found in ancient and contemporary religious symbolism and artifacts. We are still uninformed of the physiological and spiritual function of this vital organ, the very first part of the human embryo that develops.

BOTH PHYSICALLY AND SPIRITUALLY, the sun en-lightens us. Spiritually speaking, light is consciousness. It is with light that we can see. It is a logical universe. Once we grasp the reflective, multi-layered, and fractal nature of life, it makes total sense that since the sun feeds our existence on a physical level, it is the same energetically. Picture it as a Being of vast consciousness, our own consciousness, the "male" consort of mother Earth which responds to its life-giving light-information with bountiful fertility and creativity. See the sun as our spirit, the Earth as our body. You are not far off. The sun gives the matter of Earth the kiss of life, the gift of consciousness.

The center of our galaxy, our core, our source, transmits light-intelligence far and wide through a network of stars. When we recognize that our sun transmits evolutionary light data from our source to our very cells, then the current and predicted increase of solar activity is not alarming.

It has also since long been foreseen that the far greater energy of the photon belt will neutralize Earth's current electro-magnetic field. I see Earth's shield as our eggshell, our seed capsule. It is similar to the left brain, the current matrix of the planet ~ that which binds us in 3D with a linear view of time and space. It is now monitored to be rapidly "weakening." The box is opening.

Now it appears to be, due to the interactive nature of our world, that the collective power of our hearts is instrumental in this change. We cannot transcend what we condemn. It is our growing in approval and appreciation of ourselves, others and the world ~ the expansion of our hearts ~ that dissolves all bonds and enables us to see beyond this fear-based dimension. As our feelings shift, so does our worldly reflection.

We caught a glimpse in chapter eight of how our feelings and wishpower affect our own electro-magnetic vibration, which is also part of our planetary field. Gregg Braden, a former scientist and aerospace senior engineer, now a down-to-earth, broad-spectrum researcher and visionary, confirms that Earth's field is influenced by the emissions of the human heart.

> In our society we've been conditioned to believe that
> feelings and emotions are ineffective. Men have largely been
> told not to have them, and women have been told, 'If you
> are going to have them, go have them somewhere else where
> it won't bother anyone!'
>
> ~ Gregg Braden

However, we can well testify that what most influences our daily lives is not truly the weather, our knowledge, social position or bank account, but really *how we feel*. Gregg presents scientific data that shows the human heart to be the largest generator of electrical and magnetic fields in the body. Our heart's electrical field is about 100 times stronger than that of our brain, while its magnetic field is *5000 times stronger*. This is why it is our feelings, far more than our thoughts, that influence what we attract into our lives. We now discover that they affect not only our own reality but, on a larger scale, the very fabric of our physical world.

> *Our world is made of electromagnetic fields of information…*
> *Our own physics textbooks say that if you want to change the*
> *atoms of physical matter, you have to change either the electrical*
> *field or the magnetic field; the heart does both.*
> ~ *Gregg Braden*

The human heart is a programmer of our physical reality. As we change the magnet, the iron filings follow its shape. That is how our own core beliefs, our own core feelings, create our world paradigm. This is the extent of our power, and of our responsibility.

~∿

WHATEVER WE HEAR ABOUT NEW phenomena ~ solar flares[1], Earth's electro-magnetic field collapsing, the poles consequently shifting[2], a period of darkness[3], the event horizon, and black holes ~ bear in mind these are all physical manifestations of a spiritual reality that is beyond our *conceptual* comprehension. Although the physicists and astronomers are indeed the first to grasp the scope of things, and to verify the current changes, we do not want to limit our view to *only* the physical picture.

---

[1] The current transmission of increased energy and consciousness to our planet.

[2] A polarity shift from the outgoing to the ingoing cycle, from left to right brain, from the head to the heart.

[3] See Drunvalo's video: *The Maya of Eternal Time*

Have trust. These physical events all stem from the same creative life force that is our own inner existence: they are outer expressions of our own transformation. As we are growing in trust and love of ourselves *we are, as the pinnacle of our inner relationship, now reuniting with that very essence,* with the cosmic life energy that we all are. Our identity expands from trying to understand the secrets of our universe and our spiritual essence, to feeling part of it all. From this reunion, this reconnection, our life unfolds very differently to before.

OUR WORLD IS HOLOGRAPHIC: The same patterns repeat in all levels from the smallest to the largest scale. Life is a relationship ~ within us, between us and others, between us and our expanded spirit self, and between matter and consciousness. Every relationship is a gradual dropping of fear and resistance, a gradual increase of trust and of love. It is a courtship, a growing together, a bonding.

It is out of love that we dove again and again, ever deeper into the density of physical life, eventually uplifting and transforming it. On a certain level, the resistant patterns we experience within come from the density of the matter we chose to inhabit, to work with. It is not, strictly speaking, anyone's personal resistance. It is what we took on our shoulders, to enlighten through *the power of the human heart.*

Finally all mistrust, all separation, is dissolved as love triumphs over doubt and hurt. And yet, it is not a conquest, not a battle ~ it is a courtship, a seduction, it is a love affair. In trusting surrender, matter becomes imbued with the loving embrace of consciousness.

Our species, the HU-man race, is a bridge between Earth and the divine, the link that brings awareness into the physical plane. We are the living channels through which our own life force ~ the spirit of life itself, consciousness ~ inhabits, enlivens, and finally enlightens matter. That is why to nurture our own inner relationship is the best we can do. Discover yourself. Love yourself. You are creating a new world.

With all my heart,
Amber

True security comes not from clinging to the known and predictable but from trusting the process of life, welcoming change and growth at all times.

~ Read on the back of a motor home

Afterword

MY DAUGHTER wrote this poem in Fiji in 2005, interestingly expressing concepts that we had not, at the time, spoken about.

Places in our Dreams

Now I can hear the rain is falling
and I can feel the angels calling
I've got so many dreams yet to live
and a lot of loving still to give
A million things unseen to see
Oh, won't you come discover life with me?

It's our choice who we want to be
Only we can set ourselves free
We realize when we've had enough
that no one else can do it for us
So let's turn the visions that we see
into everyday reality
Be beautiful, sacred and free
In balance and in harmony

There's too much hurt and too much pain
Too many lies told again and again
Many will filter what they see
Deny to feel the urgency
Believe that things will stay the same
involuntarily playing the game

Yet we all know deep in our heart
That we are here to do our part
It's up to each to find which way
We can help start the brand new day
Won't you come discover life with me?
Oh, won't you come discover life with me?

You can take others by the hand
and guide them towards the new land
But even if their dreams you can touch
you can really only do so much
'Cause when you finally come to the door ~
a space so different than before ~
it's up to each to walk on through
and be trusting in something so new

In this time we chose to be alive
given the strength and vision now to thrive
We'll reach the dimension above
a space built on the foundation of love
the place they call "the promised land"
I want to be there holding your hand

So won't you come discover life with me?
Oh, won't you come discover life with me?

~Chandra

Moon Nodes in Astrology

THE MOON NODES describe our major life theme, the basic track we are on in this life. You may find this knowledge helpful for better understanding yourself, others, and your lives' circumstances.

The following descriptions are just an outline, a snapshot. Most books on this topic will have a few pages of detailed information on each sign. You can discover your moon node sign by finding your birth date within the given periods.

1. Libra to Aries:

Nov. 8, 1911 - May 26, 1913	*Sept. 11, 1967 - April 3, 1969*
June 19, 1930 - Jan. 6, 1932	*April 21, 1986 - Nov. 8, 1987*
Jan. 29, 1949 - Aug. 17, 1950	*Nov. 30, 2004 - Jun 18, 2006*

Coming from a place of over-emphasis on others, you are encouraged to nurture your own identity. Being naturally diplomatic for acceptance, you widen by expressing yourself in a direct manner, trusting your own impulses and developing courage and willingness to take risks. Life steers you towards a more individual and self-decisive sense of accomplishment, which then allows you to build relationships with greater independancy.

2. Scorpio to Taurus:

April 19, 1910 - Nov. 7, 1911	*Feb. 22, 1966 - Sept. 10, 1967*
Nov. 29, 1928 - June 18, 1930	*Oct. 2, 1984 - April 20, 1986*
July 12, 1947 - Jan. 28, 1949	*May 13, 2003 - Nov. 29, 2004*

You move from a life of intensive, conflicting emotions towards tranquillity and agreement within. From emotional chaos and an attraction to crisis situations towards loyalty, kindness, patience and forgiveness. From a need for intimacy and dependency towards more self sufficiency and the ability to value your own gifts and talents. Eventually, Taurean peace and contentedness create the channel through which your Scorpionic power and emotions can be focussed and grounded.

3. Sagittarius to Gemini:

Sept. 30, 1908 - April 18, 1910   Aug. 6, 964 - Feb. 21, 1966
May 13, 1927 - Nov. 28, 1928   Mar. 15, 1983 - Oct. 1, 1984
Dec. 24, 1945 - July 11, 1947   Oct. 23, 2001 - May 12, 2003

Life guides you from great attachment to your own viewpoints towards becoming wider, more flexible and tactful by asking what other people think rather than assuming to know. From a surrounding of seclusion, wilderness, and inner reflection towards a more involved, cultivated and interactive environment. It is when you develop, through empathy, Gemini's communication skills that you can really share your innate Sagittarian wisdom.

4. Capricorn to Cancer:

Mar. 14, 1907 - Sept. 29, 1908   Jan. 14, 1963 - Aug. 5, 1964
Oct. 23, 1925 - May 12, 1927   Aug. 26, 1981 - Mar. 14, 1983
June 4, 1944 - Dec. 23, 1945   April 5, 2000 - Oct. 22, 2001

You are led from an all-responsible, all-controlling superiority towards more empathy and nurture for yourself and others. Through noticing and validating your own feelings and those of others you become more allowing, receptive and serviceable. From relying on strength and being accustomed to giving materially, you grow through love and acceptance towards the ability to support in a personal and emotional way. It is through Cancerian warmth and service that you can make your Capricornian knowledge available to others.

5. Aquarius to Leo:

Aug. 24, 1905 - Mar. 13, 1907   July 4, 1961 - Jan. 13, 1963
April 5, 1924 - Oct. 22, 1925   Feb. 6, 1980 - Aug. 25, 1981
Nov. 16, 1942 - June 3, 1944   Sept. 18, 1998 - April 4, 2000

Being content to merge into community, life steers you towards being comfortable and willing to take the center stage. You develop will, often strengthening through self imposed isolation. Feeling a deep sense of dedication to others, you discover now your own, more personal enjoyment. Following your heart's desire you experience increased willpower, playfulness and creativity. It is by taking on Leo's strength and leadership that you can best dedicate your Aquarian humanitarian qualities.

6. Pisces to Virgo:

Feb. 5, 1904 - Aug. 23, 1905   Dec. 9, 1959 - July 3, 1961
Sept. 16, 1922 - April 4, 1924   July 20, 1978 - Feb. 5, 1980
April 28, 1941 - Nov. 15, 1942   Feb. 28, 1997 - Sept. 7, 1998

Having an indifferent, all encompassing, and non-involved viewpoint you evolve towards a desire for participation, dedication and service to others. From a desire to escape your surroundings towards an interest to transform them. From a deeply immersed and interconnected, non verbal understanding of the human psyche you expand through the ability to single out and express aspects, making them clearly understandable and practical to others. Once you develop Virgo's sense for detail and focus, you can bring the cosmic understanding of Pisces into the material plane.

7. Aries to Libra:

July18, 1902 - Feb. 4, 1904   May 22, 1958 - Dec. 8, 1959
Feb. 21, 1921 - Sept. 15, 1922   Dec. 30, 1976 - July 19, 1978
Oct. 10, 1939 - April 27, 1941   Aug. 12, 1995 - Feb. 27, 1997

Life encourages you to add to your self centred point of view, sensitivity and objectivity for others. Having a desire for intensity and action, you become increasingly comfortable and content with

tranquillity and quietness. You learn to balance your sense of individual independence and a need for aggression through com-
panionship and sharing, embracing a mellow, loving way of life.
Through Libran awareness of the needs of others you develop a
feeling for diplomacy, cooperation and win-win situations ~ where
you can use your Arian individualism to build confidence and self
esteem in others.

8. Taurus to Scorpio:

Dec. 29, 1900 - July 17, 1902   *Nov. 5, 1956 - May 21, 1958*
Aug. 10, 1919 - Feb. 26, 1921   *June 13, 1975 - Dec. 29, 1976*
Mar. 22, 1938 - Oct. 9, 1939   *Jan.22, 1994 - Aug.11, 1995*

From a feeling for stability and security, you find yourself having
a growing interest in spontaneous and unpredictable change, evolution and transformation. As you let go with possesiveness, deca-
dence, complacency, stagnation and emotional isolation, you
develop a passionate desire for a meaningful life, deeper emotions,
and intimacy with others. Finally, the total transformation of Scor-
pio results in your rebirth into a fully new self.

9. Gemini to Sagittarius:

June 10, 1899 - Dec. 28, 1900   *April 13, 1955 - Nov. 4, 1956*
Jan. 20, 1918 - Aug. 9, 1919   *Nov. 23, 1973 - June 12, 1975*
Sept. 2, 1936 - Mar. 21, 1938   *July 5, 1992 - Jan. 21, 1994*

Coming from a logical, rational viewpoint and intellectual, theoretical approach, you broaden through active experience and increasing reliance on intuition. You move from being busy, diplomatic and
sophisticated to what is natural and real. As indecisiveness, trivialities, superficiality and hypocrisy give way to tranquility, reflection,
patience and self trust you discover a direct and uncensored communication that speaks from your higher consciousness. Eventually,
your Sagittarian north node combines your Gemini interests in
wordly communication with spiritual authenticity.

10. Cancer to Capricorn:

July 3, 1916 - Jan. 19, 1918   May 6, 1972 - Nov. 22, 1973
Feb. 13, 1935 - Sept. 1, 1936   Dec. 16, 1990 - July 4, 1992
Oct. 3, 1953 - April 12, 1955   Jan. 9, 2011 - 29 July, 2012

From contentment with homely comforts and being provided for, you are encouraged towards going out into the world and feeling capable by yourself. Continuously overcoming the shambles in your life, you develop strength and a sense of self accomplishment. Coming from a feeling of fragility and over sensitivity that can result in emotional control of others and avoidance of personal risk, you grow by encompassing a self disciplined, self respecting and self reliant attitude. Capricornian reliability and sense of accomplishment make your Cancerian heart qualities dependable and available for others.

11. Leo to Aquarius:

Dec. 14, 1914 - July 2, 1916   Oct. 16, 1970 - May 5, 1972
July 26, 1933 - Feb. 12, 1935   May 29, 1989 - Dec. 15, 1990
Mar. 5, 1952 - Oct. 2, 1953   July 22, 2009 - Jan. 8, 2011

Having a strong sense of self satisfaction, pride, and desire to be the centre of attention, you are led towards participating in and making decisions for the group; towards friendship and contributing to others. You move from a need for others approval towards an independent sense of self worth and self trust. It is through the Aquarian sense of brotherhood that you can contribute Leo's qualities of leadership towards humanity's progress and evolution.

12. Virgo to Pisces:

May 27, 1913 - Dec. 13, 1914   April 4, 1969 - Oct. 15, 1970
Jan. 7, 1932 - July 25, 1933   Nov. 9, 1987 - May 28, 1989
Aug. 18, 1950 - Mar. 7, 1952   Jan. 4, 2008 - July 21, 2009

Life guides you to widen from detail awareness and precision towards encompassing the whole and all its imperfections. When your logical common sense, structured approach to life, and desire for rigidness and discipline expand towards intuition and spirituality, you experience creativity, relaxation, and enjoyment of spontaneity. Similarily you broaden from a place of rational theory towards a compassionate, non judgmental approach and heartfelt actions. Your doubts and your feelings that you have to manage alone turn to trust and you become fully supported. You are here to bring the brightness of the spirit into this reality, anchoring it, and making it solid through your Virgo qualities.

David Wilcock on 2012 and Human Evolution

David Wilcock is an extensive scientific researcher and psychic, with striking similarities to Edgar Cayce. The following are a few essential extracts from his presentation "2012 and Human Evolution" that can be found on his website, divinecosmos.com:

I WORKED WITH Richard C. Hoagland and combined together well over one hundred different references from mainstream scientific sources, like NASA, showing that, in fact, our solar system is experiencing climate change: it's not just the Earth.

...What if these energetic increases in the solar system were also related to consciousness?

That might seem far-fetched, at first, until you start looking back at what we now know from quantum mechanics and many other types of information like that where consciousness, the observer (the person observing your experiment in quantum mechanics) has a noticeable effect on the outcome of the experiment....

And if consciousness and energy are interconnected, then quid pro quo, the change in the solar system also refers to a change in consciousness.

THE EVOLUTION OF SPECIES

And here's another thing I've been writing about quite a bit that you can research more on my website, divinecosmos.com — the evolution of species on this planet.

We have a fossil record that goes back some 542 million years. And during that time, if you didn't know better, you would think that evolution has been gradual: that the fossils show gradual changes from one species to another, and you get this ongoing, slow evolutionary process. Well, believe it or not, that's actually not what happens. Instead what we see is really remarkable changes in short periods of time, geologically speaking.

These really remarkable changes include irreconcilable gaps in the fossil record. You have advancements that occur in the species where they evolve and there's no intermediate step. In other words they basically jump from one sort of creature to another.

One experience that I've had is coming into contact with a scientist from Russia named Peter Gariaev, who's actually done some phenomenal research on DNA.

One of the most phenomenal points that he raises — which I continue to bring up over and over again — involves two hermetically-sealed containers, with a salamander embryo in one container and a frog embryo in the other. That's all you have. Then he took a non-burning laser, shined it through the salamander embryo, and re-directed that light to where the frog embryo was.... The frog embryo completely metamorphosed. As the cells kept dividing and the embryo kept growing, it grew into a salamander!

All it ever received was the light code — the DNA vibration, or DNA harmonic, that had gotten into that light beam — and was then conveyed from one area to the other.

... Apparently, we're seeing that DNA has a receptive quality much like an antenna for consciousness. And it's able to receive that information and be re-written....

Another study I haven't had the chance to publish actually came out of National Geographic, regarding a very primitive form of life called a "sea squirt." There are just single-tube hearts inside these sea squirts; they're very, very primitive organisms. Imagine a straw, and the straw has some muscular contractions that pump the blood through the body of this creature.

Well, in this case, these scientists were able to shine a particular frequency of light into a developing sea squirt, and trigger a spontaneous metamorphosis. It developed a double-chambered heart, and actually evolved spontaneously through nothing more than the burst of light!

CYCLES OF EVOLUTION

Getting back to Robert Rohde [of U.C. Berkely] and the scientists who have been looking at the evolutionary record, what we're seeing is that species are evolving on Earth, not all at once, but in sudden spurts. And these sudden spurts don't just happen randomly and sporadically; they happen in cycles.

Dr. David Raup and Dr. James Sepkoski, two University of Chicago paleontologists, discovered evolutionary jumps that occurred in 26-million-year intervals....

Dr. Robert Rohde found another cycle in it, which exists at the same time as the 26 million year cycle.... This other cycle, which is a 62-million-year cycle with a +/- 3-million-year variation, goes all the way back to the dawn of evolution of life on Earth as we know it — 542 million years ago. What's prior to that point is called the Pre-Cambrian Era, and all you see is rock — there's no critters in it. But then, from that point forward, you get these very clean, very nice and neat 62-million year intervals in which everything on Earth is transforming. And that's pretty cool.

What's even more cool is that when you actually start crunching the numbers, you discover pretty quickly that there are neat cycles of how the 26 and 62 million-year cycles mesh with the orbit of the galaxy....

We are dealing with a galactic energy field. It's a full-halo, expanding energy field that goes throughout the entire galaxy. When it reaches us, it causes changes in our solar system. It causes activation — intelligent repatterning — of our DNA molecules.

And THAT, my friends, is what's causing these 62- and 26-million-year cycles of species evolution in the fossil record! ...

The other important point is that our climate change right now would be akin to an energetic charge that's increasing, much in the same way that the energy beam of the laser shines through the salamander embryo into the frog embryo.

It's an increase in energy; it's an increase in charge that causes evolution to occur. That's where it's coming from....

THE FEAR IS THE ILLUSION

If, however, you start reading material that is describing fear and doom and gloom, they're on the wrong track.

This material tells you that you're not protected: this is all sort of leading up to some sort of cataclysm or Armageddon — plagues, famines, diseases, economic collapse, Illuminati, government conspiracy, bread lines — oh my gosh, there's so much of this stuff out there, isn't there?... Again, if someone is telling you all of the stuff that you're seeing is leading up to a mass extinction, or a mass death, it's JUST NOT TRUE! One thing after another, you just read: Oh, they're gonna put you in a concentration camp, they're gonna give you a microchip under your skin and you're not gonna be able to eat unless you have this microchip. Honestly — I have to tell you — NONE of this stuff is going to happen....

We're dealing with the multi-dimensional evolution of the solar system....

EDUCATE YOURSELF ABOUT YOUR OWN EVOLUTION

Study more of the information, hear more of the stuff that I've done — particularly The Science of Peace series. I think you'll find that very useful.

Go to my website: www.divinecosmos.com; read David's Blog; read the Articles section. There's a lot of stuff in there.... Educate yourself about the fact that this is not doom and gloom — this is a real change that's happening. It's evolving us.

It's the most grandiose moment in human history. It's happening now. You can be a part of it just by tuning in, taking some deep breaths, having a positive outlook about the future and realizing this is the single greatest moment in our history.

We are moving into something unprecedented. All the shadow material is coming up at this time to be cleansed, healed and renewed. You don't have to live in fear. You don't have to live in a sense of foreboding. If you tune into a positive reality, that will become your reality.

DAVID'S VAST, *stunning interdisciplinary research is summarized in* The Source Field Investigations, *due for release in August 2011 with Dutton Books. David's upcoming movie* Convergence *also reveals many of these mysteries, and is co-authored with Jim Hart, who worked with Carl Sagan for two years to write* Contact. *David's four-part* Access Your Higher Self *video series provides cutting-edge instruction in how to cultivate ESP, dream recall, lucid dreams and even direct telepathic contact with your own Higher Self.*

Acknowledgments

To all those who have inspired me, who have lit my way with confirmations and reminders, pushes and prods, love, song and laughter…this book is in gratitude.

Thanks to my wonderful family and friends for assisting the birthing.

Especially to my beautiful editor Jessica Bergsman Rockenbach who flew halfway around the world to do an excellent job setting the tone ~ both on my first draft and on her tan by the poolside!

To my partner ~ shadow, anchor, and companion ~ for his support, cooking, and meticulous editing; without whom I would likely have starved long ago, and who pushed me so much further in life than I thought I was willing to go.

And to the strong, bright spirit that chose me as her mother and opened my heart.

Thanks too to Jarrah, Mitch, and Jodie for their openness and inspiration;
To Paul[1] for pointing the way;
To Cleo whose courage enhanced mine;
To Miro for the craniosacral sessions that brought me back to life;
To Jane and to Jaiv, both for their technical and personal talents;
And eternal gratitude to my dear friend Anthony ~ for the table and chair.

A big thank-you to those readers who do not mind for any oversights and repetitions, knowing them to be a natural part of life.

My heartfelt appreciation to the powerfully transformative spirit of Ubud, Bali where I spent 2010 writing this book.

And to the faithful Wayan for the cleaning and the coconuts.

---

[1] www.paulsix.com

www.ingramcontent.com/pod-product-compliance
Lightning Source LLC
Chambersburg PA
CBHW031825090426
42741CB00005B/132